Achieving your Assessment and Quality Assurance Units (TAQA)

Achieving your Assessment and Quality Assurance Units (TAQA)

Second edition

Ann Gravells

Los Angeles | London | New Delhi
Singapore | Washington DC

Learning Matters
An imprint of SAGE Publications Ltd
1 Oliver's Yard
55 City Road
London EC1Y 1SP

SAGE Publications Inc.
2455 Teller Road
Thousand Oaks, California 91320

SAGE Publications India Pvt Ltd
B 1/I 1 Mohan Cooperative Industrial Area
Mathura Road
New Delhi 110 044

SAGE Publications Asia-Pacific Pte Ltd
3 Church Street
#10–04 Samsung Hub
Singapore 049483

Editor: Amy Thornton
Development editor: Jennifer Clark
Production controller: Chris Marke
Project management: Deer Park Productions,
  Tavistock, Devon, England
Marketing manager: Catherine Slinn
Cover design: Wendy Scott
Typeset by: C&M Digitals (P) Ltd, Chennai, India
Printed and bound by CPI Group (UK) Ltd,
  Croydon, CR0 4YY

MIX
Paper from
responsible sources
FSC
www.fsc.org   FSC™ C013965

© Ann Gravells 2014

First published by Learning Matters SAGE 2014

Apart from any fair dealing for the purposes of research or private study, or criticism or review, as permitted under the Copyright, Designs and Patents Act, 1988, this publication may be reproduced, stored or transmitted in any form, or by any means, only with the prior permission in writing of the publishers, or in the case of reprographic reproduction, in accordance with the terms of licences issued by the Copyright Licensing Agency. Enquiries concerning reproduction outside those terms should be sent to the publishers.

Library of Congress Control Number: 2013953928

British Library Cataloguing in Publication data

A catalogue record for this book is available from the British Library

ISBN: 978-1-4462-7444-6
ISBN: 978-1-4462-7445-3 (pbk)

CONTENTS

ACKNOWLEDGEMENTS

I would like to give special thanks to the following people who have helped me with this edition of the book. They have freely given their time, knowledge and advice, which have resulted in some excellent contributions.

Adele Sewell	Mac Macdonald
Andrea Lavender	Marie Falconer
Angela Faulkener	Mel Page
Bronia Davis	Dr Susan Mullins
Gill Payne	Suzanne Blake

I would also like to thank the following people who have supported me with the previous edition of this book:

Angela O'Leary	Joan Willison
Bob Freeman	Peter Adeney
Johanna Hurren	Vickie Prince
Jacklyn Williams	

Special thanks go to my father Bob Gravells, who is so good at proofreading and pointing out my typing errors.

I would like to thank my editor Jennifer Clark for her continued support and excellent guidance, and Belbin Associates for permission to reproduce copyright material.

I would especially like to thank Amy Thornton from Learning Matters (part of SAGE Publications Ltd) for her advice, encouragement and tremendous patience with all my questions, e-mails and telephone calls.

Particular thanks go to readers of previous editions of this book who have taken the time to give valuable feedback, which has greatly assisted me when preparing this edition.

Every effort has been made to trace the copyright holders and to obtain their permission for the use of copyright material. The publisher and author will gladly receive any information enabling them to rectify any error or omission in subsequent editions.

Ann Gravells
www.anngravells.co.uk

Ann is a director of her own company, *Ann Gravells Ltd*, an educational consultancy based in East Yorkshire. She specialises in teaching, training and quality assurance for the Further Education and Skills Sector.

Ann creates resources for teachers and learners such as PowerPoints and handouts for the TAQA units and the Award in Education and Training. These are available via her resource website: www.anngravells.co.uk/resources.

Ann is a consultant to the University of Cambridge's Institute of Continuing Education. She has worked for several awarding organisations producing qualification guidance, policies and procedures, and carrying out quality assurance of teacher training qualifications. She has been teaching in further education colleges since 1983.

Ann holds a Masters in Educational Management, a PGCE, a Degree in Education, and a Medal of Excellence for teaching. Ann is a Fellow of the Institute for Learning and holds QTLS status.

She is often asked how her surname should be pronounced. The 'vells' part of Gravells is pronounced like 'bells'.

She is the author of:

- *Achieving your Assessor and Quality Assurance Units*
- *Delivering Employability Skills in the Lifelong Learning Sector*
- *Passing Assessments for the Award in Education and Training*
- *Passing PTLLS Assessments*
- *Preparing to Teach in the Lifelong Learning Sector*
- *Principles and Practice of Assessment in the Lifelong Learning Sector*
- *The Award in Education and Training*
- *What is Teaching in the Lifelong Learning Sector?*

She is co-author of:

- *Equality and Diversity in the Lifelong Learning Sector*
- *Passing CTLLS Assessments*
- *Passing the Award in Education and Training*
- *Planning and Enabling Learning in the Lifelong Learning Sector.*
- *The Certificate in Education and Training*
- *Passing the Certificate Education and Training*

She has edited:

- *Study Skills for PTLLS.*

The author welcomes any comments from readers; please contact her via her website.

www.anngravells.co.uk

PREFACE

This book was first published in 2012 and was called *Achieving your TAQA Assessor and Internal Quality Assurer Award.* TAQA stands for training, assessment and quality assurance. It was successful due to its use of language which new assessors and internal quality assurers could understand.

Due to demand from readers, this edition has been updated to take into account developments within the Further Education and Skills Sector, and to include chapters regarding the external quality assurance role. Even if you are not taking these units as part of a qualification, reading the chapters will help you understand how the external role impacts upon the assessment and internal quality assurance roles.

The book is also appropriate to anyone taking units from the Award, Certificate and Diploma in Education and Training, as some of the assessment and quality assurance units can be used towards achievement of these qualifications. It is also appropriate to anyone just wanting to know what it is like to become an assessor or a quality assurer in education and training.

In this chapter you will learn about:

- the structure of the book and how to use it
- TAQA units and qualifications
- how to achieve your units
- Qualifications and Credit Framework
- abbreviations and acronyms.

The structure of the book and how to use it

Whether you are a new or an experienced practitioner, this book will guide you through the terminology, processes and practices to enable you to improve your role and/or work towards a relevant qualification in assessment and quality assurance.

The book has been specifically written for assessors as well as internal and external quality assurers who are working towards the Training, Assessment and Quality Assurance units (often known by the acronym TAQA). The content is also applicable to anyone requiring further information to assist their job role, or for continuing professional development (CPD).

The book is structured in chapters which relate to the eight assessment and quality assurance units. However, as some of the units' content is very similar, more than one chapter will need to be read to ensure full coverage of the unit content.

Due to the terminology used throughout the subject areas, you will find lots of acronyms within the book. A list of the most commonly used ones can be found at the end of this chapter.

The book is also relevant to anyone taking units from the:

- Award in Education and Training

- Certificate in Education and Training

- Diploma in Education and Training.

If you take one of these qualifications at some point in the future, you will find that some of the assessment and quality assurance units will be accepted towards achievement.

This book is structured in chapters which relate to the content of the three assessments, the three internal quality assurance (IQA) and the three external quality assurance (EQA) units. You can work logically through the chapters or just read relevant aspects relating to the units you are working towards or areas relating to your job role. Some aspects within one unit might also be applicable to another unit. Therefore, rather than duplicate text, there will be a statement referring you to a particular chapter for more information.

There are activities and examples within each chapter which will assist your understanding of the assessment and quality assurance processes. At the end of each chapter section is an extension activity to stretch and challenge your learning further. If you are working towards a TAQA unit, completing the activities will help you to gather suitable materials. At the end of each chapter is a list of possible evidence which you could provide towards your achievement of the TAQA units.

A cross-referencing grid at the end of each chapter shows how the content contributes towards the TAQA units' assessment criteria, as well as the National Occupational Standards for Learning and Development. There is also a theory focus with relevant references, further information and websites that you might like to refer to.

Throughout the chapters there are examples of completed templates that could be used or adapted for assessment and quality assurance purposes. However, do check with your organisation in case they have particular documents they require you to use.

Chapter 8 relates to the management of others and as such contains various leadership, management and communication theories. The qualification unit this chapter relates to is part of the management standards as well as being a TAQA unit.

The appendices contain the learning outcomes and assessment criteria for the Assessment, Internal and External Quality Assurance units. You could use these like a checklist to mark off your progress and achievement.

The index will help you to quickly locate useful topics within the book.

TAQA units and qualifications

The assessment, internal and external quality assurance units form part of the Learning and Development qualifications, often known as the TAQA suite of qualifications for England, Wales and Northern Ireland; separate standards are available in Scotland.

The units are suitable for anyone assessing, internally or externally quality assuring qualifications, programmes of learning, or competence in the work environment. You can take the units whether you are employed full time or part time, are self-employed, or are employed on a voluntary or peripatetic (working for several organisations) basis.

The qualifications are made up of a combination of units according to job roles. There is a *knowledge* unit, which can be taken whether you are performing the job role or not, and then one or two *performance* units depending upon the specific requirements of your job role.

The qualifications are based on standards which have been produced by a Sector Skills Council (SSC). These are known as National Occupational Standards and should exist for every subject area where a formal qualification can be achieved. SSCs aim to increase the skills and productivity of their sector's workforce and influence the development of qualifications and apprenticeships. They have a major impact on the delivery of publicly and privately funded training throughout the UK. There will be a SSC or a similar Standard Setting Body (SSB) for the subject you will assess or quality assure. It would be useful to find out who they are, as they create the assessment strategy and guidance (i.e. the required qualifications and/or experience which assessors and quality assurers should have) for each qualification. The SSC for TAQA was the Learning and Skills Improvement Service (LSIS), which ceased operating in August 2013. The Education and Training Foundation came into effect in September 2013.

> *The Education and Training Foundation has been set up to improve professionalism and standards in the further education and skills sectors. Established by sector bodies and funded by The Department for Business, Innovation and Skills (BIS), the Foundation sets professional standards and provides support to ensure learners benefit from a well-qualified, effective and up-to-date professional workforce supported by good leadership, management and governance.*

www.et-foundation.co.uk/ (accessed 27.09.13)

When National Occupational Standards are approved, an awarding organisation will turn them into qualifications. Any organisation which is approved by them (often called a *centre*) can apply to offer the qualifications. Several different awarding organisations can offer the same qualification; the content will not differ, but the way it is assessed might.

Assessment qualifications

There are three units at level 3: the first is knowledge based and the other two are performance based (see Appendices 1, 2 and 3). As the first unit (Unit 1) is purely knowledge based, it can be taken prior to or at the same time as a performance unit. The knowledge unit is ideal for anyone wanting to know what it is like to be an assessor, without having to carry out assessment activities. The units can be achieved in any order and each has a credit value on the Qualifications and Credit Framework (QCF).

Unit 1 Understanding the principles and practices of assessment (3 credits)
This is a knowledge-based unit for new and existing assessors or anyone who wishes to know about the theory of assessment. You don't need to carry out any assessment activities with learners to achieve this unit.

Unit 2 Assess occupational competence in the work environment (6 credits)
This is a performance unit for anyone who assesses in the work environment using methods such as asking questions, examining products of work and observing practice. The assessments might be towards a qualification, a programme of learning, or to confirm an employee's competence towards their job specification.

Unit 3 Assess vocational skills, knowledge and understanding (6 credits)
This is a performance unit for anyone who assesses in any environment using methods such as assignments, projects, simulations and tests. The assessments might be towards a

qualification, a programme of learning, or to confirm an employee's knowledge and skills towards their job specification.

Table 0.1 Assessment qualification titles and units

Level 3 Award in Understanding the Principles and Practices of Assessment		
Unit 1 Understanding the principles and practices of assessment		
Level 3 Award in Assessing Competence in the Work Environment		
Unit 1 Understanding the principles and practices of assessment	Unit 2 Assess occupational competence in the work environment	
Level 3 Award in Assessing Vocationally Related Achievement		
Unit 1 Understanding the principles and practices of assessment	Unit 3 Assess vocational skills, knowledge and understanding	
Level 3 Certificate in Assessing Vocational Achievement		
Unit 1 Understanding the principles and practices of assessment	Unit 2 Assess occupational competence in the work environment	Unit 3 Assess vocational skills, knowledge and understanding

Internal quality assurance qualifications

There are three units at level 4: the first is knowledge based and the other two are performance based (see Appendices 4, 5 and 8). As the first unit (Unit 4) is purely knowledge based, it can be taken prior to or at the same time as a performance unit. It is ideal for anyone wanting to know what it is like to be an IQA, without carrying out any quality assurance activities. The units can be achieved in any order and each has a credit value on the QCF.

Unit 4 Understanding the principles and practices of internally assuring the quality of assessment (6 credits)
This is a knowledge-based unit for new and existing internal quality assurers or anyone who wishes to know about the theory of internal quality assurance. You don't need to carry out any internal quality assurance activities with assessors to achieve this unit.

Unit 5 Internally assure the quality of assessment (6 credits)
This is a performance unit for anyone who internally quality assures the work of assessors, for example observing their practice, sampling their judgements and decisions, giving support and advice. It can be achieved in any environment by internally quality assuring qualifications, programmes of learning or workplace competence.

Unit 8 Plan, allocate and monitor work in own area of responsibility (5 credits)
This is a performance unit for anyone who leads the internal quality assurance process within an organisation, for example, co-ordinating the work of other internal quality assurers. The role will include having a responsibility for managing the quality and performance of assessors and/or other internal quality assurers . Developing systems and liaising with external inspectors might also be part of this role. This unit can also be taken by external quality assurers who lead a team. The unit is based on the National Occupational Standards for Management and Leadership.

Table 0.2 Internal quality assurance qualification titles and units

Level 4 Award in Understanding the Internal Quality Assurance of Assessment Processes and Practice		
Unit 4 Understanding the principles and practices of internally assuring the quality of assessment		
Level 4 Award in the Internal Quality Assurance of Assessment Processes and Practice		
Unit 4 Understanding the principles and practices of internally assuring the quality of assessment	Unit 5 Internally assure the quality of assessment	
Level 4 Certificate in Leading the Internal Quality Assurance of Assessment Processes and Practice		
Unit 4 Understanding the principles and practices of internally assuring the quality of assessment	Unit 5 Internally assure the quality of assessment	Unit 8 Plan, allocate and monitor work in own area of responsibility

External quality assurance qualifications

There are three units at level 4: the first is knowledge based and the other two are performance based (see Appendices 6, 7 and 8). As the first unit (Unit 6) is purely knowledge based, it can be taken prior to, or at the same time as, the performance unit. It is ideal for anyone wanting to know what it is like to be an external quality assurer. The units can be achieved in any order and each has a credit value on the QCF.

Unit 6 Understanding the principles and practices of externally assuring the quality of assessment (6 credits)
This is a knowledge-based unit for new and existing external quality assurers or anyone who wishes to know about the theory of external quality assurance. You don't need to carry out any external quality assurance activities to achieve this unit.

Unit 7 Externally assure the quality of assessment (6 credits)
This is a performance unit for anyone who externally quality assures the work of assessors and internal quality assurers, for example observing their practice, sampling their judgements and decisions, giving support and advice. It can only be achieved by practising external quality assurers who are working for an awarding organisation.

Unit 8 Plan, allocate and monitor work in own area of responsibility (5 credits)
This is a performance unit for anyone who manages and leads the external quality assurance process within an awarding organisation, for example co-ordinating the work of other external quality assurers. Developing systems, policies and liaising with awarding organisation personnel might also be part of this role. This unit can also be taken by internal quality assurers.

Table 0.3 External quality assurance qualification titles and units

Level 4 Award in Understanding the External Quality Assurance of Assessment Processes and Practice		
Unit 6 Understanding the principles and practices of externally assuring the quality of assessment		
Level 4 Award in the External Quality Assurance of Assessment Processes and Practice		
Unit 6 Understanding the principles and practices of externally assuring the quality of assessment	Unit 7 Externally assure the quality of assessment	
Level 4 Certificate in Leading the External Quality Assurance of Assessment Processes and Practice		
Unit 6 Understanding the principles and practices of externally assuring the quality of assessment	Unit 7 Externally assure the quality of assessment	Unit 8 Plan, allocate and monitor work in own area of responsibility

How to achieve your units

First of all, you need to decide which units are relevant to your job role; you can then locate and enrol at a suitable training centre or college. You will be registered with an awarding organisation, which accredits the units and issues certificates upon successful completion.

Once you have learnt the theory and begun to put it into practice, you will be assessed, for example by an assignment, observation, questions and/or a professional discussion. Although the assessment activities may differ depending upon where you are taking your units, the content of the units remains the same.

You could use the Appendices as a checklist to see what you currently know and can already provide evidence for, or to identify what you need to learn and work towards within the relevant units. The units beginning with the word *understanding* are the knowledge based units and can usually be evidenced by an assignment, written statements or a professional discussion. The other units are performance units, which means they have to be evidenced by you actually performing the requirements for real as part of your job role. You can take the units in any order or at the same time. If you take them at the same time, your assessor might be able to assess you holistically. This means some aspects for one unit can be cross-referenced to other relevant units rather than be repeated.

You will be allocated an assessor who should explain how they will assess you, for example by visiting you in your work environment to observe you in action. You should gather evidence of your achievement in the form of completed assignments, responses to questions and products of your work such as completed assessment or quality assurance records. There is guidance at the end of each chapter as to possible evidence you could provide.

You will need to keep all your work in a file or folder, often referred to as a *portfolio*, which can be manual or electronic. Copies of your assessor's records, such as observation and feedback reports, will also need to be included. If you quote from any textbooks, journals or the internet when producing written work, you will need to reference your work accordingly, otherwise it could be considered as plagiarism. Your assessor should be able to give you advice on the best way to do this as it is usually a requirement if you are working towards units at level 4.

While you are working towards the units, you might need to be countersigned by another qualified person in the same subject area as yourself. For example, if you are assessing a hairdressing qualification, another qualified hairdressing assessor will need to confirm your decisions. This is to ensure that you are carrying out the requirements of the qualification and units correctly. How long it takes you to complete will depend upon the time it takes for you to generate all the required evidence. However, you should be given a realistic target date for achievement as part of an action plan with your own assessor.

Your work will be assessed and a sample might also be internally and externally quality assured. When you have met all the requirements, the training centre or college you have enrolled with will apply for your certificate from the awarding organisation. Once you have your certificate, you will no longer need to be countersigned.

Qualifications and Credit Framework

Ofqual, together with its partner regulators in Wales (DCELLS) and Northern Ireland (CCEA), is responsible for the regulation of the QCF. There is a separate framework for Scotland. The frameworks will eventually contain all available qualifications in the country.

The QCF is a system for recognising skills and qualifications by awarding credit values to the units. A credit value of 1 equates to 10 learning hours. These values enable you to see how long it would take an average learner to achieve a unit. For example, the *Understanding the principles and practices of assessment* unit is 3 credits, which equates to 30 hours. The total hours include *contact time* with a trainer and assessor, and *non-contact time* for individual study, assignment work and the production of your evidence.

There are three sizes of qualifications with titles and associated credit values:

- Award (1 to 12 credits)
- Certificate (13 to 36 credits)
- Diploma (37 credits or more).

The terms Award, Certificate and Diploma don't relate to progression, i.e. you don't start with an Award, progress to the Certificate and then to the Diploma. The terms relate to how big the qualification is (i.e. its size), which is based on the total number of credits. By looking at the title and credit value, you will be able to see how difficult it is and how long it will take to complete.

The difficulty of the qualification is defined by its level. The QCF has nine levels: entry level plus levels 1 to 8 (there are 12 levels in Scotland).

A rough comparison of the levels to existing qualifications is:

1 – GCSEs (grades D–G)

2 – GCSEs (grade A*–C)

3 – A levels

4 – Vocational Qualification (VQ) level 4, Higher National Certificate (HNC)

5 – VQ level 5, Degree, Higher National Diploma (HND)

6 – Honours Degree

7 – Masters Degree

8 – Doctor of Philosophy (PhD).

All qualifications on the QCF use the terms *learning outcomes* and *assessment criteria*. The learning outcomes state what the learner *will do*, and the assessment criteria what the learner *can do*. Units are either *knowledge based* (to assess understanding) or *performance based* (to assess competence). You can see the content of all the TAQA units in the appendices.

Abbreviations and acronyms

All working environments seem to use jargon such as abbreviations and acronyms at some point. Assessment and quality assurance is no different and the ones used seem to be continually updated and added to. Throughout this book, the first occurrence of any acronym in each chapter will always be in full, followed by the acronym in brackets. The following table lists most of those you will come across as a new assessor or quality assurer.

Table 0.4 Abbreviations and acronyms

ACL	Adult and Community Learning
ADD	Attention Deficit Disorder
ADHD	Attention Deficit and Hyperactivity Disorder
ADS	Adult Dyslexia Support
AELP	Association of Employment and Learning Providers
AI	Awarding Institution
AO	Awarding Organisation
AoC	Association of Colleges
ASD	Autism Spectrum Disorder
ATL	Association of Teachers and Lecturers
ATLS	Associate Teacher Learning and Skills
BEd	Bachelor of Education
BIS	Department for Business, Innovation and Skills
BME	Black and Minority Ethnic
CCEA	Council for the Curriculum, Examinations and Assessment (Northern Ireland)
Cert Ed	Certificate in Education
CETT	Centre for Excellence in Teacher Training
CL	Community Learning
CLA	Copyright Licensing Authority
COSHH	Control of Substances Hazardous to Health
CPD	Continuing Professional Development
CQFW	Credit and Qualification Framework for Wales
CRB	Criminal Records Bureau (now DBS)
DBS	Disclosure and Barring Service
DCELLS	Department for Children, Education, Lifelong Learning and Skills (Wales)
DSO	Designated Safeguarding Officer
E&D	Equality and Diversity
EBD	Emotional and Behavioural Difficulties
ECDL	European Computer Driving Licence
EDAR	Experience, Describe, Analyse and Revise
EDIP	Explain, Demonstrate, Imitate and Practice
EHRC	Equality and Human Rights Commission
EI	Emotional Intelligence
EQA	External Quality Assurance/Assurer
ESOL	English for Speakers of Other Languages
FAQ	Frequently Asked Questions
FE	Further Education
FHE	Further and Higher Education
GCSE	General Certificate of Secondary Education
GLH	Guided Learning Hours
H&S	Health and Safety
HEA	Higher Education Academy
HEI	Higher Education Institution
IAG	Information, Advice and Guidance
IAP	Individual Action Plan
ICT	Information and Communication Technology
IfL	Institute for Learning
IIP	Investors in People
ILA	Individual Learning Account
ILP	Individual Learning Plan
ILT	Information and Learning Technology
IQ	Intelligence Quotient
IQA	Internal Quality Assurance/Assurer
ISA	Independent Safeguarding Authority
IT	Information Technology
ITE	Initial Teacher Education
ITP	Independent Training Provider

(Continued)

Table 0.4 (Continued)

ITT	Initial Teacher/Trainer Training
IWB	Interactive Whiteboard
LA	Local Authority
LAR	Learner Achievement Record
LDD	Learning Difficulties and/or Disabilities
LLUK	Lifelong Learning UK (no longer operational)
LSA	Learner Support Assistant
LSCB	Local Safeguarding Children Board
LSIS	Learning and Skills Improvement Service (no longer operational)
MLD	Moderate Learning Difficulties
NEET	Not in Education, Employment or Training
NIACE	National Institute of Adult Continuing Education
NLH	Notional Learning Hours
NLP	Neuro Linguistic Programming
NOS	National Occupational Standards
NQT	Newly Qualified Teacher
NRDC	National Research and Development Centre for adult literacy and numeracy
NTA	Non-teaching Assistant
NVQ	National Vocational Qualification
Ofqual	Office of Qualifications and Examinations Regulation
Ofsted	Office for Standards in Education, Children's Services and Skills
PAT	Portable Appliance Testing
PCET	Post-Compulsory Education and Training
PGCE	Postgraduate Certificate in Education
PLTS	Personal Learning and Thinking Skills
POCA	Protection of Children Act (1999)
PPP	Pose, Pause, Pick
PSHE	Personal, Social and Health Education
QCF	Qualifications and Credit Framework
QTLS	Qualified Teacher Learning and Skills
QTS	Qualified Teacher Status (schools)
RARPA	Recognising And Recording Progress and Achievement in non-accredited learning
RLJ	Reflective Learning Journal
RPL	Recognition of Prior Learning
RWE	Realistic Working Environment
SCN	Scottish Candidate Number
SCQF	Scottish Credit and Qualifications Framework
SEAL	Social and Emotional Aspects of Learning
SFA	Skills Funding Agency
SL	Student Loan
SLC	Subject Learning Coach
SMART	Specific, Measurable, Achievable, Relevant and Time bound
SoW	Scheme of Work
SP	Session Plan
SSB	Standard Setting Body
SSC	Sector Skills Council
SWOT	Strengths, Weaknesses, Opportunities and Threats
T&L	Teaching and Learning
TAQA	Training, Assessment and Quality Assurance
UCU	University and College Union
ULN	Unique Learner Number
VACSR	Valid, Authentic, Current, Sufficient and Reliable
VARK	Visual, Aural, Read/write and Kinaesthetic
VB	Vetting and Barring
VLE	Virtual Learning Environment
WBL	Work-Based Learning
WEA	Workers' Educational Association
WWWWWH	Who, What, When, Where, Why and How

Summary

In this chapter you have learnt about:

- the structure of the book and how to use it
- TAQA units and qualifications
- how to achieve your units
- Qualifications and Credit Framework
- abbreviations and acronyms.

Theory focus

References and further information

Gravells, A (2013) *The Award in Education and Training*. London: Learning Matters SAGE.

LLUK (2010) *National Occupational Standards for Learning and Development.* London: Lifelong Learning UK.

Websites

Ann Gravells (information regarding teaching, assessment and quality assurance): www.anngravells. co.uk

CCEA Northern Ireland: www.rewardinglearning.org.uk

DCELLS Wales: www.wales.gov.uk/topics/educationandskills

Department for Business, Innovation and Skills: www.bis.gov.uk

Education and Training Foundation: www.et-foundation.co.uk

Institute for Learning: www.ifl.ac.uk

Job sites for assessors and quality assurers:

www.eatjobs.co.uk

www.fecareers.co.uk

www.fejobs.com

www.jobs.ac.uk

www.tes.co.uk/jobs

Ofqual: www.ofqual.gov.uk

Qualifications and Credit Framework: http://tinyurl.com/447bgy2

Scottish Credit and Qualifications Framework: www.scqf.org.uk

Sector Skills Councils: www.sscalliance.org

1 PRINCIPLES AND PRACTICES OF ASSESSMENT

Introduction

In this chapter you will learn about:

- the role of assessment
- key concepts and principles of assessment
- minimising risks
- types of assessment
- methods of assessment.

Within the chapter there are activities and examples which will help you to reflect on the above and to develop and enhance your understanding of the principles and practices of assessment. Completing the activities will help you to gather evidence towards the *Principles and practices of assessment* unit. At the end of each section is an extension activity to stretch and challenge your knowledge and understanding.

At the end of the chapter is a list of possible evidence which could be used towards the *Principles and practices of assessment* unit.

A cross-referencing grid shows how the content of this chapter contributes towards the relevant TAQA units' criteria and the National Occupational Standards. There is also a theory focus with relevant references, further information and websites to which you might like to refer.

The role of assessment

What is assessment?

Assessment is a way of finding out if learning has taken place. It enables you, as the assessor, to ascertain if your learner has gained the required skills, knowledge, understanding and/or attitudes needed at a given point in time. It also provides your learners with an opportunity to demonstrate what progress they have made and what they have learnt so far. If you don't plan for and carry out any assessment with your learners, you will not know how well or what they have learnt.

Assessment should not be in isolation from the teaching and learning process. You can assess that learning is taking place each time you are with your learners. This can simply be by watching what they are doing and/or asking questions. If you don't formally teach, you might at some point be carrying out short coaching or training sessions with your learners. However, there are some assessors who don't teach or train, but will just assess, make decisions and give feedback. This might be where competent staff are demonstrating their skills, knowledge and understanding towards their job role, or an aspect of a qualification in the workplace.

If your learners are taking a qualification, you will need to use formal methods of assessment such as an assignment or a workplace observation. However, you can devise informal methods to use with your learners to check their progress at any time, such as asking a few questions. Assessment should focus on improving and reinforcing learning as well as measuring achievements. It should help your learners realise how they are progressing and what they need to do to improve and/or develop further.

Example

Hardeep has devised a quiz based on a popular television programme which he uses with his group of learners at the end of sessions. This is to assess their ongoing progress and knowledge of the subject of Geography. He then uses the formal activities provided by the awarding organisation (AO) to assess their achievement.

Assessment should be a regular and continual process; it might not always be formalised, but you will be watching what your learners are doing, asking them questions and reviewing their progress whenever you are in contact with them. If you also teach or train, your learners will be demonstrating their skills, knowledge and understanding regularly, for example through tasks, discussions and ongoing activities. It is good practice to give your learners feedback when assessing them informally to help them realise what progress they are making. If they have not reached a certain standard, you should still give feedback on what they have done well so far, and how they can improve and develop further.

You are therefore constantly making judgements and should be aware of the impact that your comments can have on your learners' confidence when you give feedback. Imagine how you feel when you receive feedback, perhaps elated because the comments are good, but demoralised if not. Comments which specifically focus on the activity or work produced, rather than the individual, will be more helpful and motivating to your learners. Assessment should not become a personal or *subjective* judgement, but should be *objective* and relate to the activity or criteria being assessed.

Assessment should not be confused with evaluation; assessment is of the *learner*, evaluation is of the *programme* that the learner is taking, for example a qualification. Assessment is specific towards a learner's progress and achievements, as well as how they can improve.

Evaluation is a quality assurance monitoring tool. It includes obtaining feedback from your learners and others, for example employers, line managers and quality assurers, to help you improve the overall learner experience as well as your own practice.

There is a difference between assessment *for* learning, and assessment *of* learning. Assessment *for* learning is usually a formative process. It will ascertain progress so far in order to plan further learning and development. Assessment *of* learning is usually summative and confirms that learning and achievement have taken place.

The starting point for assessment

If you are going to assess accredited qualifications, the starting point should be the programme *syllabus*, often known as a *qualification handbook*. This should state how your subject should be assessed and quality assured and will be available from the AO which accredits the qualification and issues the certificates. It will give information and guidance in the form of an *assessment strategy*. The assessment strategy should state the experience, professional development and qualifications that assessors and internal quality assurers (IQAs) should have. It will also state how the subject should be assessed, and whether assessment activities are provided for you or you need to create your own. Alternatively, you might be assessing non-accredited qualifications, which are programmes of learning which don't lead to a formal qualification issued by an AO. However, a company certificate of achievement might be issued as proof of success.

Activity

If you are assessing learners who are working towards a qualification, find out who the AO is for your particular subject and access their website. Locate the qualification handbook and review the assessment strategy to ensure you can meet the requirements. If you are going to assess accredited or non-accredited programmes of learning, familiarise yourself with what you will assess and what activities you can use.

The purpose of the assessment strategy is to ensure the subject is assessed in accordance with relevant guidance and regulations, to give a quality service to your learners and to maintain the reputation of your organisation, the qualification and the AO (if applicable).

If you are going to assess competence and performance in the work environment, the starting point should be the company standards or job specifications. This will help you plan effective activities to assess skills, knowledge and understanding based on what the learners know already. If the standards or job specifications have not been written in a way that clearly states what someone has to *know* and what someone has to *do* then they could easily be misinterpreted. You will need to discuss them with your learner and their supervisor to ensure you all interpret the requirements in the same way. They might also change; therefore you would need to ensure you are working with the latest version.

The assessment process

The assessment process is a systematic procedure which should be followed to give your learner a positive experience. Depending upon the subject you are assessing and whether it is academic (theory or knowledge based) or vocational (practical or performance based), you will usually follow the assessment cycle (see Figure 1.1). The cycle will continue until all aspects of the programme or qualification have been achieved by your learner.

Throughout the cycle, standardisation of assessment practice between assessors should take place; this will help ensure the consistency and fairness of decisions, and that all assessors interpret the requirements in the same way. Internal quality assurance (IQA) will also take place throughout as part of the quality assurance process (see Chapters 3 and 4 for further information).

Figure 1.1 Assessment cycle

- **Initial assessment** – ascertaining if your learner has any previous knowledge and/or experience of the subject, topic or unit to be assessed. This information can be obtained through application forms, interviews and discussions. The results of initial assessment activities will give you information regarding your learners, for example any specific assessment requirements they may have or any further training and support they may need. This process might not always be carried out by you, but the information obtained must be passed onto you. Initial assessment is known as assessment *for* learning, as it helps prepare learners *for* assessment and identifies their potential.

- **Assessment planning** – agreeing suitable types and methods of assessment with learners, setting appropriate target dates, involving others as necessary (such as colleagues or supervisors) and following relevant organisational guidelines.

- **Assessment activity** – using relevant methods, approaches and activities, for example observation, questioning, assignments, or gathering appropriate evidence of competence. Assessment can be formative (usually ongoing and informal to check progress, for example a discussion) and/or summative (usually at the end and formal, for example a test). Summative assessment is often known as assessment *of* learning as it counts towards the achievement *of* something.

- **Assessment decision and feedback** – making a judgement of success or otherwise, giving constructive feedback and agreeing any further action that may be necessary. Records of what was assessed and the decisions made should always be maintained.

- **Review of progress** – reviewing progress and achievement, discussing any other issues that may be relevant to the learning and assessment process.

Records should be maintained throughout all aspects of the assessment cycle and quality assurance activities should take place on an ongoing basis. The cycle will then begin again with an initial assessment regarding the next subject, topic or unit of the qualification the learner is working towards.

The need for assessment

Assessment can be separated into the needs of the learner, yourself as the assessor, your organisation and the AO (if applicable).

Table 1.1 Examples of the need for assessment

Learner – to:	Assessor – to:
<ul><li>clarify what is expected of them</li><li>enable discussions with assessors</li><li>evaluate their own progress</li><li>have something to show for their achievements, for example a certificate</li><li>plan and achieve their aim</li><li>know how well they are progressing</li><li>know they are achieving the correct standard or level</li><li>know what they have to do to improve and progress further</li><li>learn from their mistakes</li></ul>	<ul><li>adapt teaching, learning and assessment activities</li><li>ascertain learners' progress and achievement so far</li><li>carry out all aspects of the assessment cycle and keep records</li><li>develop learners' self-assessment skills</li><li>diagnose any learner needs or particular learning requirements</li><li>empower learners to take control of their learning</li><li>follow the requirements of the AO or programme</li><li>improve motivation and self-esteem</li><li>make decisions and give feedback</li><li>prepare learners for further assessments</li><li>prove they can assess effectively</li><li>standardise judgements and practice with others</li></ul>
Organisation – to:	**Awarding organisation – to:**
<ul><li>achieve funding (if applicable)</li><li>analyse enrolment, retention, success and achievement rates</li><li>ensure adequate resources are available</li><li>ensure consistency of assessors' practice</li><li>ensure there is an effective IQA system</li><li>give references for learners if requested</li><li>identify gaps in learning</li><li>justify delivery of programmes</li><li>maintain records</li><li>promote a learner-centred approach</li><li>satisfy external requirements</li></ul>	<ul><li>accredit achievements</li><li>ensure compliance with regulations and qualification requirements</li><li>ensure staff follow the assessment strategy</li><li>sample assessment and IQA activities</li><li>give guidance to assessors and IQAs</li><li>issue certificates</li><li>formulate qualifications from recognised National Occupational Standards (NOS)</li><li>provide written reports regarding quality and compliance</li></ul>

Roles and responsibilities of an assessor

Your main role will be to plan and carry out assessments according to the requirements of the qualification, or of a programme or job specification. You might also need to teach or train your learners if required. You should choose appropriate assessment methods, make decisions and give feedback to your learners.

You should have a job description; however, if you don't have one, following the requirements of the assessor units will ensure you are performing your role adequately (see Appendices 1, 2 and 3). Your roles and responsibilities might include far more than those stated in the assessment cycle.

For example, your role may involve:

- attending meetings, exhibitions, award ceremonies and presentation events

- checking the authenticity of any witness statements

- completing and maintaining safe and secure records

- countersigning other assessors' judgements (if they are not yet qualified and you are)

- following organisational and regulatory authorities' procedures

- giving constructive, supportive and developmental feedback to your learners regarding progress and achievement

- identifying and dealing with any barriers to fair assessment

- implementing internal and external quality assurance action points

- liaising with others involved in the assessment process

- making judgements based on the assessment requirements

- maintaining your own occupational competence and professional development

- negotiating and agreeing assessment plans with learners

- making best use of different assessment types and methods

- providing statistics to managers and others

- reflecting upon your practice to ensure you are meeting all relevant requirements

- responding to any appeals made against your assessment decisions

- reviewing learner progress

- standardising practice with other assessors

- supporting learners with special assessment requirements and dealing with sensitive issues in a supportive manner

- teaching or training learners

- working towards relevant assessment qualifications.

If you are unsure of any aspect of your assessor role, make sure you ask a colleague or your manager. You may be the only assessor for your particular subject within your organisation; therefore it is important that you liaise with your manager or IQA to ensure you are interpreting the requirements correctly. If you are a member of a team of assessors, you will need to ensure you all work together to give your learners equal and fair access to assessment opportunities. If there are several assessors for the same subject, there will be a co-ordinating or lead assessor who will manage the team and give support and advice regarding the assessment process.

Your role will require you to use various assessment activities, which can take place in different environments depending upon what is being assessed and why.

Example

- *Classroom or training room – practical and theoretical tasks, tests, discussions, role plays, projects, presentations.*

- *Lecture theatre or hall – exams, multiple-choice and written questions and answers.*

- *Library or home – assignments, research and reading.*

- *Outside environment – practical activities.*

- *Work environment – observations, questions and reviewing products and evidence produced by learners.*

- *Workshop – practical tests and simulations.*

Wherever you are assessing you will need to ensure both you and your learners are suitably prepared, and that you follow the assessment requirements and relevant organisational and regulatory guidelines. If you have not been told what these are, you will need to ask someone you work with.

Your role as an assessor will also be to inspire and motivate your learners. If you are enthusiastic and passionate about your subject, this will help to encourage, motivate and further challenge your learners. Your learners may already be motivated for personal reasons and be enthusiastic and *want* to perform well. This is known as *intrinsic* motivation. They may be motivated by a *need* to learn, for example to gain a qualification, promotion or pay rise at work. This is known as *extrinsic* motivation. If you can recognise the difference between a learner's wants and needs, you can appreciate why they are motivated and ensure you make their experience meaningful and relevant. Whatever type of motivation your learners have will be transformed, for better or worse, by what happens during their assessment experience with you.

There will be certain records and documents that you will need to maintain. These will include assessment plans, feedback records, reviews of progress and overall tracking sheets. Records must be maintained to satisfy organisational and regulatory requirements. You should also safely store confidential documents and audio/digital/video recordings that include images of learners. Record keeping will be explained in detail in Chapter 2.

Activity

What do you consider your roles and responsibilities to be as an assessor? Make a list and place them in order of importance.

Boundaries

There are two aspects to boundaries: those between your assessing role and other professional roles, and other factors you are *bound by* which might hinder or challenge your role.

- Professional boundaries are those within which you need to work and it is important not to overstep these, for example by becoming too personal or friendly with your learners. Boundaries are about knowing where your role as an assessor stops. You should be able to work within the limits of that role, but know that it is okay to ask for help. Don't try to take on too much, or carry out something which is part of someone else's role.

- Other boundaries include the things you are bound by, for example policies and procedures, the amount of administrative work you are expected to complete, or a lack of funding or resources. These boundaries can often be interpreted as the negative aspects of your roles and responsibilities.

You might have other professional roles besides assessing, for example you might interview learners and have to decide whether they can attend a programme or not. You might have difficult decisions to make; however, you should always be able to get the support of other staff at your organisation. If you make a decision not to accept a learner, you will need to justify your reasons. Never feel you are on your own; find out who can give help and advice when you need support. You should find out and follow your organisation's policies and procedures. If you are a new assessor, you might have been allocated a *mentor* and/or someone to countersign your decisions. They should support you as necessary and you will find it helpful to keep in touch with them and ask for advice.

When you are with learners, you need to remain in control, be fair and ethical with your practice, and not demonstrate any favouritism towards particular learners, for example by giving one more support than another. You might feel it sensible to make a telephone call to a learner who has been absent but making regular calls would be inappropriate. Giving your personal telephone number to learners could be seen as encouraging informal contact, and you may get calls or texts which are not suitable or relevant. You might not want to take your break with your learners or join their social networking sites as you could become more of a friend than an assessor. It is unprofessional to use bad language, to touch learners in an inappropriate way and to let your personal problems affect your work. Always remain professional and objective.

Policies and procedures
You will need to follow your organisation's policies and procedures, which should include:

- access and fair assessment

- appeals and complaints

- confidentiality of information

- copyright and data protection

- equality and diversity

- health, safety and welfare (including safeguarding)

- plagiarism and authenticity

- quality assurance.

There may be other requirements such as a dress code, acceptable use of computer equipment, a behaviour code and regulations such as the Control of Substances Hazardous to Health (COSHH) that you will need to follow.

Activity

Identify and list the policies, procedures and regulations which will relate to your role as an assessor for your particular subject. Which are the most important and why?

Equality and diversity

All learners should have equality of opportunity throughout the assessment process, providing they are taking a programme they are capable of achieving. There is no point setting learners up to fail, just because you need a certain number of learners for your programme to go ahead, perhaps due to targets or funding. When designing and using assessment activities, you need to ensure you meet the needs of all your learners and reflect the diverse nature of your group. Never let your own attitudes, values and beliefs interfere with the assessment process. You could design activities which will challenge more able learners and/or promote the motivation of learners who are not progressing so well. You need to differentiate your activities to ensure you are meeting the needs of all your learners, for example using less challenging activities for those who are struggling. However, you will need to check what you can adapt to ensure you are not changing the assessment criteria.

The National Occupational Standards for Learning and Development (2010) give the following definitions of equality and diversity:

Equality – A state of fair treatment that is the right of all people regardless of difference in, for example, culture, ability, gender, race, religion, wealth, sexual orientation, or any other group characteristic.

Diversity – Acknowledging that each individual is unique, and recognising our individual differ- ences in, for example, culture, ability, gender, race, religion, wealth, sexual orientation, or any other group characteristic.

(LLUK, 2010, p35)

Your organisation should have an equality and diversity or equal opportunities policy with which you should become familiar. You might have a learner who achieves tasks quickly; hav- ing more in-depth and challenging activities available would be beneficial to them. If you have learners who are not achieving the required assessment tasks, you could design an activity that you know they will achieve to raise their motivation and encourage them to progress further. However, don't oversimplify activities as this will leave learners thinking they were too easy. You could always give your learners a choice of, for instance, a straightforward, a challenging or a very challenging activity. Their choice may depend upon their confidence level and you will have to devise such activities beforehand if they are not provided for you. If you have different levels of learners within the same group, this can work quite well as they will usually want to attempt something they know they can achieve. However, it can also have the opposite effect in that learners feel they are more capable than they actually are. These types of activities are more suited for formative assessment which checks progress. You might need to arrange assessments in other languages, for example Welsh, or use a bilingual approach.

Assessment activities should always reflect the diverse nature of your learner group, for example culture, language and ethnicity. They should not be biased according to the person producing them, as this could mean aspects such as terminology or jargon might not be those of the learners but those of the producer, placing the learner at a disadvantage. You also need to be careful not to discriminate against a learner in any way.

The Equality Act (2010) replaced all previous anti-discrimination legislation and consoli- dated it into one Act (for England, Scotland and Wales). It provides rights for people not to be discriminated against or harassed, for example because they have an association with a disabled person or are wrongly perceived as disabled. In this example, reasonable adjust- ments must take place during assessment activities to lessen or remove the effects of a disadvantage to a learner with a disability.

The Act contains nine *protected characteristics*:

- age
- disability
- gender reassignment
- marriage and civil partnership
- pregnancy and maternity
- race
- religion or belief
- sex
- sexual orientation.

There are seven different *types of discrimination*:

1. associative discrimination: direct discrimination against someone because they are associated with another person with a protected characteristic

2. direct discrimination: discrimination because of a protected characteristic

3. indirect discrimination: when a rule or policy which applies to everyone can disadvantage a person with a protected characteristic

4. discrimination by perception: direct discrimination against someone because others think they have a protected characteristic

5. harassment: behaviour deemed offensive by the recipient

6. harassment by a third party: the harassment of staff or others by people not directly employed by an organisation, such as an external consultant or visitor

7. victimisation: discrimination against someone because they made or supported a complaint under equality legislation.

It is important to take the protected characteristics into account when planning and carrying out assessment activities, and to ensure discrimination does not take place by anyone involved in the assessment process. Try to focus on the positive and always ask what your learner *can do*, not what they *cannot do*.

Further details regarding equality and diversity can be found in the companion book *Equality and Diversity in the Lifelong Learning Sector* (Gravells and Simpson, 2012).

Safeguarding

Safeguarding is a term used to refer to the duties and responsibilities that those providing a health, social or education service have to perform to protect individuals and vulnerable people from harm. Following the publication of the Safeguarding Vulnerable Groups Act in 2006, a vetting and barring scheme was established in autumn 2008. This Act created an Independent Barring Board to take all discretionary decisions on whether individuals should be barred from working with children and/or vulnerable adults. As an assessor, you will be bound by this Act if you work with children (those under the age of 18 years in training) and/or vulnerable adults. You might need to attend safeguarding training every three years (every two years for some staff depending upon their safeguarding involvement). You might be required to have a criminal record check via the Disclosure and Barring Service (DBS) before you can work as an assessor.

A vulnerable adult is defined as *a person aged 18 years or over, who is in receipt of or may be in need of community care services by reason of 'mental or other disability, age or illness and who is or may be unable to take care of him or herself, or unable to protect him or herself against significant harm or exploitation'* (Bonnerjea, 2009, p9).

This could be anyone needing formal help to live in society, for example a young mother, someone with a learning disability or a recently released prisoner. If your organisation is inspected by Ofsted, your learners will be asked how safe they feel and whether they are able to give you feedback regarding any concerns they may have.

You have a duty of care and a personal responsibility towards all your learners and should apply six key elements of appropriate service provision:

- respect
- dignity
- independence
- individuality
- choice
- confidentiality.

There are four key processes that should be followed to ensure your learners are safe:

1. an assessment of their needs;
2. planning services to meet these needs;
3. intervention if necessary when you have a concern;
4. reviewing the services offered.

If you have any concerns regarding a learner, for example if you feel they are being bullied or may be at risk of harm or abuse, you must refer to your Designated Safeguarding Officer (DSO) immediately. It would be useful to find out who this person is if you don't already know. Never be tempted to get personally involved with your learner's situation.

Activity

How will aspects of equality and diversity, and safeguarding impact upon your role as an assessor?

Health and safety

Your role as an assessor will require you to follow various regulations, for example the Health and Safety at Work etc Act (1974). This places a legal responsibility upon you, as well as upon your organisation and your learners. If you see a potential hazard, it is your responsibility to do something about it before an accident occurs, even if this is just reporting it to the relevant person within your organisation. The health and safety of yourself, your colleagues and your learners is of paramount importance.

You might have to carry out a risk assessment to ensure the area and assessment activities are safe for all concerned. It can normally be achieved by a walk-through of the area and a discussion with those involved. However, a formal record must be kept in case of any incidents. You probably unconsciously carry out a risk assessment whenever you do anything, for example when crossing the road, you would automatically check the traffic flow before stepping out.

Have a look at the units in Appendices 1, 2 and 3. Look at the learning outcomes and assessment criteria to see what an assessor should know and do. Compare these to your job description or contract of employment. Appendix 1 relates to knowledge, Appendices 2 and 3 to performance. If you are working towards one or more of these units, use the assessment criteria as a checklist and note down what you currently know or can do to meet them.

Key concepts and principles of assessment

Key concepts of assessment relate to ideas, whereas principles are how the ideas are put into practice. For the purpose of this chapter, they have been separated for clarity; however, some concepts could also be classed as principles depending upon your interpretation.

Key concepts

Think of concepts as the aspects involved throughout the assessment process.

They include the following (which are then explained in detail):

- accountability
- achievement
- assessment strategies
- benchmarking
- evaluation
- internally or externally devised assessment methods (formal and informal)
- progression
- transparency
- types of assessment, for example initial (at the beginning), formative (ongoing) or summative (at the end).

Accountability

You need to be *accountable* to your learners and your organisation to ensure you are carrying out your role as an assessor correctly. Your learners should know why they are being assessed and what they have to do to meet the assessment criteria. You should not be assessing your learners unless they are ready to be assessed. You will also be accountable to the AO if you assess their accredited qualifications. You might be accountable to employers if you are assessing their staff in the work environment.

Achievement

You may be required to analyse *achievement* data and compare this to national or organisational targets. The funding your organisation receives might also be related to your learners' achievements. It is always a useful evaluation method to keep a record of how many learners you start with, how many successfully achieve and in what timescale.

Assessment strategies

Following the *assessment strategy* for your subject will ensure you are carrying out your role correctly and hold, or are working towards, the required assessor qualifications if applicable.

Benchmarking

Benchmarking involves comparing what is the accepted standard for a particular subject area against the current position of your own learners' performance. Using benchmarking data can help inform target setting for individuals or groups. If learners don't achieve the benchmark, an evaluation will need to take place and improvements will need to be implemented. Benchmarking can also be used to compare organisations that provide a similar service, or to compare performance in different locations within the same organisation.

Evaluation

Evaluation of the assessment process should always take place to inform current and future practice. All aspects of the assessment cycle should be evaluated on an ongoing basis and feedback obtained from all involved.

Internally or externally devised assessment methods

Internally devised assessments might be produced by you or other staff at your organisation, such as assignments, projects or questions which will also be marked internally. These should always be appropriate, relevant and at the right level for your learners. *Externally devised assessments* are usually produced by an AO, for example an examination. *Formal* assessments usually count towards achievement of a qualification, whereas *informal* assessments are used to monitor ongoing progress and development.

Progression

Progression should be taken into account when assessing learners, i.e. what they are going to do next. It could be another unit of the current qualification or a different aspect of a job description, either at your organisation, in the work environment or elsewhere. Progression opportunities should always be discussed with your learner to ensure they are on the right route and that they are capable of achieving.

Transparency

To assist *transparency*, you need to ensure that everyone who is involved in the assessment process clearly understands what is expected and can see there is nothing untoward taking place. That includes your own interpretation and understanding of the assessment requirements as well as each learner's understanding. You should be honest with your learners and not let them feel they have achieved more than they have. Transparency is also about having nothing to hide and being open to scrutiny, i.e. keeping auditable records which must be maintained throughout the assessment process.

Types of assessment

Types of assessment include initial, formative and summative as well as diagnostic tests which ascertain a learner's current skills, knowledge, understanding and experience. Some types of diagnostic tests can also identify learners with dyslexia, dyspraxia, dysgraphia, dyscalculia and other needs. Initial assessment is carried out prior to, or at the beginning of, a programme to identify your learner's starting point, potential and level. Formative assessment is ongoing, and summative assessment is at the end. Types of assessment will be explained in more detail later in this chapter.

Key principles

Think of principles as *how* the concepts are put into practice.

One important principle is known by the acronym VACSR; you will need to ensure all assessed work is:

- **V**alid – the work is relevant to what is being assessed and is at the right level

- **A**uthentic – the work has been produced solely by the learner

- **C**urrent – the work is still relevant at the time of assessment

- **S**ufficient – the work covers all the requirements at the time

- **R**eliable – the work is consistent across all learners, over time.

If the above are not ensured, you might make an incorrect judgement and a learner might appeal against your decision. Conversely, you might not notice a learner has plagiarised someone else's work or done something incorrectly.

Other key principles of assessment include:

- communication – communicating regularly with learners, other assessors, IQAs, employers and others who are involved

- continuing professional development (CPD) – maintaining the currency of skills, knowledge and understanding to ensure your assessment practice and subject knowledge are up to date

- equality and diversity – ensuring all assessment activities embrace equality, inclusivity and diversity and represent all aspects of society

- ethics – ensuring the assessment process is honest and moral, and takes into account confidentiality and integrity

- fairness – ensuring assessment activities are fit for purpose, and planning, decisions and feedback are justifiable; all learners should have an equal chance of an accurate assessment decision

- health and safety – ensuring these are taken into account throughout the full assessment process, carrying out risk assessments as necessary

- motivation – encouraging and supporting your learners to reach their maximum potential at an appropriate level

- quality assurance – ensuring assessment activities and decisions meet the required standards

- record keeping – ensuring accurate records are maintained throughout the teaching, learning and assessment process

- responsibility – making objective decisions, following all organisational guidelines, keeping records and producing reports as required

- SMART – ensuring all assessment activities are specific, measurable, achievable, relevant and time bound (see Chapter 2 for further details)

- standardisation – ensuring the assessment requirements are interpreted accurately and that all assessors are making comparable and consistent decisions.

Quality assurance should be carried out throughout the assessment process. The purpose is to ensure assessors are performing accurately and fairly. IQA is carried out by a member of staff in the same subject area as the assessors. However, an IQA cannot quality assure their own assessment decisions. External quality assurance (EQA) is carried out by a member of staff from the AO with whom the learners are registered (see Chapters 4 and 5 for details of the IQA process and Chapters 6 and 7 for details of the EQA process).

Following the key concepts and principles of assessment will ensure you are performing your role as an assessor according to all relevant regulations and requirements.

Extension Activity

Look at the bulleted lists of key concepts and key principles of assessment on pages 24 and 26 and describe how each will impact upon your role as an assessor. You may need to research some aspects further or speak to relevant staff at your organisation.

Minimising risks

When planning to assess your learners you need to be aware of potential risks. This applies not only to those regarding the health, safety and welfare of all concerned, but also to the types of risks that may be involved in your own area of responsibility for your particular subject. Just ask yourself what could possibly go wrong, and if you think of something, then there is a risk to the assessment process.

You need to minimise risks such as putting unnecessary stress upon learners, over-assessing, under-assessing or being unfair and expecting too much too soon. Some learners might not be ready to be observed for a practical skill, or feel so pressured by target dates for a theory task that they resort to colluding or plagiarising work from others or the internet. If learners are under pressure, or have any issues or concerns that have not been addressed, they might decide to leave.

Being aware of any risks to the assessment process, and taking opportunities to discuss any issues your learners might have should help alleviate any concerns. Other risks could include giving a learner more of an advantage over another learner, or using inappropriate assessment activities.

There are also risks on your part as an assessor, for example pressure to pass learners quickly due to funding and targets, or favouritism and bias towards some learners over others. Another risk could be if you carry out assessments in the work environment and visit places with which you are not familiar. You might need to travel early or late in the dark, find locations on foot, take public transport or drive to areas you are not familiar with. If you are visiting places on your own, you will be classed as a lone worker and your organisation should have a policy for your protection. If you feel uncomfortable or unsafe at any time, you should get in touch with your supervisor. Having a mobile phone is helpful in such situations. If you don't have one, note where the nearest public phone is should you need it. You may find it useful to search the internet for the postcode you are visiting. This will give you a street map and pictures of the local area to enable you to visualise where you are going beforehand.

If you are assessing in the work environment, you might come across employers who are not supportive of their staff and may put barriers in their way. For example, someone might make it difficult for you to visit at a certain time to carry out a formal assessment. Careful planning and communication with everyone concerned will be necessary.

It could be that if you have close friends or relatives whom you are required to assess, you might not be allowed to, or if you do, your decisions would need to be countersigned by another impartial assessor and go through the IQA process. If the qualification is accredited, the AO will give you guidance on this.

If you have any concerns regarding risks to yourself, your learners or your assessment decisions, you must discuss these with your supervisor or manager.

Extension Activity

What risks do you feel you will encounter as an assessor and how will you overcome them? Have you ever been placed in a risky situation? If so, what would you do differently next time?

Types of assessment

Different subjects will require different types of assessment, which can be carried out formally or informally depending upon the requirements. Assessment types are different from assessment methods. A method is how the assessment type will be used and can be formal or informal. Formal assessments are to confirm achievement and are usually planned and carried out according to the assessment requirements or criteria. Informal assessments can occur at any time to check ongoing progress.

Table 1.2 Formal and informal assessment methods (note: some can occur in both depending upon the situation)

Formal	Informal
• assignments • case studies • essays • examinations • multiple-choice questions • observations • professional discussions and questions • projects • tests • witness statements	• crosswords • discussions • gapped handouts (sentences with missing words) • journals/diaries • peer and self-assessment • puzzles and crosswords • practical activities • questions: oral, written, multiple choice • quizzes • role plays • worksheets

You may be familiar with some types of assessment such as initial (at the beginning), formative (ongoing) and summative (at the end). Initial assessment helps you ascertain information before your learner commences the programme. Formative assessment can happen at any time during the programme and is usually informal as you can devise your own activities to check progress. Summative assessment is to confirm achievement and is usually formal. You must follow the requirements of the AO if the programme is accredited by them.

You will probably use different methods depending upon whether you are assessing knowledge or performance. Knowledge is usually assessed by assignments, essays and tests. Performance is usually assessed by observation, questions and discussions. However, these will vary depending upon the subject you are assessing and where you are assessing. Formal assessment activities are usually provided by the AO (if you are assessing an accredited qualification). You will be able to devise your own informal methods to check ongoing progress.

All assessment types and methods should be suitable to the level of your learners. A level 1 learner might struggle to maintain a journal of their progress and a level 2 learner may not be mature enough to accept peer feedback. A level 3 learner may feel a puzzle is too easy and so on (see Introduction for details of levels). Some learners may respond better to informal than formal assessment. You need to consider the assessment requirements for your subject and how you can best implement these without changing the assessment criteria.

Example

Maria sees her group of learners once a week for an Art and Design programme. Each week, she commences the session by asking some questions regarding the topics covered in the previous week. This is formative assessment to ensure her learners have understood the topics taught. Towards the end of term, she will issue a summative assessment in the form of an assignment, which will formally test their skills, knowledge and understanding.

You might have all the details of assessment types and methods provided for you. If not, you will need to carefully select these to suit your subject, the situation and your learners. You might decide to assess your learners on a formative basis throughout their time with you to check progress and use a summative test at the end to confirm achievement. This would enable you to see how they are progressing and whether or not they will be ready for the formal test. You might be provided with tests or assignments for your learners to complete at set times during the programme. To be sure your learners are ready you could use activities, quizzes and smaller tasks for them to carry out beforehand. This would make the assessment process more interesting and highlight any areas that need further development. If you are assessing a programme whereby the activities are provided for you, for example tests or exams, there is often the tendency to teach purely what is required to achieve a pass. Learners may therefore not gain valuable additional skills and knowledge. Teaching to pass tests does not maximise your learners' ability and potential.

Table 1.3 briefly explains assessment types and the terminology of assessment. The types you use will be based on whether you assess occupational competence in the work environment or vocational skills, knowledge and understanding.

Extension Activity

Refer to Table 1.3 and choose four types of assessment that you might use with your learners. How will you use them for your particular subject?

Table 1.3 Assessment types and terminology

Assessment type/ terminology	Description
Academic	Assessment of theory or knowledge.
Adaptive	Questions are selected during the test on the basis of their difficulty, in response to an estimate of the learner's ability.
Analytic scoring	A method of scoring grades for tests such as speaking and writing, for example a writing test would have an analytic score based on grammar and vocabulary.
Aptitude	A diagnostic test to assess a learner's ability for a particular job or vocation.
Assessor led	Assessment is planned and carried out by the assessor, for example an observation.
Benchmarking	A way of evaluating learner performance against an accepted standard. Once a standard is set, it can be used as a basis for the expectation of achievements with other groups/learners.
Blended	Using more than one assessment method in different locations, for example observation in the work environment backed up with online assessments.
Competence based	Criteria that learners need to perform in the work environment.
Criterion referencing	Assessing prescribed aspects a learner must achieve to meet a certain standard.

Assessment type/ terminology	Description
Diagnostic	A specific assessment relating to a particular topic or subject and level, which builds on initial assessment. Sometimes called a skills test. The results determine what needs to be learnt or assessed in order to progress further. Some types of diagnostic assessments can also identify learners with dyslexia, dyspraxia, dysgraphia, dyscalculia, etc.
Differentiation	Organising teaching, learning and assessment to suit learners' abilities and needs.
Direct	Evidence provided by a learner towards their qualification, for example products from their work environment.
Evidence	Assessment based upon items a learner provides to prove their knowledge and competence.
External	Assessments set and marked externally by an AO.
Formal	Assessment that involves the recognition and recording of achievement, often leading to certification of an accredited qualification.
Formative	Ongoing, interim or continuous assessment. Can be used to assess skills and/ or knowledge in a progressive way, to build on topics learnt and plan future learning and assessments. Often referred to as assessment for learning, allowing additional learning to take place prior to further assessments.
Holistic	Assessing several aspects of a qualification, programme or job specification at the same time.
Independent	An aspect of the qualification is assessed by someone who has not been involved with the learner for any other part of their learning or assessment.
Indirect	Evidence provided by others regarding a learner's progress, for example a witness statement from their supervisor.
Informal	Assessment that is in addition to formal assessment, for example questioning during a review of progress with a learner or an observation during a group activity.
Initial	Assessment at the beginning of a programme or unit, relating to the subject being learnt and assessed, to identify a learner's starting point and level. Initial assessment can also include learning preferences tests as well as English, maths, and information and communication technology (ICT) tests. The latter can be used as a basis to help and support learners.
Integrated	Information acquired in a learning context is put into practice and assessed in the learner's work environment.
Internal	Assessments carried out within an organisation that are either internally set and marked or externally set by the relevant AO and internally marked.
Ipsative	A process of self-assessment to recognise development. Learners match their own achievements against a set of standards or their own previous achievements. This is useful for learners to consider their progress and development. However, they do need to work autonomously and be honest with themselves.
Learner led	Learners produce evidence and let their assessor know when they are ready to be assessed.
Norm referencing	Comparing the results of learner achievements to one another, for example setting a pass mark to enable a certain percentage of a group to achieve or not.

(Continued)

Table 1.3 (Continued)

Assessment type/ terminology	Description
Objective	An assessment decision that is based around the criteria being assessed, not a personal opinion or decision.
Predictive	An indication of how well a test predicts future performance in a relevant skill.
Process	The assessment of routine skills or techniques, for example to ensure a learner is following a set process or procedure.
Process (as in teaching)	Teaching more than is required for the learner to achieve, for example teaching keyboard skills to a learner who is taking a word-processing qualification (i.e. it is not in the syllabus but it is helpful).
Product	The outcome is assessed, not the process of making it, for example a painting or a working model.
Product (as in teaching)	Only teaching the minimum amount required to pass an assessment.
Proficiency	An assessment to test ability or skills without reference to any specific programme of learning, for example riding a bicycle.
Profiling	A way of recording learner achievements for each individual aspect of an assessment. Checklists can be a useful way to evidence these. More than one assessor can be involved in the process.
Psychometric	A test of psychological qualities, for example intelligence and personality.
Qualitative	Assessment based upon individual responses to open questions given to learners. Clear criteria must be stated for the assessor to make a decision as questions can be vague or misinterpreted.
Quantitative	Assessment based upon yes/no or true/false responses, agree/disagree statements or multiple-choice tests, giving a clear right or wrong answer. Totals can be added to give results, for example 8 out of 10. Learners could pass purely by guessing the correct answers.
Screening	A process to determine if a learner has a particular need, for example in English or maths.
Subjective	A personal decision by the assessor, where the assessment criteria might not be clearly stated. This can be unfair to a learner.
Summative	Assessment at the end of a programme or unit, for example an exam. If a learner does not pass, they will usually have the opportunity to retake. Often known as assessment of learning, as it shows what has been achieved from the learning process.
Triangulation	Using more than one assessment method, for example observation, oral questioning and a test. This helps ensure the reliability and authenticity of a learner's work and makes the assessment process more interesting.
Vocational	Job-related practical assessment, usually in a learner's work environment.

Methods of assessment

Assessment can only take place once learning has occurred, but how do you know that learning has occurred? You might be able to answer this by saying, 'I'll ask questions', or 'I'll see my learner performing a task'. That is fine, if you know what questions to ask and how your learner should respond, or what you expect to see when your learner performs. If you don't know this, you will need to plan and use suitable methods to assess your learners when you know they are ready.

To effectively plan how you will assess your learners, besides adhering to the principle of VACSR, you will need to use methods which are ethical, fair and safe.

- Ethical: the methods used take into account confidentiality, integrity, safety, security and learner welfare.

- Fair: the methods used are appropriate to all learners at the required level, taking into account any particular needs. All learners should have an equal chance of an accurate assessment decision.

- Safe: there is little chance of plagiarism, the work can be confirmed as valid and authentic, confidentiality is taken into account, learning and assessment are not compromised in any way, nor the learner's experience or potential to achieve. (Safe in this context does not relate to health and safety but to whether the assessment methods are sufficiently robust to make a reliable decision.)

Example

If you give learners the information to answer questions, this is unethical. If you allow your learners to copy text from the internet to answer questions without quoting their source, it will be deemed unsafe. If you give some learners more help than others, this is unfair. If you set a test which does not accurately reflect the assessment criteria, it is invalid. If you devise a set of questions and use them with different groups of learners, they may discuss them among themselves, therefore rendering their responses unreliable.

There are several different assessment methods you could use, for example observations, questioning, tests and exams. If assessment activities are not provided for you, you will need to devise your own. Always take into account a learner's needs, the level of achievement they are aiming for and the subject requirements before planning to use any assessment activities. The methods you choose will depend upon what you will assess, where and how. If you are assessing units that are on the Qualifications and Credit Framework (QCF) these are known as *knowledge* units (to assess understanding) and *performance* units (to assess skills) (see Introduction for details regarding the QCF).

Assessment should never be just for the sake of assessing. There should always be a reason for any assessment activity you carry out, the main one being to find out if learning has taken place and whether the learner is ready to progress further.

Never be afraid to try something different, particularly with formative assessments that you can design yourself. You could use puzzles, quizzes or crosswords as a fun and active way of informally assessing progress. Try searching the internet for free software to help you create these; a few sites are listed at the end of the chapter.

Table 1.4 starting on page 37 lists the assessment methods, approaches and activities you could use, along with a brief description, and their strengths and limitations. When using any activity, you need to ensure it is inclusive, and to differentiate for individual needs, learner difficulties and/or disabilities. Always follow health and safety guidelines and carry out any relevant risk assessments where applicable. Make sure your learners are aware of the reason why they are being assessed, and don't overcomplicate your activities.

Extension Activity

Think about the learners you have at present or those whom you will be assessing in the future. How do you know that learning has taken place? Look at Table 1.4 starting on page 37, decide which methods you could use for formative and summative purposes, and state the strengths and limitations of their use for your subject.

Summary

In this chapter you have learnt about:

- the role of assessment
- key concepts and principles of assessment
- minimising risks
- types of assessment
- methods of assessment.

Evidence

Evidence from the completed activities within this chapter, plus the following, could be used towards the *Principles and practices of assessment* unit, for example:

- written statements cross-referenced to the unit's assessment criteria
- answers to questions/assignments issued by your assessor
- records of discussions with your assessor.

Cross-referencing grid

This chapter contributes towards the following assessment criteria, along with aspects of the National Occupational Standards for Learning and Development. Full details of the learning outcomes and assessment criteria for each unit can be found in the Appendices.

Unit	Assessment criteria
Understanding the principles and practices of assessment	1.1, 1.2, 1.3, 1.4 2.1 3.4, 3.5 4.1, 4.4 5.1, 5.2 6.1, 6.2 7.1 8.1, 8.3
Assess occupational competence in the work environment	1.1 2.1 4.1, 4.2
Assess vocational skills, knowledge and understanding	1.1 4.1, 4.2
National Occupational Standards	**Reference**
9 – Assess learner achievement	KU1, KU3, KU7, KU8, KU9, KU10 9.3, 9.4
11 – Internally monitor and maintain the quality of assessment	KU2, JU3, KU4, KU10, KU12 11.3, 11.5
12 – Externally monitor and maintain the quality of assessment	KU1, KU3, KU12

Theory focus

References and further information

Bonnerjea, L (2009) *Safeguarding Adults: Report on the Consultation on the Review of 'No Secrets'*. London: Department of Health.

Department for Education and Skills (DfES) (2006) *Safeguarding Children and Safer Recruitment in Education*. London: DfES.

Ecclestone, K (2005) *Understanding Assessment and Qualifications in Post-Compulsory Education and Training* (2nd edition). Ashford: NIACE.

Gardner, J (2006) *Assessment and Learning*. London: SAGE Publications.

Gravells, A and Simpson, S (2012) *Equality and Diversity in the Lifelong Learning Sector* (2nd edition). London: Learning Matters SAGE.

LLUK (2010) *The National Occupational Standards for Learning and Development*. London: Lifelong Learning UK.

Read, H (2011) *The Best Assessor's Guide*. Bideford: Read On Publications Ltd.

Tummons, J (2011) *Assessing Learning in the Lifelong Learning Sector* (3rd edition). London: Learning Matters SAGE.

Websites

Chartered Institute for Educational Assessors: www.ciea.org.uk

COSHH: www.hse.gov.uk/coshh

Disability and the Equality Act: http://tinyurl.com/2vzd5j

Disclosure and Barring Service: www.gov.uk/government/organisations/disclosure-and-barring-service/about

Equality and Human Rights Commission: www.equalityhumanrights.com

Health and Safety Executive: www.hse.gov.uk

Health and Safety resources: www.hse.gov.uk/services/education/information.htm

Initial assessment tools: www.excellencegateway.org.uk/toolslibrary

Office safety and risk assessments: www.officesafety.co.uk

Ofsted: www.ofsted.gov.uk

Puzzle software: www.about.com

www.crossword-compiler.com

www.educational-software-directory.net/game/puzzle

http://hotpot.uvic.ca

www.mathsnet.net

Table 1.4 Assessment methods, approaches and activities: strengths and limitations

Method/approach/activity	Description	Strengths	Limitations
Activities – group or individual	Different tasks carried out by learners to demonstrate their skills, knowledge, understanding and/or attitudes	Can be individual, paired or group tasks Ideal as a formative assessment approach to establish progress at a given point during a session, or as a summative approach for workplace tasks	If paired or grouped, assessor must establish achievement of individuals Can be time consuming for the assessor to devise
Assignments	Can be practical or theoretical tasks which can assess various aspects of a subject or qualification over a period of time	Consolidates learning Several aspects of a qualification can be assessed Some assignments are set by the awarding organisation who will give clear marking criteria Learners might be able to add to their work if they don't meet all the requirements first time	Everything must have been taught beforehand or be known by the learner Questions can be misinterpreted Can be time consuming for learners to complete Must be individually assessed and written feedback given Assessor might be biased when marking
Blended assessments	Using more than one method of assessment, usually including technology	Several methods of assessment can be combined, enabling all learning preferences to be reached	Not all learners may have access to the technology
Buzz groups	Short topics to be discussed in small groups	Allows learner interaction and focuses ideas Checks understanding Does not require formal feedback	Learners may digress Specific points could be lost Checking individual learning may be difficult

(Continued)

Table 1.4 (Continued)

Method/ approach/ activity	Description	Strengths	Limitations
Case studies/ Scenarios	Can be a hypothetical situation, a description of an actual event or an incomplete event, enabling learners to explore the situation	Can make topics more realistic, enhancing motivation and interest Can be carried out individually or in a group situation Builds on current knowledge and experience	If carried out as a group activity, roles should be defined and individual contributions assessed Time should be allowed for a debrief Must have clear outcomes Can be time consuming to prepare and assess
Checklists	A list of criteria which must be met to confirm competence or achievement	Can form part of an ongoing record of achievement or job profile Assessment can take place when a learner is ready Ensures all criteria are documented	Learners may lose their copy and not remember what they have achieved
Controlled assessment	An activity or test which occurs in a number of stages with varying levels of control to ensure reliability Usually timed	Can be formative to assess progress or summative to assess achievement Can be used for knowledge and/or performance Is flexible and modification is possible Ensures the same conditions for everyone Makes assessment activities manageable	Can be stressful to learners Learners might study just to pass the requirements

Method/approach/activity	Description	Strengths	Limitations
Discussions with learners *also known as a professional discussion*	A one-to-one conversation between the assessor and learner based around the assessment criteria	Ideal way to assess aspects which are more difficult to observe, are rare occurrences, or take place in restricted or confidential settings Useful to support observations to check knowledge Learners can describe how they carry out various activities	A record must be kept of the discussion, for example audio/digital/visual along with notes Needs careful planning as it is a discussion not a question and answer session Learners need time to prepare Assessor needs to be experienced at questioning and listening skills Assessor needs to be experienced at using open and probing questions, and listening carefully to the responses
Discussions/debates	Learners talk about a relevant topic either in groups or pairs	Allows freedom of viewpoints, questions and discussions Can contribute to meeting assessment criteria	Easy to digress Assessor needs to keep the group focused and set a time limit Some learners may not get involved; others may dominate Assessor needs to manage the contributions of each individual and know what has been achieved by whom Can be time consuming Learners may need to research a topic in advance Can lead to arguments
e-assessments/online assessments	*Electronic assessment* – assessment using ICT *Synchronous* – assessor and learner are simultaneously present, communicating in real time *Asynchronous* – assessor and learner are interacting at different times	Teaching, learning and assessment can take place in a virtual learning environment (VLE) Assessment can take place at a time to suit learners Participation is widened Results and feedback can be instantly generated Ensures reliability	Learners need access to a computer or suitable device and need to be computer literate Reliable internet connection needed Self-discipline is needed Clear targets must be set Authenticity of learner's work may need validating Technical support may be required

(Continued)

Table 1.4 (Continued)

Method/ approach/ activity	Description	Strengths	Limitations
		Less paperwork for the assessor Improves computer skills Can be blended with other assessment methods Groups, blogs, forums and chat rooms can be set up to improve communication	
Essays	A formal piece of written text, produced by a learner, for a specific topic	Useful for academic subjects Can check a learner's English skills at specific levels Enhances a learner's knowledge by using research and reading	Not suitable for lower level learners Marking can be time consuming Plagiarism can be an issue Does not usually have a right or wrong answer therefore difficult to grade Learners need good writing skills
Examinations	A formal activity which must be carried out in certain conditions	Can be *open book* or *open notes*, enabling learners to have books and notes with them Some learners like the challenge of a formal examination and cope well	Invigilation required Security arrangements for examination papers to be in place prior to the examination and afterwards Learners may have been taught purely to pass expected questions by using past papers, therefore they may forget everything afterwards Some learners may be anxious Can be *closed book* or *closed notes*, not allowing learners to have books and notes with them Results might take a while to be processed If a learner fails, they may have to wait a period of time before a retake

Method/ approach/ activity	Description	Strengths	Limitations
Group work	Enables learners to carry out a specific activity, for example problem solving Can be practical or theoretical	Allows interaction between learners Encourages participation and variety Rotating group members enables all learners to work with each other	Careful management by the assessor is required regarding time limits, progress and ensuring all group members are clear about the requirements Could be personality problems with team members or large groups One person may dominate Difficult to assess individual contributions Time is needed for a thorough debrief
Holistic	Enables learners to demonstrate several aspects of a programme or qualification at the same time	Similar criteria from different units can be assessed at the same time Makes evidence collection and demonstration of achievement and competence much more efficient	Could confuse the learner if aspects are assessed which were not planned for
Homework	Activities carried out between sessions, for example answering questions to check knowledge	Learners can complete at a time and place that suits them Maintains interest between sessions Encourages learners to stretch themselves further Consolidates learning so far	Clear time limits must be set Learners might not do the activity, or might get someone else to do it for them Must be marked/assessed and individual feedback given
Interviews	A one-to-one discussion, usually before a learner commences a programme, or part way through to discuss progress	Enables the assessor to determine how much a learner knows Enables the assessor to get to know each learner and discuss any issues	Not all learners may react well when interviewed Needs careful planning and consistency of questions between learners

(Continued)

Table 1.4 (Continued)

Method/ approach/ activity	Description	Strengths	Limitations
Learner statements	Learners write how they have met the assessment criteria	Enables learners to take ownership of their achievements	Learners might misinterpret the assessment criteria and/or write too much or too little Another assessment method should be used in addition to confirm practical skills
Learning journal/diary or reflective account	Learners keep a record of their progress, their reflections and thoughts, and reference these to the assessment criteria	Helps assess English skills Useful for higher level programmes	Should be specific to the learning taking place and be analytical rather than descriptive Contents need to remain confidential Can be time consuming and/or difficult to read
Observations	Watching learners perform a skill	Enables skills to be seen in action Learners can make a mistake (if it is safe) enabling them to realise their errors Learners can be observed again if they did not fully achieve the requirements Can assess several aspects at the same time (holistic assessment)	Timing must be arranged to suit each learner Communication needs to take place with others (if applicable) No permanent record unless visually recorded Questions must be asked to confirm knowledge and understanding Assessor might not be objective with decision Learner might put on an act for the assessor which is not how they normally perform
Peer assessments	Learners give feedback to their peers after an activity	Promotes learner and peer interaction and involvement Learners may accept comments from peers better than those from the assessor Enables learners to assess each other Activities can often correct misunderstandings and consolidate learning without intervention by the assessor	Everyone needs to understand the assessment criteria and requirements Needs to be carefully managed to ensure no personality conflicts or unjustified comments Assessor needs to confirm progress and achievements as they might differ Some peers may be anxious about giving feedback Should be supported with other assessment methods Needs careful management and training in how to give feedback

Method/ approach/ activity	Description	Strengths	Limitations
Portfolios of evidence	A formal record of evidence (manual or electronic) produced by learners towards a qualification	Ideal for learners who don't like formal exams Can be compiled over a period of time Learner centred therefore promotes autonomy Evidence can be left in its natural location to be viewed by the assessor	Authenticity and currency to be checked Computer access required to assess electronic portfolios Tendency for learners to produce a large quantity of evidence All evidence must be cross-referenced to the relevant criteria Can be time consuming to assess Confidentiality of documents within the portfolio must be maintained
Practical activities/tasks	Assesses a learner's skills in action	Actively involves learners Can meet all learning preferences if carefully set	Some learners may not respond well to practical activities Can be time consuming to create Questions must be asked to ascertain knowledge and understanding
Presentations	Learners deliver a topic, often using ICT	Can be individual or in a group Can assess skills, knowledge, understanding and attitudes	If a group presentation, individual contributions must be assessed Some learners may be nervous or anxious in front of others
Products	Evidence produced by a learner to prove competence, for example paintings, models, video, audio, photos, documents	Assessor can see the final outcome Learners feel a sense of achievement, for example by displaying their work in an exhibition	Authenticity needs to be checked if the work has not been seen being produced
Projects	A longer-term activity enabling learners to provide evidence which meets the assessment criteria	Can be interesting and motivating Can be individual or group led Can meet all learning preferences Encourages research skills Learners could choose their own topics and devise tasks	Clear outcomes must be set, along with a time limit, and must be relevant, realistic and achievable Progress should be checked regularly If a group is carrying out the project, ensure each individual's input is assessed Assessor might be biased when marking

(Continued)

Table 1.4 (Continued)

Method/approach/activity	Description	Strengths	Limitations
Puzzles, quizzes, word searches, crosswords, etc.	A fun way of assessing learning in an informal way	Fun activities to test skills, knowledge and/or understanding Useful backup activity if learners finish earlier than planned Useful way to assess progress of lower level learners Good for assessing retention of facts	Can seem trivial to mature learners Does not assess a learner's level of understanding or ability to apply their knowledge to situations Can be time consuming to create and assess
Questions	A key technique for assessing understanding and stimulating thinking; can be informal or formal Questions can be closed, hypothetical, leading, open, probing, multiple choice	Can be short answer or long essay style Can challenge and promote a learner's potential A question bank can be devised which could be used again and again for all learners Can test critical arguments or thinking and reasoning skills Oral questions suit some learners more than others, for example a learner who is dyslexic might prefer to talk through their responses	Closed questions only give a yes or no response which does not demonstrate knowledge or understanding Questions must be written carefully, i.e. be unambiguous, and can be time consuming to prepare If the same questions are used with other learners, they could share their answers Written responses might be the work of others, i.e. copied or plagiarised Expected responses or grading criteria need to be produced beforehand to ensure consistency and validity of marking May need to rephrase some questions if learners are struggling with an answer
Recognition of prior learning (RPL)	Assessing what has previously been learnt, experienced and achieved to find a suitable starting point, or to claim equivalent or exemption units on the QCF	Ideal for learners who have achieved aspects of the programme prior to commencement No need for learners to duplicate work, or be reassessed Values previous learning, experiences and achievements	Checking the authenticity and currency of the evidence provided is crucial Previous learning, experiences and achievements might not be relevant in relation to current requirements Can be time consuming for both the learner to prove and the assessor to assess

Method/ approach/ activity	Description	Strengths	Limitations
Reflective account	Learners reflect upon how they have put theory into practice and link this to the criteria being assessed	Formally assessed, therefore can count towards achievement as well as progress Useful for higher level learners A type of self-assessment	Can be time consuming to assess Learners need the skills of reflective writing and cross-referencing Learners might feel they have achieved more than they have
Reports, research and dissertations	Learners produce a document to inform, recommend and/or make suggestions based on the assessment criteria	Useful for higher level learners Encourages the use of research techniques	Learners need research and academic writing skills Can be time consuming to assess Plagiarism and authenticity can be an issue
Role plays	Learners act out a hypothetical situation	Enables the assessor to observe learners' behaviour Encourages participation Can lead to debates Links theory to practice	Can be time consuming Clear roles must be defined Not all learners may want, or be able, to participate Some learners may get too dramatic Individual contributions must be assessed Time needed for a thorough debrief
Self-assessment	Learners decide how they have met the assessment criteria, or how they are progressing at a given time	Promotes learner involvement and personal autonomy Encourages learners to check their own work Encourages reflection	Learners may feel they are doing better or worse than they actually are Assessor needs to discuss progress and achievements with each learner to confirm their decisions Learners need to be specific about what they have achieved and what they need to do to complete any gaps Difficult for the learner to be objective when making a decision

(Continued)

Table 1.4 (Continued)

Method/ approach/ activity	Description	Strengths	Limitations
Skills tests	Designed to find out the level of skill or previous experience/knowledge towards a particular subject or vocation	Could be online or computer based to enable a quick assessment, for example English Results can be used as a starting point for learning or progression	Learners might be apprehensive of formal tests Feedback might not be immediate
Simulation	Imitation or acting out of an event or situation	Useful when it is not possible to carry out a task for real, for example to assess whether learners can successfully evacuate a building in the event of a fire	Only enables an assessment of a hypothetical situation; learners may act very differently in a real situation Not usually accepted as demonstration of competence
Team building exercises/ energisers	A fun and light-hearted way of re-energising learners after a break Can be used to informally assess skills, knowledge and attitudes	A good way of learners getting to work with each other Can revitalise a flagging session	Not all learners may want to take part Some learners may see them as insignificant and time wasting Careful explanations are needed to link the experience to the topic being assessed
Tests	A formal assessment situation	Cost-effective method as the same test can be used with large numbers of learners Some test responses can be scanned into a computer for marking and analysis Other tests can be taken at a computer or online which gives immediate results	Needs to be carried out in supervised conditions or via a secure website Time limits usually required Can be stressful to learners Does not take into account any formative progress Feedback might not be immediate Learners in other groups might find out the content of the tests from others Identity of learners needs confirming

Method/ approach/ activity	Description	Strengths	Limitations
Tutorials	A one-to-one or group discussion between the assessor and learner with an agreed purpose, for example assessing progress so far	A good way of informally assessing a learner's progress and/or giving feedback An opportunity for learners to discuss issues or for informal tuition to take place	Needs to be in a comfortable, safe and quiet environment as confidential issues may be discussed Time may overrun Records should be maintained and action points followed up
Video/audio	Recorded evidence of actual achievements	Direct proof of what was achieved by a learner Can be reviewed by the assessor and internal quality assurer after the event	Can prove expensive to purchase equipment and storage media Can be time consuming to set up and use Technical support may be required Storage facilities are required
Walk and talk	A spoken and visual way of assessing a learner's competence	Enables a learner to *walk and talk* through their product evidence within their work environment Gives an audit trail of the evidence relating to the assessment criteria Saves time as no need to produce a full portfolio of evidence; the walk and talk can be recorded as evidence of the discussion Useful where sensitive and confidential information is dealt with	Can be time consuming Difficult for quality assurers to sample the evidence

(Continued)

Table 1.4 (Continued)

Method/ approach/ activity	Description	Strengths	Limitations
Witness statements/ testimonies	A statement from a person who is familiar with the learner (they could also be an expert in the standards being assessed and the occupation of the learner in the work environment)	The witness can confirm competence or achievements for situations which might not regularly occur, or when the assessor cannot be present	The assessor must confirm the suitability of the witness and check the authenticity of any statements Learners could write the statement and the witness might sign it not understanding the content
Worksheets and gapped handouts	Interactive handouts to check knowledge (can also be electronic) Blank spaces can be used for learners to fill in the missing words	Informal assessment activity which can be done individually, in pairs or groups Useful for lower level learners Can be created at different degrees of difficulty to address differentiation	Mature learners may consider them inappropriate Too many worksheets can be boring Learners might not be challenged enough

2 ASSESSING OCCUPATIONAL COMPETENCE IN THE WORK ENVIRONMENT

Introduction

In this chapter you will learn about:

- assessment planning in the work environment
- making assessment decisions
- providing feedback
- standardising practice
- record keeping – assessment.

Within the chapter there are activities and examples which will help you to reflect on the above and to develop and enhance your knowledge of assessing occupational competence in the work environment. Completing the activities will help you to gather evidence towards the *Assessing occupational competence in the work environment* unit. At the end of each section is an extension activity to stretch and challenge your knowledge and understanding.

At the end of the chapter is a list of possible evidence which could be used towards the *Assessing occupational competence in the work environment* unit.

A cross-referencing grid shows how the content of this chapter contributes towards the relevant TAQA units' criteria and the National Occupational Standards. There is also a theory focus with relevant references, further information and websites to which you might like to refer.

Assessment planning in the work environment

Assessing learners, employees or apprentices in the work environment will help you confirm their competence towards a new skill, a qualification or their job role. For the purpose of this chapter, the term *learner* will be used for anyone who is being assessed in the work environment. Planning what to assess, and when, is a crucial phase of the assessment process. However, before you commence the planning process, you need to be fully conversant with what you are going to assess, where this will be, and any particular requirements and regulations for your subject.

If you are assessing towards a qualification which is accredited through an awarding organisation (AO), a certificate will be issued upon successful completion. The AO will monitor the delivery, assessment and quality assurance of the qualification to ensure all their requirements are being met. If you have not already done so, you will need to obtain a copy of the qualification handbook which will contain all the details regarding the assessment requirements.

If you are assessing an employee's competence towards their job role or a new skill they are putting into practice, this is known as *non-accredited* as a certificate will not be issued by an AO. However, a *record of achievement* might be given to the employee once they have proved their competence. This could be issued by their employer or the organisation you are working for.

Vocational qualifications are an excellent way for competent learners to demonstrate their skills, knowledge and understanding in their work environment and to gain an accredited certificate. However, if there are aspects of the qualification with which they are not familiar, training will need to take place. An initial assessment would greatly help to identify what may need to be learnt before any formal assessment takes place. If you are not familiar with how to teach or train, there are relevant qualifications you can take such as the Award in Education and Training, which is the first step in the teacher training process.

When assessing learners in their place of work, it is best to plan ahead to arrange your visits according to location, for example assessing learners in close proximity to ease the time and cost spent travelling. Out of courtesy, notify your learner's employer in advance, in case there is any reason why they cannot accommodate you on a particular day. You will also need to check travel, transport and/or parking arrangements.

Activity

When you are planning to assess in the work environment, will you use public transport or is there a company vehicle you can use? If you use your own vehicle, find out how you can reclaim any expenses. Are there any protocols you need to follow when visiting other organisations? If you are not sure, find out, as you may need to confirm dates and times, and carry appropriate photo identification.

If your learner works shifts or during the weekend, you will need to visit when they are working, as it is not fair to ask them to change their work patterns just to suit you. If for any reason an assessment is cancelled, make sure a revised date is scheduled as soon as possible and inform all concerned. Always confirm your visit one or two days beforehand, just in case there is any reason you cannot go.

At some point in your assessment career, you might find you are assessing a colleague, a friend or a relative. It is always best to inform your internal quality assurer (IQA) to enable them to carry out a further sample of your work to ensure nothing untoward is taking place. The external quality assurer (EQA) from the AO might also need to be informed.

If you are currently working towards an assessment qualification yourself, you may need to have some or all of your decisions and records countersigned by another assessor who is qualified in your subject area. This could be your supervisor or manager, who might also observe your practice to ensure they have confidence in your role as an assessor.

You might find the following checklist useful to ensure you are performing your role as an assessor correctly.

Assessor checklist

☑ Do I need to achieve certain assessor qualification units? If so, do I know which ones and who will countersign my decisions until I am qualified?

☑ Do I need to participate in any continuing professional development? If so, what and when?

☑ Is there an assessment strategy which states what qualifications and experience I must have? If so, do I meet the requirements or is there anything I need to do?

☑ Do I have a copy of the qualification handbook for the subject I will be assessing? If not, do I know how to obtain one and use it effectively?

☑ Do I understand the awarding organisation's requirements for the qualification I will assess? If not, who can I ask?

☑ What meetings do I need to attend and when?

☑ Do I have the opportunity to standardise my practice with that of other assessors? If so, when is the next event?

☑ When will my internal quality assurer observe my practice? Do I know who they are and how I can get in touch with them?

☑ Have all my learners been registered with the awarding organisation (if applicable)?

☑ What is the induction procedure I go through with a new learner?

☑ Do I know the procedure for claiming certificates or issuing records of achievement/attendance? If not, is there anything I need to do or anyone I need to communicate with?

☑ Am I familiar with all relevant policies and procedures? If not, how do I find out about them?

☑ Do I need to carry out initial or diagnostic assessments with my learners? If so, what do I need to do?

☑ Do I have an assessment tracking sheet which shows the achievement of all my learners? If not, can I create one?

☑ Can I complete individual assessment plans with each learner, with suitable dates, times and assessment methods, taking into account any particular individual needs? Is there a facility to give each learner a copy, either manual or electronic?

☑ Do I need to liaise with anyone else, for example workplace supervisors? If so, how do I go about this?

☑ Can I differentiate the assessment activities if necessary? Do I need to inform anyone such as the awarding organisation?

☑ How can I utilise new and emerging technologies?

☑ Do I need to produce questions or assignments with expected responses? Should I standardise these with anyone else?

☑ What specific assessment records will I need to complete and why?

☑ Do I feel confident making assessment decisions, giving feedback and completing the relevant records?

☑ How can I ensure the assessed work meets standards of validity, authenticity, currency, sufficiency and reliability?

☑ Do I know the requirements for keeping records? If not, what are the requirements?

☑ Do I know what to do if a learner appeals against my decision?

Initial assessment

Using initial assessments will help you to find out about your learners and to identify any particular aspects which might otherwise go unnoticed. It is best to do this prior to the programme commencing. This will allow time to deal with any issues that might arise or to guide learners to a different, more appropriate programme if necessary.

Initial assessment can:

- allow for differentiation and individual requirements to be planned for and met

- ascertain why your learner wants to take the programme along with their capability to achieve

- find out the expectations and motivations of your learner

- give your learner the confidence to negotiate suitable targets

- identify any information which needs to be shared with colleagues

- identify any specific additional support needs.

Example

Jennifer had applied to take a Conflict Management qualification and was attending an interview with the trainer. After discussing her current skills and knowledge, and her aspirations for using the qualification to improve her career, she decided it was not for her at that time. She felt she lacked confidence. The trainer therefore referred her to the National Careers Service where she could get further advice.

Diagnostic assessment

Diagnostic assessments can be used to evaluate a learner's skills, knowledge, strengths and areas for development in a particular subject area. It could be that your learner feels they are capable of achieving at a higher level than the diagnostic assessments determine. The results will give a thorough indication of not only the level at which your learner needs to be placed for their subject, but also which specific aspects they need to improve on. Skills tests can be used for learners to demonstrate what they can do; knowledge tests can be used for learners to demonstrate what they know and understand.

Diagnostic tests can also be used to ascertain information regarding English, maths, and information and communication technology (ICT) skills. Information gained from these tests will help you plan to meet any individual needs and/or to arrange further training and support if necessary.

Diagnostic assessment can:

- ascertain learning preferences, for example visual, aural, read/write and kinaesthetic (VARK)

- enable learners to demonstrate their current level of skills, knowledge and understanding

- ensure learners can access support

- identify an appropriate starting point and level for each learner

- identify gaps in skills, knowledge and understanding to highlight areas to work on

- identify previous experience, knowledge, achievements and transferable skills

- identify specific requirements, for example English, maths and ICT skills.

Activity

Find out what initial and diagnostic assessments are used at your organisation. Will it be your responsibility to administer these, or is there a specialist person to do this? If possible, carry out an initial assessment with a learner. How will you use the results to help plan what your learner will do and when?

Many different types of initial and diagnostic tests are available. Some organisations design and use their own while others purchase and use widely available tests, for example the system called *Basic Key Skills Builder* (BKSB) to diagnose English, maths and ICT skills.

The results of initial and diagnostic assessments should help you negotiate appropriate assessment plans with your learners, ensuring they are on the right programme at the right level with the support they need to succeed.

It could be that your learner has achieved some units of a qualification elsewhere and might just need to provide their certificate as evidence of prior achievement. If the achieved units are listed on the QCF, they should automatically be recognised and classed as an equivalent unit. The learner therefore does not need to retake them.

Example

Sharron has completed a diagnostic assessment process which was designed to assess her skills and knowledge towards the level 2 Diploma in Travel and Tourism. Sharron had started the qualification at another organisation prior to moving to the area. Her current assessor was able to see her evidence for three units which she had completed fairly recently. Sharron was therefore accredited with these units once her assessor had confirmed all the requirements had been met. She therefore did not need to be reassessed for these units.

Once you have the information you need from the initial and diagnostic assessment process, you can agree an assessment plan with your learner. The template in Table 2.1 is a form which could be used or adapted for initial and diagnostic assessment purposes. It should be supported with appropriate skills tests for English, maths and ICT.

Assessment planning

Assessment planning should be short term and long term, to allow formative and summative assessment to take place. Including your learners in the planning process will help identify what they have learnt, how and when they will be assessed, and will allow for communication to take place to clarify any points or concerns.

Assessment requirements are usually written in specific terminology, for example:

- ability outcomes

- aims and objectives

- assessment criteria

- evidence requirements

- learning outcomes

- performance criteria

- standards

- statements of competence.

All qualifications on the QCF use the terms *learning outcomes* and *assessment criteria*. The learning outcomes state what the learner *will do*, and the assessment criteria state what the learner *can do*. The methods you use to assess your learners will depend upon whether you are assessing knowledge or performance. Assessing knowledge will be covered in more detail in Chapter 3, whereas this chapter mainly focuses on assessing performance.

Table 2.1 Example initial and diagnostic assessment template

Initial and diagnostic assessment		
Separate skills tests in English, maths and ICT should be taken		
Name:	**Date:**	
What experience do you have in this subject area?		
What relevant qualifications do you have? *If you have achieved any units on the Qualifications and Credit Framework, please state them here.*		
Have you completed a learning preference questionnaire? If YES, what is your preferred style of learning? If NO, please complete the questionnaire at www.vark-learn.com and note your results here:	YES/NO Learning preference results: V: A: R: K:	
Do you have any particular learning needs or requirements? If YES, please state here, or talk to your assessor in confidence.	YES/NO	
Are you confident using a computer? If YES, what experience or qualifications do you have?	YES/NO	Skills test results: ICT:
What help would you like with written/spoken English?		Skills test results: English:
What help would you like with maths?		Skills test results: Maths:
Why have you decided to take this programme/ qualification? (*continue overleaf*)		

Units on the QCF are either *knowledge based* (to assess understanding) or *performance based* (to assess competence). Usually, the *knowledge* units will state what the learner *will do* in sentences beginning with *understand*. What the learner *can do* is stated in sentences beginning with verbs such as *explain*. The *performance* units are slightly different and will state what the learner *will do* in sentences beginning with *be able to*. What the learner *can do* is stated in sentences beginning with verbs such as *demonstrate*. The different verbs help differentiate between theory and practice. However, there are some units which combine knowledge and performance into one unit, particularly if the qualification is small.

Activity

Look at Appendices 1 and 2 at the back of this book. You will see that Appendix 1 is a knowledge unit and Appendix 2 is a performance unit. You can tell this by the different verbs used for the learning outcomes and assessment criteria. If you are working towards these units yourself, you will probably complete an assignment for the knowledge unit (theory) and be observed for the performance unit (practice). If so, speak to your assessor and find out how you will be assessed and when.

If you are assessing performance in the work environment, the most commonly used methods include:

- observations

- examining work products and evidence produced by your learner

- asking questions – written or oral

- holding discussions with your learner, often known as professional discussions

- obtaining witness statements, for example from a learner's supervisor

- reading your learner's written statements of how they perform certain tasks

- recognising your learner's prior learning (RPL).

If you are assessing a qualification, the methods might be stated by the AO. If not, you will need to decide on what is most appropriate. Try to use a mixture of at least two or three different activities to keep the process interesting, for example observation, oral questions and looking at work produced by the learner. In this way, you are ensuring you are assessing not only learner performance, but knowledge and understanding too.

Assessment should be a two-way process between you and your learner; you need to plan what you are going to do, and they need to know what is expected of them and when. It could be that you will assess units or aspects in a different order to those stated in the qualification requirements. For example, instead of assessing Unit 1 before any others, you might decide with your learner that Unit 3 could be assessed first as they are already performing the requirements which are included in that unit.

The way you plan to assess your learners will depend upon the:

- assessment type and method

- assessment strategy from the AO (if applicable)

- dates, times and duration of assessment activities

- individual learner and qualification/employment level

- location and environment

- organisational budget

- requirements for making decisions and giving feedback

- resources and materials available

- special requirements or particular learner needs

- staff availability and expertise

- subject or qualification, i.e. workplace competence or a vocational qualification.

The planning process should involve a discussion between you and your learner, with the chance to set realistic dates and targets. However, it could be that when you do assess your learner, they are not quite as ready as anticipated.

Example

Megan is assessing the Level 2 Award in Floristry. She visits each learner once a month in their place of work to observe their competence, and asks questions to check their knowledge. While carrying out an assessment with Ben, she realises he is not quite competent in the area she had planned to assess. Megan demonstrates how to perform one of the tasks expected and then Ben attempts it on his own. Megan asks Ben to practise this over the next few days and arranges to return the following month to carry out a formal assessment.

In this example, Megan has carried out an impromptu training session with Ben by demonstrating the task. She then encouraged him to do it himself while she was still present, and then on his own afterwards. Megan could assess other aspects of the qualification while she is there if Ben feels confident. In this way, the visit can still lead to an achievement and the assessment plan can be updated as necessary. You will need to be patient with your learners as it takes time for them to consolidate learning and put theory into practice. At times you might just be assessing progress rather than achievement. However, don't let this demoralise your learner; try to keep them motivated to work towards achieving something.

If you carry out training sessions and demonstrate something in front of learners, always check if they are left- or right-handed as this could change the way they view things. When they look at you, your right hand will be on their left. If you are demonstrating on a one-to-one basis, try to stand or sit next to your learner rather than facing them.

Assessment planning should be specific, measurable, achievable, relevant and time bound (SMART).

- **S**pecific – the activity relates only to what is being assessed and is clearly stated.

- **M**easurable – the activity can be measured against the assessment requirements, allowing any gaps to be identified.

- **A**chievable – the activity can be achieved at the right level.

- **R**elevant– the activity is realistic, relates to what is being assessed and will give consistent results.

- **T**ime bound – target dates and times can be agreed.

Planning SMART assessment activities will help ensure all the assessment requirements will be met by your learners, providing they have acquired the necessary skills and knowledge beforehand.

Always ask your learners if there is anything you can do to help make their assessment experience a positive one. For example, ensure you face your learners when speaking to assist anyone hard of hearing, or use written questions instead of asking oral questions (or vice versa). If you use printed handouts make sure they are in a font, size and colour to suit any particular learner requirements.

Assessment planning should provide opportunities for both you and your learners to obtain and use information regarding progress and achievement. It should also be flexible in order to respond to any emerging skills and new ideas, for example the use of technology. The way you plan should include strategies to ensure that your learners understand what they are working towards and the criteria that will be used for assessment. You should also plan how and when you will give feedback. It could be verbally immediately after the assessment, the next time you see your learner, or by e-mail or other written means. However, the sooner the better, while everything is fresh for both of you.

Holistic assessment planning

Learners might be able to demonstrate several criteria from different aspects or units at the same time. These can be assessed together, which is known as *holistic* assessment. You may be able to observe naturally occurring situations in addition to what has originally been planned. Rather than planning to assess individual aspects or units on different occasions, you could discuss your learner's job role with them to identify which assessment criteria from other units could be demonstrated at the same time. You could also involve the learner's manager as they might be aware of situations where the learner can demonstrate their competence. While the assessment might take longer, it would reduce the number of assessment activities and therefore the inconvenience to all involved. Your learner would need to be ready to demonstrate their competence; don't plan to assess them unless they are ready. Never arrange to assess your learner if they are not ready, as this could demoralise them and waste time. Holistic assessment should make evidence collection and demonstration of competence much more efficient.

Example

Rafael is due to assess Sheila for the Level 3 Certificate in Assessing Vocational Achievement, which consists of the following three units:

1. *Understanding the principles and practice of assessment*

2. *Assess occupational competence in the work environment*

3. *Assess vocational skills, knowledge and understanding.*

Units 2 and 3 have almost identical assessment criteria for learning outcomes 3 and 4. Rafael is therefore able to plan to assess these on the same day, providing Sheila can demonstrate them with her learners.

Holistic assessment is beneficial to all concerned when assessing occupational competence, particularly in a work environment. It could be that you carry out a holistic assessment and find your learner is competent at most but not all of the criteria you planned to assess. If this is the case, you can still sign off what they have achieved and then update the assessment plan to assess the remaining criteria on another occasion. Alternatively, you might be able to ask questions or hold a discussion with your learner to evidence the gaps, if this is acceptable. If so, you would need to keep a record of what was asked and the responses your learner gave. Without records, there is no proof of what has occurred.

Involving witnesses
You could involve witnesses: these are other people the learner is in contact with, for example their supervisor, who can give a statement as to their competence. They will write about how your learner has met the requirements. However, you will need to liaise with them to confirm the authenticity of their statements. If witnesses are involved, they will need to be briefed as to what they are expected to do, and they must be familiar with the subject and criteria being assessed. You might also need to check a copy of the witness's certificates and curriculum vitae.

Assessment plans

The assessment plan is like a written contract between you and your learner towards the achievement of their qualification, programme or job role. It can be reviewed, amended and updated at any time. Careful assessment planning and prior knowledge of your learner's previous achievements are the key to ensuring everyone involved understands what will take place and when. Table 2.2 is an example of a completed *assessment plan and review record*. The plan can be reviewed and updated at any time to take into account progress as well as achievement. Rather than completing a separate feedback form when a learner has achieved something, the form could perform a dual function. It could be used for planning what will be assessed, reviewing progress and documenting feedback and achievement. This is particularly useful when holistic assessment is carried out.

Table 2.2 Example assessment plan and review record

Assessment plan and review record				
Learner: Irene Jones			**Assessor:** Jenny Smith	
Qualification: Level 1 Certificate in Hospitality & Catering			**Registration number:** 1234ABCD	
Date commenced: 6 January			**Expected completion date:** 17 December	
Date agreed	**Aspects to be assessed**	**Date achieved**	**Assessment details** *Planning* – *methods of assessment, activities and SMART targets* *Review and feedback* – *revisions to plan, issues discussed, feedback given regarding progress and achievement*	**Target/ review date**
10 Jan	Unit 101 Maintenance of a safe, hygienic and secure working environment		**Planning** An observation will take place in February at the County Leisure Centre to assess competence in the workplace for Unit 101. The awarding organisation's checklists will be used for this purpose. An observation will take place, oral questions will be asked and a discussion will take place based on the knowledge requirements. A witness statement will be obtained from Irene's supervisor. Irene has a copy of the assessment criteria and we have discussed the requirements of the following learning outcomes of Unit 101 today. 1. Be able to maintain personal health and hygiene. 2. Know how to maintain personal health and hygiene. 3. Be able to help maintain a hygienic, safe and secure workplace. 4. Know how to maintain a hygienic, safe and secure workplace.	Target: 6 February Review: 6 April

Assessment planning is a crucial part of the teaching and learning process. If it is not carried out correctly and comprehensively, problems may occur which could disadvantage your learners and prevent them from being successful. When planning assessments, you will need to take into account equality of opportunity, inclusivity and differentiation within the assessment process. Never assume everything is fine just because your learners don't complain. Always include your learners in the assessment planning and review process in case there is something you don't know that you need to act upon.

Informal assessments, for example peer feedback, puzzles and quizzes, will not require an assessment plan if they are just to check ongoing progress. However, you must always be SMART when using any formal assessment activities to ensure they have a purpose.

Assessment rationale

When planning to assess, you should have a rationale, i.e. you need to consider who, what, when, where, why and how (WWWWWH) assessment will take place. This information should always be agreed with your learners beforehand so that everyone is aware of what will occur. If you are assessing on an individual basis, the assessment planning process should still be formalised, and an assessment plan completed and agreed. When the assessment has taken place or when you review your learner's progress, the plan can be updated.

Extension Activity

Consider the WWWWWH of the assessment planning process for your particular subject and, if possible, agree an occupational competence assessment plan with a learner. Ensure you are familiar with the assessment criteria you will be assessing towards. Who else will you need to involve when creating the assessment plan (besides your learner), what will you assess, when, where, why and how will you do it?

Making assessment decisions

To know that learning has taken place, some form of assessment must happen which results in a decision. The decision relates to what has or has not been achieved. Decisions should be in accordance with the assessment requirements and full records must be maintained, usually for at least three years. It is quite a responsibility to confirm an achievement (or otherwise) as it can affect your learner's personal and professional development. Your learner may need to meet certain criteria to achieve a promotion at work, or they may want to achieve a qualification for personal fulfilment. To make a decision as to what your learner has achieved, you need to ensure all the relevant assessment requirements have been met. You also need to be confident yourself that you understand what you are assessing. When assessing, you must always remain *objective*, i.e. by making a decision based on your learner's competence towards set criteria. You should not be *subjective*, i.e. by making a decision based on your own opinions or other factors such as the learner's personality. However, some qualifications or job roles might require the learner to demonstrate the correct attitude and manners if, for example, this is part of their job role.

You could observe your learner's skills and then ask questions to check their knowledge and understanding. Don't be tempted to give them a grade, for example a distinction or a merit; they have either met or not met the requirements. If your learner did not perform according to the requirements, or answered questions incorrectly, they will need to do it again. You might need to rephrase your instructions or questions. It could be that your learner does know the correct response, but your question was vague or ambiguous.

Any written work your learners carry out must always be their own and they may have to show photo identification, sign an authentication statement or complete a declaration form to prove this. If you have several learners all working towards the same outcomes, you will need to ensure they have not colluded on any formal assessment activities. Otherwise, you might be accrediting them with something their peers have done, or even something they have copied from someone else or the internet.

Activity

Ask a colleague if you can observe an assessment activity they are due to carry out. Look at their assessment plan and the materials they use. Observe how they communicate with their learner and others, reach their decisions, give feedback and complete their records.

Seeing how other assessors plan and assess will help you develop your own skills.

Your decisions should always be valid, authentic, current, sufficient and reliable (VACSR) (see Chapter 1 for further details). You should also be fair and ethical when assessing your learners, making a decision and giving feedback.

- Fair – the assessment activity was appropriate to all learners at the required level, is inclusive, i.e. available to all, and differentiates for any particular needs. All learners should have an equal chance of an accurate assessment decision.

- Ethical – the assessment process takes into account confidentiality, integrity, safety, security and learner welfare.

You may find, when assessing, that your learners have not achieved everything they should have. When making a decision, you need to base this on all the information or evidence available to you at the time. If your learner has not met all the requirements, you need to give constructive feedback, discuss any inconsistencies or gaps, and give advice on what they should do next. If your learner disagrees with the assessment process or your decision, they are entitled to follow your organisation's appeals procedure. Don't get so tied up with your administrative work or form filling when making a decision that you forget to inform your learner what they have achieved.

If you are having difficulty making a decision, discuss this with your line manager or another assessor to obtain a second opinion. You need to be fully confident when making a decision to confirm that what you have assessed does meet the requirements. You are not doing your learners any favours by saying they have achieved something when they have not. You might also notice skills your learners have that they can use in other situations. It is useful to point out any such transferable skills to help them realise other contexts in which they could work. You might also see other aspects demonstrated in addition to those planned. If this is the case, make sure you include them in your decision, inform your learner what else they have achieved, and update your records.

If you are assessing work from learners who hand it to you for assessment at a later time, it would be a good idea to have a system of signing it in and out. Your learner will have put a lot of effort into their work and would like to know that you will take reasonable care with it. When you have made your decision, given feedback and returned their work, you could ask your learner to sign that they have received it back. If your learner was to lose it, you will have your original assessment records to prove that assessment has taken place. If you are assessing work which has been e-mailed to you or uploaded via a website for you to access, there will be the facility for you to add electronic comments to it. This will therefore create a record of what was submitted and when, and what comments and feedback were given and when.

Recognition of prior learning

Recognition of prior learning (RPL) is about assessing a learner's existing skills, knowledge and understanding towards what they are hoping to achieve. It should save them having to duplicate anything unnecessarily. However, it can be time consuming to judge whether it meets the criteria. It could be that you have a learner who has achieved an aspect of a qualification or programme elsewhere. Depending upon the evidence they can produce in support of it, they might not have to repeat some or all of the requirements. You would need to compare what they have achieved already against the assessment requirements. You can then agree an assessment plan of how to fill the gaps, for example by a discussion or an observation.

There are occasions where a learner will not have to repeat anything, particularly if they are taking a qualification which is on the QCF and they have been accredited with some units already. This is known as an *equivalent unit*. Details of qualifications and units achieved on the QCF will be held centrally and your learner will be able to prove this via their electronic learner record or certificate if necessary.

Example

> Roberto had achieved the Equality and Diversity unit as part of the Certificate in Education and Training which is on the QCF. His job role changed the following year and he decided to take the Diploma in Education and Training which is also on the QCF. As the Equality and Diversity unit was also in the Diploma, he did not have to retake it.

There might be occasions where a learner will have an *exempt* qualification or unit. This means the qualification or unit was on the previous National Qualifications Framework (NQF) and is similar to a qualification or unit on the current QCF. There is therefore no need for a learner to take the newer version if the older version is still acceptable. Your learner will have a certificate to prove their achievement; however, you should always check the authenticity of these.

Factors which could influence your judgement and decision

When making a judgement or decision regarding your learner's achievement, you must always follow the assessment requirements, as well as your organisation's quality assurance measures. You must remain objective and not let any factors influence your decision if they are not relevant to what is being assessed. If you are influenced for any reason, then there is a strong risk your learner will not achieve based on their own merit.

The following are factors to consider when making a decision.

- Appeals – if a learner has made an appeal about a decision made by you or another assessor, you should not feel you must pass them for other assessments if they have not met the requirements. Make sure you follow your organisation's procedures and keep records of your decisions.

- Complaints – if a learner has made a complaint about a particular assessment method or the way you have treated them, you must remain objective and not take anything personally. You should not let this influence any future decisions. However, you could ask if another assessor could take on this learner if you feel uncomfortable with the situation.

- Consistency – are you being fair to all your learners or are you biased towards some learners more than others for any reason?

- Methods of assessment – have you used appropriate or alternative methods, for example, asking oral questions rather than issuing written questions for a learner who has dyslexia?

- Plagiarism – have any learners copied work from others or the internet, or not referenced their research adequately? You could type a sentence of their work into a search engine to see if it already exists elsewhere.

- Pressure – do you feel under pressure to pass learners who are borderline, perhaps due to funding measures, targets, inspectors or employer expectations?

- Risk assessments – are any of your learners likely to leave, or do they need extra support for any reason? Don't feel obliged to give so much support that your work becomes your learner's.

- The assessment requirements – have both you and your learner interpreted these in the same way? Was the activity too easy or too hard?

- Trends – is there a pattern, i.e. are most learners making the same mistakes? If so, it could be that they have misinterpreted something, or you have misinformed them or been vague or ambiguous. If this is the case, you could summarise the trends and discuss them with your learners. You could also discuss aspects of good practice to further their development.

- Type of assessment (i.e. formal or informal assessments) – you might be more lenient with informal assessments to encourage progress. However, you do need to be fair and ethical with all your assessment methods and decisions.

- VACSR – is your learner's evidence valid, authentic, current, sufficient and reliable? How can you ensure their work meets all these requirements? If you are assessing group work, how do you know what each individual has contributed? If you don't know, you might be attributing achievement to those who have not contributed much.

If you are in any doubt, you must talk to someone who is a specialist in your subject area such as another assessor. Samples of your decisions should be checked by your IQA to ensure you are assessing correctly, consistently and fairly. However, this usually takes place after you have made a decision and it might be too late if you have made a positive judgement. You will then need to explain to your learner that they have not passed and that they need to do further work. If you are assessing an accredited qualification, an EQA from the AO for your subject may also sample your decisions along with the learner's work. If your learners are working towards an accredited qualification, you will need to ensure they have been registered with the appropriate AO first. It might not be your responsibility to carry out this task, but you should communicate the details of your learners to the relevant staff. You should then receive a list of their registration numbers which can be added to your assessment documentation.

Ensuring you choose the right method of assessment to carry out with your learners, and making a decision which is fair and ethical, will help support your learners towards their achievement.

Extension Activity

Consider what could influence you when making an assessment decision. Are the assessment requirements explicit, enabling you to be totally objective, or could they be misinterpreted, making it difficult for you to make a judgement? What would you do if you felt under pressure to pass a learner who had not met the criteria?

If possible, agree an assessment plan with a learner, assess them and make a decision. Then consider if you would do anything differently and why.

Providing feedback

All learners need to know how they are progressing and what they have achieved at regular points. Feedback will help encourage, motivate and develop them further. It can be given after an assessment activity, perhaps verbally to your learner; however, it should always be formally documented. When giving feedback in writing, it should be written on the correct document, not just on your learner's work in case they lose it. You can, of course, make developmental notes on your learner's work, for example to correct spelling errors or to make annotations to show you have read it. You must keep records of feedback to show who has achieved what, as well as to satisfy internal and external organisation requirements.

Feedback should be based on facts which relate to what has been assessed; they should not be based purely on your personal opinions. The former is known as *objective*, the latter *subjective*. However, you can mix the two. For example, *Well done Hannah, you have met the criteria and I felt the way you handled the situation was really professional.*

The advantages of giving feedback are that:

- it creates opportunities for clarification, discussion and progression

- it emphasises progress rather than failure

- it can boost your learner's confidence and motivation

- it identifies further learning opportunities or actions required

- your learner knows what they have achieved

- your learner knows what they need to do to improve or change.

If you are writing feedback to be read by learners at a later date, you need to appreciate that how you write it may not be how they read it. It is easy to interpret words or phrases differently to what is intended; therefore, if you can, read the feedback to them at the time of returning their work to allow a two-way discussion to take place. If you don't see your learners regularly, you could e-mail feedback to them. If so, don't get too personal; keep to the facts but be as positive as possible to retain their motivation. If you are giving individual verbal feedback, consider when and where you will do this, so as not to embarrass your learner in any way and to allow enough time for any questions they may have.

Consider your tone of voice when speaking and take into account your learner's non-verbal signals as well as your own body language. You might give feedback to a group regarding an activity. If you do, make sure your feedback is specific to the group and/or each individual's contributions. Your learners will like to know how they are progressing and what they need to do to improve or develop further. Simple statements such as *well done* or *good* don't tell your learner *what* was well done or good about their work or how they can improve it. Using your learner's name makes the feedback more personal. Being specific enables your learner to appreciate what they need to do to improve, and smiling while giving feedback can be encouraging.

Example

Rashid sees his learners once a month in their work environment to assess their performance. He also sees them once a fortnight in college to support them with their knowledge. Between these times, he marks their assignments and e-mails informal feedback to them. A typical e-mail reads:

Paula, you have passed your assignment. I particularly liked the way you compared and contrasted the two theories. Do be careful when proofreading – you tend to use 'were' instead of 'where'. I will return your assignment when I next see you, along with more detailed written feedback. Do get in touch if you have any questions.

This feedback is specific and developmental and will help Rashid's learners to stay motivated until he next sees them. Giving feedback in this way is a good method of keeping in touch if you don't see your learners frequently. It also gives your learners the opportunity to communicate with you if necessary. E-mails and written feedback enable you to maintain records, if required, for audit purposes. Feedback can lose its impact if you leave it too long, and learners may think you are not interested in their progress if they don't hear from you.

Feedback should always be:

- based on facts and not opinions

- clear, genuine and unambiguous

- constructive, supportive and developmental

- documented – records must be maintained

- focused on the activity, not the person

- helpful and honest

- specific and detailed regarding what was or was not achieved, and what needs improving or developing further.

Activity

Think of an instance where you have given feedback recently. How did you do this and could you have improved it in any way? What did you find difficult about giving feedback and why? What records did you maintain and why?

There could be issues such as not having enough time to write detailed feedback, not being very good with eye contact when giving verbal feedback, or not being able to turn negative points into constructive points. Giving feedback which is constructive and helpful to your learners will come with practice. Coffield states:

If rich feedback is to be given to all learners, then tutors need the time to read and reflect on their assignments, time to write encouraging and stretching comments, and time to discuss these face to face.

(2008, p36)

If you don't take the time to support your learners with encouraging feedback, you will not be helping them to improve in the long term.

The role of questioning in feedback

The role of questioning in feedback allows your learner to consider their achievements before you tell them. A good way to do this is to ask your learner how they feel they have done straight after you have assessed them. This gives them the opportunity to recognise their own mistakes or reflect on what they could have done differently. You could then build on this through feedback and discuss what needs to be improved and achieved next.

Having good listening skills will help you engage your learners in a conversation by hearing what they are saying and responding to any questions or concerns. Giving your learners time to talk will encourage them to inform you of things they might not otherwise have said, for example if something has had an effect upon their progress. Listening for key words will help you focus upon what is being said, for example *I struggled with the last part of the assignment.* The key word is 'struggled' and you could therefore ask a question such as, *What was it that made you struggle?* This would then allow a conversation to take place, giving you the opportunity to help and support your learner.

When questioning:

- allow enough time for your questions and your learners' responses

- ask open questions, i.e. those beginning with who, what, when, where, why and how

- avoid trick or complex questions

- be aware of your posture, gestures and body language

- be conscious of your dialect, accent, pitch and tone

- don't ask more than one question in the same sentence

- involve everyone if you are talking to a group

- make sure you don't use closed questions which just elicit a *yes* response, for example *'Did you understand what I just said?'*; learners may feel that is what you want to hear but it does not confirm knowledge,

- try not to say *erm, yeah, okay, you know,* or *does that make sense?*

- use eye contact and smile

- use learners' names

- watch your learners' reactions.

Questioning and feedback should always be adapted to the level of your learners. You will not help your learners if you are using higher level words or jargon when their level of understanding is lower. You should also be aware of where you give the feedback in case you are interrupted or are in a noisy environment. You should always give feedback in a way that will make it clear how your learner has met the requirements, what they have achieved and what they need to do next.

Example

Marcela is working towards the Certificate in Customer Service. She has just been observed by her assessor Geoff, who has also marked her responses to the written questions. Geoff gave her verbal feedback stating: Marcela, you've done really well and passed all the criteria for the observation and written questions. You dealt with the irate customer in a pleasant and calm way. However, I would recommend you use the customer's name a bit more when speaking with them to appear friendly. You've met all the requirements; we can now sign that unit off and plan for the next one.

In this example, the assessor was constructive, specific and developmental with his feedback. Marcela knew that she had achieved the unit, and what she could do to improve for the future. The use of the word *however* is much better than the word *but*, which can sound negative. The feedback was also worded at the right level for the learner.

Table 2.3 Example feedback and action record

Feedback and action record			
Learner: Irene Jones		**Assessor:** Jenny Smith	
Qualification: Level 1 Certificate in Hospitality & Catering		**Date:** 6 February	
Aspects assessed	**Feedback**	**Action required**	**Target date**
Unit 101 Maintenance of a safe, hygienic and secure working environment	I observed Irene on 6 February at the County Leisure Centre to assess her competence in the workplace. I used the awarding organisation's checklists to ensure all the requirements were met and made additional comments regarding what was seen. Irene successfully performed all the requirements of Unit 101 and I am pleased to say she has passed. I also asked some oral questions to check her knowledge and have digitally recorded these as evidence of achievement. I held a discussion with Irene based on the knowledge requirements, which was also digitally recorded. Irene obtained a witness statement from her supervisor, which confirmed she had successfully covered the criteria over a period of time.	Irene and I will meet on 6 April to complete an assessment plan for Unit 102 and review her progress to date. In the meantime, Irene will read the supporting handouts for Unit 102 and put theory into practice at the Leisure Centre.	6 April
Achievements	**Learning outcomes**	**Assessment criteria**	
Unit 101	1. Be able to maintain personal health and hygiene. 2. Know how to maintain personal health and hygiene. 3. Be able to help maintain a hygienic, safe and secure workplace. 4. Know how to maintain a hygienic, safe and secure workplace.	1.1 – 1.5 2.1 – 2.5 3.1 – 3.5 4.1 – 4.19	

Often, the focus of feedback is likely to be on mistakes rather than strengths. If something positive is stated first, any negative comments are more likely to be listened to and acted upon. Starting with a negative point may discourage your learner from listening to anything else that is said. If possible, start with something positive, then state what could be improved and finish on a developmental note. This sandwiches the negative aspect between two positive or helpful aspects. You will need to find out if your organisation has any specific feedback methods they wish you to use that will ensure a standardised approach across all assessors to all learners. Whatever method you use to give feedback, it should always be backed up by a written record.

The example in Table 2.3 is of a completed *feedback and action* record. It clearly shows what was carried out, what action needs to be taken and what has been achieved. A copy should be given to the learner and the original kept by the assessor. However, you could use the original assessment plan as in Table 2.2 to add the feedback and achievements, therefore only using one form instead of two. This will depend upon your organisation's requirements.

Different feedback methods

There are many ways you can give feedback to your learners. These include being the following:

- Descriptive – describes examples of what could be improved and why, and is usually formal. Using this method lets you describe what your learner has done, how they have achieved the required assessment requirements and what they can do to progress further.

- Evaluative – usually just a statement such as *well done* or *good*. This method does not offer helpful or constructive advice and is usually informal. It does not give learners the opportunity to know what was done well or how they could improve.

- Constructive – is specific and focused to confirm your learner's achievement or to give developmental points in a positive and helpful way.

- Destructive – relates to improvements which are needed and is often given in a negative way which could demoralise the learner.

- Objective – clearly relates to specific assessment requirements and is factual regarding what has and has not been met.

- Subjective – is often just a personal opinion and can be biased, for example, if the assessor is friendly with the learner. Feedback might be vague and not based on the assessment requirements.

When giving feedback to learners you need to be aware that it could affect their self-esteem and whether they continue or not. The quality of feedback received can be a key factor in their progress and their ability to learn new knowledge and skills. Ongoing constructive and developmental feedback which has been carefully thought through is an indication of your interest in your learner and of your intention to help them develop and do well in the future.

When giving feedback:

- own your statements by beginning with the word *I* rather than *you* (however, written feedback could be given in the third person if your organisation prefers)

- start with something positive, for example *I really liked the confident manner in which you delivered your presentation*

- be specific about what you have seen, for example *I felt the way you explained that topic was really interesting due to your knowledge and humour* or *I found the way you explained that topic rather confusing*

- offer constructive and specific follow-on points, for example *I feel I would have understood it better if you had broken the subject down into smaller stages*

- end with something positive or developmental, for example *I enjoyed your presentation – you had prepared well and came across as very organised and professional. Or, I enjoyed your session. However, a handout summarising the key points would be really helpful to refer to in future.*

Being constructive, specific and developmental with what you say, and owning your statements by beginning with the word *I*, should help your learner focus upon what you are saying and listen to how they can improve. If you don't have any follow-on points then don't create them just for the sake of it. Conversely, if you do have any negative points or criticisms, don't say *My only negative point is …* or *My only criticisms are …* It is much better to replace these words and say *Some areas for development could be …* instead.

If assessment decisions count towards the achievement of a qualification, it is crucial to keep your feedback records along with any action identified for each learner. Records must always be kept safe and secure; your car boot or home is not a good idea, nor is a corner of the staffroom or an open-plan office. AOs expect records to be securely managed, whether they are manual or electronic.

You might need to give feedback to other people, for example your learner's supervisor in their work environment. You need to be careful of what you say and how you say it. It could be that your feedback is used as part of the staff appraisal process to monitor your learner's performance and job prospects.

Extension Activity

Compare and contrast different feedback methods such as descriptive and evaluative, constructive and destructive, objective and subjective. Which do you feel you use when giving feedback and why?

Standardising practice

Standardisation of assessor practice ensures consistency and fairness regarding planning, decisions and feedback. It should also give a consistent experience to all learners from the time they commence to the time they achieve or leave. You should standardise your decisions with other assessors, particularly where more than one assessor is involved in the same subject area. It is also an opportunity to ensure all assessors are interpreting the qualification and assessment requirements accurately and completing records appropriately.

However, assessors need to take into account the individual needs of their learners and the settings in which assessment takes place. For example, if a learner is being assessed in a health and social care setting with a client, it might be more appropriate to obtain a reflective account or a witness statement. An observation carried out by an assessor could upset the client in this situation. Therefore, the number of observations or pieces of evidence from different learners for the same aspect of a qualification could differ. Unless there are written requirements as to the type of evidence and number of observations required, assessors can make their own decisions depending upon the situation.

Activity

Find out when the next standardisation activity is, along with what will be discussed. Prior to this, ensure you are fully familiar with what will be standardised. Think of some questions to ask your colleagues regarding the assessment planning and feedback process.

Attending a standardisation event will give you the opportunity to share good practice and compare your assessment decisions with your colleagues by looking at their assessed work and vice versa. You can then discuss your findings as a team. This will ensure you have interpreted the requirements accurately, that the learner evidence is appropriate and that the assessment records are completed correctly. Even if you don't learn anything new, it will confirm you are doing things right.

Table 2.4 is an example of a completed template used by assessors for standardising assessed work.

The benefits of standardisation

Standardisation events are not team meetings: the latter are to discuss issues relating to the management of the programme, for example AO updates, targets, success rates and learner issues. Activities to standardise practice could be carried out electronically as well as in person.

The benefits of standardisation are:

- a consistent experience for all learners
- a contribution to CPD
- accountability to AOs and regulatory authorities
- all assessment decisions are fair and ethical for all learners
- an opportunity to discuss changes and developments
- clearly defined roles and responsibilities of staff

Table 2.4 Example standardisation record for assessed work

Standardisation record for assessed work			
Learner: Ann Bex			**Registration No/ULN:** 0123456789
Qualification/programme: Customer Service			**Level:** 2
Standardising assessor: M Singh			**Original assessor:** J Smith
Aspect/s standardised: Unit 101			**Date:** 16 February
Checklist	**Yes**	**No**	**Comments/Action required**
Is there an agreed assessment plan with SMART targets?	Y		Your plan had very clear SMART targets with realistic dates for achievement.
Are the assessment methods appropriate and sufficient? Which methods were used?	Y		Observation, questioning, products and witness statements have been used. You can reduce the number of observations in the workplace if you can rely on the witness statements.
Does the evidence meet *all* the required criteria?	Y		All assessment criteria have been met through the various assessment methods.
Does the evidence meet VACSR?	Y		You have ensured all these points are included; you also took into consideration an aspect that you had not planned to assess but that naturally occurred during an observation.
Is there a feedback record clearly showing what has been achieved? (Is it adequate and developmental?)	Y		Your feedback is very thorough and confirms your learner's achievements. However, you could be more developmental to guide your learner towards ways of improving her current practice.
Has subsequent action been identified (if applicable)?		N	The feedback record shows what has been achieved and what feedback has been given. However, no further action has been identified. You need to plan which units will be assessed next and set target dates.
Do you agree with the assessment decision?	Y		I agree with the decision you made. However, I do feel you could have reduced the number of workplace observations.
Are all relevant documents signed and dated (including countersignatures if applicable)?		N	As you are still working towards your Assessor Award, you need to ensure your decisions have been countersigned by a qualified assessor.
Are original assessment records stored separately from the learner's work?		N	You have given your original copies to your learner. You need to ensure you keep the original and give your learner a copy. The original can be kept manually or electronically but must be kept secure for three years in the assessor office.

General comments:
Although there are a few 'No's' in the checklist, this does not affect my judgement as I agree with your decision for this learner. You agreed a SMART assessment plan with your learner which was followed through with assessment and feedback. All your records are in place. However, don't forget to keep originals in the office and give your learner a copy. This is part of our organisation's policy due to some learners having amended the original copy in their favour. It is harder to amend a copy as the pen colour is more prominent.

Make sure you set clear targets for future development and assessment opportunities when you give feedback. It is better to do it at this point while you are with your learner to enable a two-way conversation to take place and to agree suitable target dates.

As you are still working towards your Assessor Award, you need to ensure your decisions have been countersigned by a qualified assessor. Please do this by the end of the month.

Comments from original assessor in response to the above:
I agree with your feedback. I had forgotten about keeping original copies and only giving a photocopy to my learner. I will ensure I do this in future. I was not able to get hold of my countersignatory as he was on holiday. I will ensure he reads my records and signs them upon his return. I will then take a copy ready to use as evidence for my Assessor Certificate. I realise that I must give more developmental feedback and agree future targets when I am with my learner.

Key: SMART: specific, measureable, achievable, relevant, time bound
VACSR: valid, authentic, current, sufficient, reliable

- compliance with relevant codes of practice

- confirming your own practice

- consistency and fairness of judgements and decisions

- empowerment of assessors

- ensuring the assessment requirements are followed

- identifying trends or inconsistencies

- sharing good practice

- succession planning if assessors are due to leave

- maintaining an audit trail of aspects standardised

- giving assessors time to formally meet

- meeting quality assurance requirements

- setting action plans for the development of systems and staff.

Example

Lukas was a new assessor and was not very familiar with the standards of the qualification he was due to assess. The full team of assessors met once a month to discuss the content of each unit. This ensured they were all interpreting the requirements in the same way and making correct decisions. Lukas attended the next meeting and was given the opportunity to reassess a unit which had already been assessed by someone else. This activity helped him understand the requirements and see how the documentation was completed.

If you assess a vocational qualification, you might decide to carry out three observations with each of your learners and give them a written test, whereas another assessor might only carry out one observation and ask some verbal questions. Standardising this approach between all assessors ensures the process is fair. There are times when an individual learner's needs should be taken into account, which will lead to a difference in assessment activities. However, all learners should be entitled to the same assessment experience no matter which assessor they have been allocated.

Standardised summative assessments, marked in the same way for everyone, are necessary for any modern society, which aspires to fairness and justice for its citizens.

(Wolf, 2008, p19)

Examples of standardisation activities
Standardisation activities could include:

- comparing how documents have been completed by different assessors

- creating questions (written and oral) along with expected responses

- designing or revising documents, templates and forms

- ensuring the same documents are used by everyone

- judging evidence as a team rather than by one assessor

- looking at the qualification criteria, discussing how each assessor interprets them and what they would expect from their learners

- remarking or reassessing work to ensure the same decision is reached by different assessors

- peer observations/shadowing

- producing assessment materials as a team to ensure all learners are given a fair chance, for example assignments

- role playing aspects such as assessment planning, making a decision and giving feedback (these could be visually recorded to allow playback, pauses and discussions).

Records should be maintained of all standardisation activities. They will prove what was carried out and when, are a good reference for staff and will be requested by EQAs when they carry out a monitoring activity.

It is important to keep up to date with any changes regarding what you are assessing. If you are assessing an accredited qualification, the standards will change every few years. AOs issue regular updates, either by hard copy or electronically. Once you receive these, you need to discuss the content with your colleagues to ensure you all interpret them in the same way. It would prove useful to maintain minutes of these meetings reflecting your responses to changes and updates.

Obtaining feedback

Obtaining the views of your learners and others will greatly assist you when reflecting upon your role as an assessor and will aid the standardisation process. You could ask your learners directly after an assessment activity how they felt the process went. However, while some learners might feel confident enough to tell you, others might not. When evaluating your own practice, you need to consider the views of your learners and others in order to improve. How you do this will depend upon the type of feedback you have obtained and how useful it will be.

A survey might have ascertained that most learners felt the initial assessment process could be improved, for example using a computerised learning preference test rather than a paper-based one. You might have obtained feedback from an individual learner that their assessment plan had unrealistic target dates. In this case, you could renegotiate the plan with more suitable dates. Feedback from your learners might impact upon your role by making you aware of other aspects, for example the types of questions used in an assignment were too complex, some activities might not have been challenging enough, or a multiple-choice test confused a learner who has dyslexia as they mistook a *b* for a *d*.

Feedback will help standardise the practice of assessors by ensuring the activities used are valid and reliable, and the assessment types and methods are safe, fair and ethical. The views of your learners and others should have an impact upon your own role by helping you improve the assessment experience for your learners.

Extension Activity

Look at the standardisation form in Table 2.4. Does your organisation use something similar? If not, use a form similar to this to ensure you are standardising your judgements with other assessors the next time you meet. You would need to take along all your records as well as your learner's assessed work. After using it, consider what changes you would make to the document or the standardisation process.

Record keeping – assessment

It is important to keep records, otherwise how can you prove what progress your learners have made and exactly what they have achieved? This will usually be for a set period, for example three years, and should be the original records, not photocopies or carbon copies. It is fine to give copies to your learners, as it is harder to forge a copy than an original. Sadly, there are learners who do this; keeping the originals will therefore ensure your records are authentic. You also need to satisfy any company, quality assurance, AO or regulatory authority's audit requirements.

When learners submit work, for example an assignment, it is good practice to issue a receipt. If not, a learner might say that they have submitted their work when they have not.

Keeping full and accurate factual records is also necessary in case one of your learners appeals against an assessment decision you have made. If this happens, don't take it personally – they will be appealing against your decision, not you as a person. You will also need to pass records to your IQA if necessary as well as to any other authorised colleagues who have an interest in your learner's progress and achievement. Table 2.5 lists examples of assessment records. However, you might not need to use all of them depending upon your job role.

Table 2.5 Examples of assessment records

Assessment records	
• achievement dates and grades • action plans • appeals records • application forms • assessment plan and review records • assessment tracking sheet showing progression through a qualification for all learners • authentication declarations/statements • checklists • copies of certificates • diagnostic test results • enrolment forms • formative and summative records • feedback records	• initial assessment records • learning preference results • observation checklists • observation reports • performance and knowledge records • professional discussion records • progress reports • receipts for submitted work • records of achievement • records of oral questions and responses • retention and achievement records • standardisation records • tutorial reviews • witness statements

There might be a standardised approach to completing your records, for example the amount of detail which must be written, or whether the records should be completed manually or electronically. You will need to find out what your organisation expects you to do. Some organisations now use handheld devices to directly input assessment information. These can also be used to support learners to produce their work electronically, for example creating an e-portfolio of evidence towards a qualification.

Activity

Find out what records you are required to maintain, where you can access them and how they should be completed, i.e. the amount of information required. How long must they be kept at your organisation? Where should they be kept? Can they be completed manually or electronically, or both?

All records should be accurate and legible. If you need to make any amendments, make crossings out rather than use correction fluid. Try to keep on top of your administrative work, even if this is carried out electronically. If you leave it a while, you may forget to note important points. You will need to be organised and have a system; learner records could be stored alphabetically in a filing cabinet, or in separate electronic folders on a computer. If storing electronically, make sure you keep a backup copy in case anything gets deleted accidentally. Other records could be stored by the programme or qualification title or AO name.

Example

Andrea has a group of 12 learners working towards a Certificate in Health and Social Care. As she travels around various workplaces to carry out assessment, she maintains an A4 lever arch file, which has a tracking sheet at the front to record the dates of each learner's completed units. She then has plastic wallets for each learner, filed alphabetically, which contain their assessment plans and reviews, and feedback and action records. As she manually completes a document, she makes a copy to give to her learners. Andrea's organisation will be moving over to a web-based electronic storage system in the next few months, which will make it quicker to access the information providing there is an internet connection.

When completing any records, if signatures are required, these should be obtained as soon as possible after the event if they cannot be obtained on the day. Any signatures added later should have the date they were added, rather than the date the form was originally completed. If you are assessing your learners directly, for example by an observation, you will know who they are. If you are assessing work that has been handed to you on a different date or sent electronically, you will need to ensure it is the work of your learner. When completing documents electronically, you will need to find what the policy is in your organisation as to whether an e-mail address or electronic signature is required or not. It could be that one document is signed by all parties at the beginning or end of the programme instead of each separate document. This would confirm the learner's identity and verify work was all their own.

Record keeping and ensuring the authenticity of your learners' work is of paramount importance. To satisfy everyone involved in the assessment process you must be able to show a valid audit trail for all your decisions.

A useful record to track overall learner achievement is known as an assessment tracking sheet. Table 2.6 is an example of a completed tracking sheet for five learners taking five units of a qualification. It shows the dates and grades and is an *at-a-glance* method of seeing the achievement of all learners.

Table 2.6 Example assessment tracking sheet

Assessment tracking sheet					
Assessor: Jenny Smith	**Qualification:** Level 1 Certificate in Hospitality & Catering				
Learner name and registration number	**Aspects assessed**				
	101	102	103	104	105
Chang Hanadi 4524UDBQ	11/06/13 Pass		08/03/13 Pass	10/05/13 Refer 15/05/13 Pass	
Hamed Aamir 1674UEME		07/05/13 Pass			
Jones Irene 1234ABCD	06/02/13 Pass				
Wilson Peter 7985IENF	15/01/13 Pass	04/02/13 Pass			
Young Lou 7496UWME	10/01/13 Pass				

RARPA records

If you are assessing a programme which is not accredited by an AO, you may need to follow the requirements for *recognising and recording progress and achievement in non-accredited learning* (RARPA).

There are five processes to RARPA.

1. Aims – these should be appropriate to the individual or group of learners.

2. Initial assessment – this should be used to establish each learner's starting point.

3. Identification of appropriately challenging learning objectives – these should be agreed, renegotiated and revised as necessary after formative assessment, and should be appropriate to each learner.

4. Recognition and recording of progress and achievement during the programme – this should include assessor feedback, learner reflection and reviews of progress.

5. End of programme – this includes summative assessment, learner self-assessment and a review of overall progress and achievement. This should be in relation to the learning objectives and any other outcomes achieved during the programme.

If you use the RARPA system, you will need to check what records must be maintained; there may be a standard system for you to follow or you may need to design your own assessment records.

Legislation relating to records

All records should be kept secure and should only be accessible by relevant staff. You need to ensure you comply with organisational and statutory guidelines such as the Data Protection Act (1998) and the Freedom of Information Act (2000).

The Data Protection Act (1998) is mandatory for all organisations that hold or process personal data. The Act contains eight principles to ensure that data are:

1. processed fairly and lawfully

2. obtained and used only for specified and lawful purposes

3. adequate, relevant and not excessive

4. accurate and, where necessary, kept up to date

5. kept for no longer than necessary

6. processed in accordance with the individual's rights

7. kept secure

8. transferred only to countries that offer adequate protection.

Confidentiality should be maintained regarding all information you keep. The Freedom of Information Act (2000) gives your learners the opportunity to request to see the information public authorities hold about them. All external stakeholders, such as AOs and funding bodies, should be aware of your systems of record keeping as they may need to approve certain records or storage systems.

Some records might be maintained centrally within your organisation using a management information system. These should include:

- appeals and complaints

- assessor details: name, contact information, curriculum vitae, CPD plans and records

- AO qualification handbook

- enrolment and/or unique learner number

- equal opportunities data such as an analysis of learners by ethnic origin, disability, gender and age, etc.

- evaluation forms, questionnaire and survey results

- internal and external quality assurance reports

- learner details: name, address, date of birth, contact information, registration number

- organisational self-assessment report and records of actions taken

- regulatory and funding guidance

- schemes of work and session plans for taught programmes

- statistics such as retention, achievements and destinations.

Portfolios of evidence

Some qualifications require learners to produce a portfolio of evidence. A portfolio is a file or folder of documents and information, known as *evidence*, which proves achievement. It can be manual or electronic. It is an ideal opportunity for learners to holistically cross-reference the evidence they provide across several areas. There is no need for them to produce evidence for all the individual assessment criteria; they can just give the piece of evidence a reference number and quote this number against the other relevant assessment criteria it meets. If this is the case, your learner should have a copy of the qualification's requirements to help them see what is needed. You can both refer to these when planning the types of evidence which will be provided, and how and when you will assess the evidence.

Portfolios usually contain:

- a record of achievement or unit summary, i.e. a list of what has been achieved along with dates and signatures

- assessment plans and review records

- assessment feedback and action records

- an authentication statement by the learner that all work is their own

- written statements by the learner as to how the evidence meets the criteria

- the learner's evidence cross-referenced to the criteria

- any other documents such as witness statements to support the learner's achievements.

With any portfolio, the quality of the evidence is important, not the quantity. When you are assessing evidence, you don't want to be spending a lot of time searching for something, and your IQA or EQA will not want to either. Some qualifications might require you, as the assessor, to cross-reference the evidence rather than the learner. If this is the case, you will need to plan what is required and by when, encouraging your learner to self-assess their evidence towards the relevant assessment criteria before giving it to you. Your assessment records should be kept independently from your learners' portfolios. However, you should give copies to your learners as proof that the assessment process has taken place and of the decisions made.

Electronic portfolios, known as e-portfolios, are becoming more popular as learners can generate and upload their evidence at a time to suit them. Often the qualification criteria are already within the online system and will automatically cross-reference the learner's evidence to the criteria. Some systems also allow communication to take place between assessors and learners and track all contact. Evidence can be in the form of data files, scanned documents, video, digital and audio files, etc. Assessment of evidence can therefore take place remotely. Your assessment records and feedback can also be uploaded and managed by the system. Assessment in the form of an observation might still be necessary, although this could be digitally recorded and/or observed via a web camera. When assessing electronic evidence, you must make sure that it has been produced solely by your learner, who might have to produce photo identification at some point. If you are ever in doubt as to whether the learner is who they say they are, you will need to follow your organisation's procedure to ascertain this.

Extension Activity

Locate your organisation's forms and templates which you will be required to use for the assessment process. How do they differ to the examples in this chapter? What changes would you recommend to your documents and why? Can you discuss these changes at your next team meeting?

Summary

In this chapter you have learnt about:

- assessment planning in the work environment

- making assessment decisions

- providing feedback

- standardising practice

- record keeping – assessment.

Evidence

Evidence from the completed activities within this chapter, plus the following, could be used towards the *Assessing occupational competence in the work environment* unit, for example:

- four completed assessment plans for at least two learners (methods must include observation of performance, examining work products and questions – to be assessed in the work environment)

- four assessment activities you would use with your learners (for example, observation checklists, assignments, written questions, oral questions)

- four completed feedback records for the two learners

- minutes of assessor team meetings

- records of standardisation activities

- written statements cross-referenced to the unit's assessment criteria

- answers to questions issued by your assessor

- records of discussions with your assessor.

Cross-referencing grid

This chapter contributes towards the following assessment criteria, along with aspects of the National Occupational Standards for Learning and Development. Full details of the learning outcomes and assessment criteria for each unit can be found in the Appendices.

Unit	Assessment criteria
Understanding the principles and practices of assessment	3.1, 3.2 4.2 5.1, 5.2 6.2 7.2 8.2
Assess occupational competence in the work environment	1.1, 1.2, 1.3, 1.4 2.1, 2.2, 2.3, 2.4 3.1, 3.2, 3.3
Assess vocational skills, knowledge and understanding	1.1, 1.3 2.4, 2.5, 2.6 3.1, 3.2, 3.3
National Occupational Standards	**Reference**
9 – Assess learner achievement	KU2, KU3, KU4, KU5, KU10, KU11, KU12, KU13, KU14, KU15, KU16, KU17, KU18 9.1, 9.2, 9.3, 9.4, 9.5, 9.6, 9.7, 9.8
11 – Internally monitor and maintain the quality of assessment	KU1, KU3, KU4, KU5, KU6, KU11, KU14, KU18 11.2, 11.3, 11.4, 11.5, 11.6, 11.7, 11.8, 11.9, 11.11
12 – Externally monitor and maintain the quality of assessment	KU3, KU5, KU17 12.3, 12.5, 12.7

Theory focus

References and further information

Coffield, F (2008) *Just Suppose Teaching and Learning Became the First Priority*. London: LSN.

Ofqual (2009) *Authenticity – A Guide for Teachers*. Coventry: Ofqual.

Olin, R and Tucker, J (2012) *The Vocational Assessor Handbook* (5th edition). London: Kogan Page.

Pachler, N, Mellar, H, Daly, C, Mor, Y and Wiliam, D (2009) *Scoping a Vision for Formative E-assessment (FEASST)* JISC. London: Institute of Education.

Race, P, Brown, S and Smith, B (2004) *500 Tips on Assessment*. Abingdon: Routledge.

Read, H (2011) *The Best Assessor's Guide*. Bideford: Read On Publications Ltd.

Read, H (2013) *The Best Initial Assessment Guide*. Bideford: Read On Publications Ltd.

Tummons, J (2011) *Assessing Learning in the Lifelong Learning Sector* (3rd edition). London: Learning Matters SAGE.

Wolf, A (2008) Looking for the best result. *Make the Grade*, Summer 2008. Institute of Educational Assessors.

Websites

Assessment methods: www.brookes.ac.uk/services/ocsld/resources/methods.html

Assessment resources: www.excellencegateway.org.uk and www.questionmark. com.uk

Basic Key Skills Builder: www.bksb.co.uk

Data Protection Act (1998): www.legislation.gov.uk/ukpga/1998/29/contents

Efutures (e-assessment regulators): www.ofqual.gov.uk/how-we-regulate/90articles/7-e-assessment

Freedom of Information Act (2000): www.legislation.gov.uk/ukpga/2000/36/ contents

Health and Safety Executive: www.hse.gov.uk

Learning Records Service: www.learningrecordsservice.org.uk

Learning preferences: www.vark-learn.com

Oxford Learning Institute, Giving and receiving feedback: www.learning.ox.ac.uk/supervision/stages/feedback/

Plagiarism: www.plagiarism.org and www.plagiarismadvice.org

QCF shortcut: http://tinyurl.com/2944r8h

RARPA: www.learningcurve.org.uk/resources/learning/rarpa

3 ASSESSING VOCATIONAL SKILLS, KNOWLEDGE AND UNDERSTANDING

Introduction

In this chapter you will learn about:

- vocational assessment planning
- reviewing learner progress
- questioning techniques
- the role of ICT in assessment
- continuing professional development.

Within the chapter there are activities and examples which will help you to reflect on the above and to develop and enhance your knowledge of how to assess vocational skills, knowledge and understanding. Completing the activities will help you to gather evidence towards the *Assessing vocational skills, knowledge and understanding* unit. At the end of each section is an extension activity to stretch and challenge your knowledge and understanding.

At the end of the chapter is a list of possible evidence which could be used towards the *Assessing vocational skills, knowledge and understanding* unit.

A cross-referencing grid shows how the content of this chapter contributes towards the relevant TAQA units' criteria and the National Occupational Standards. There is also a theory focus with relevant references, further information and websites to which you might like to refer.

Vocational assessment planning

If you are not assessing competence in the workplace, you will probably be assessing an academic or a vocational programme and might also be teaching or training your learners, for example in a college or training organisation. This would enable you to get to know your learners well before you assess them. Conversely, someone else might teach the learners and you might just be responsible for assessing them. Teaching, training and assessment can take place in many contexts, for example a college, training organisation, prison, community hall or other appropriate location. If you are teaching, you will probably have a group of learners. Alternatively, you might be training individuals on a one-to-one basis.

The subject you assess will determine the assessment type and method to be used. For example, an academic programme could be assessed by an exam whereas a vocational programme could be assessed by an observation and questions. You will need to check the syllabus or qualification handbook to see what assessment activities are provided for you, or what you may have to devise.

Assessment activities can be initial (at the beginning), formative (part way through a programme), and/or summative (at the end of a unit, qualification or programme). Formative assessments will check ongoing progress and usually consist of informal activities. Summative assessments will confirm achievement and usually consist of formal activities (see Chapter 1 for a comprehensive list of types of assessment you could use). Assessment activities can be assessor led, for example observations, or learner led, for example assignments, or a mixture of both. The methods will vary depending upon whether you are assessing skills, knowledge or understanding; some methods can cover both (see Chapter 1 for a comprehensive list of assessment methods and activities).

When planning to carry out assessment activities, you will need to know when your learners are ready to be assessed. There is no point assessing them if they have not learnt everything they need to know, as you will be setting them up to fail. If you don't teach as well as assess, you will need to communicate with the person who has taught the learner to ensure the required learning has taken place beforehand. If a learner has been absent for any reason, you will need to make sure they are up to date regarding what they have missed. Carrying out a formative assessment well before a summative assessment can help both you and your learner see how ready they are.

The timing of your assessments can also make a difference: if you plan to assess on a Friday before a holiday period, your learners might not be as attentive; equally so first thing on a Monday morning. This is difficult, of course, if you only see your learners on these particular days. If you are planning a schedule of assessments throughout the year, you will need to consider any public or cultural holidays. There is no point planning to assess on Mondays if the majority of these fall on public holidays.

Activity

If you have not already done so, obtain a copy of the syllabus or qualification handbook for your subject. Ascertain what assessment activities have been provided for you and what you need to create. When will you carry these out, i.e. different dates for individual learners, or the same dates for groups of learners?

You will need to carry out some form of assessment planning with your learners, even if it is just agreeing target dates for the submission of assignments, or planning ahead for the dates of tests or exams. Your learners will need to know what they are working towards, when they will be assessed and how they will be assessed, for example by assignments or tests. This information could be in the form of an action plan rather than an assessment plan. The action plan would contain the details of the assignments or the expected test dates. It can be updated with achievement dates, and be added to or amended as necessary. An example action plan is shown in Table 3.1 (see Chapter 2 for further details regarding assessment planning).

Table 3.1 Example action plan

Action plan			
Learner: Marcia Indira		**Assessor:** Abbi Cross	
Qualification: Level 2 Business, Administration and Finance		**Registration number:** 7913PIRW	
Date commenced: 5 September		**Expected completion date:** 28 July	
Assignment	**Assignment questions**	**Target date**	**Achievement date**
Unit 1: Business Enterprise Learning outcome 2: Be able to develop a business enterprise idea	Q1 – Generate a range of ideas for a business enterprise	7 October	
	Q2 – Compare the viability of the business enterprise ideas	14 October	
	Q3 – Select and develop a business idea	21 October	

If you are teaching as well as assessing, you will need to prepare a scheme of work to show what you will teach and when, and how you will assess skills, knowledge and understanding. For example, formative assessments could include multiple-choice tests, questions, quizzes and role plays which can assess progress. Summative assessments could include assignments, exams or tests to confirm achievement. When planning your programme delivery, make sure you have taught all the required material before carrying out any summative assessments. Ongoing formative assessments will help you gauge that learning has taken place. You will need to ensure appropriate time is planned for assessment activities during your sessions or in between sessions, i.e. as homework. You will also need to plan adequate time to carry out any marking and assessment, making a decision and giving feedback to your learners. It is best to stagger the summative assessment activities so that you don't put too much pressure on your learners or on yourself.

It could be that your learners will be taking an exam and this will need to be planned and invigilated according to the awarding organisation's (AO's) requirements on a set date. Some assignments might also need to be completed under supervised conditions. You would therefore need to ensure you have taught everything in good time. You could use past exam or test papers as a formative assessment activity to check the progress of your learners beforehand. This will also give them an idea of the structure that will need to be followed in their responses.

If your learners are working towards an accredited qualification, you will need to ensure they have been registered with the appropriate AO. It might not be your responsibility to carry out this task, but you should communicate the details of your learners to the relevant staff.

If a record of attendance or an in-house certificate will be issued to your learners upon successful completion, this information should be communicated to the person who will produce them. You should inform your learners when they can expect to receive any feedback or formal recognition of their achievements, and what they can do if they disagree with any decisions.

Table 3.2 lists examples of assessment activities which could be used to assess skills, knowledge and understanding.

Table 3.2 Skills, knowledge and understanding – assessment activities

Assessment activities Skills	Assessment activities Knowledge and understanding
• assignments (practical) • case studies (practical) • creating products, i.e. working models • peer assessment of an activity • observation of practical work in a laboratory, workshop or a realistic working environment • projects (individual or team based) • recognition of prior learning (RPL) • self-assessment • simulations • skills tests	• assignments (theoretical) • case studies (theoretical) • discussions • examinations • oral and written questions • presentations • projects (individual or team based) • puzzles and quizzes • RPL • reflective learning journals • role plays • tests and multiple-choice questions • written statements

If you are responsible for devising your own assessment methods and activities, you might decide to choose ones which are easy to mark, for example multiple-choice questions. You might not have a lot of time for preparation and marking, therefore the more time you spend preparing something suitable and relevant, the easier the marking will be. There is no point making assessment activities complex unless it is a requirement of the qualification or you need to challenge higher level learners further. Lower level learners can easily become demoralised if the activities are unattainable.

If you assess group work, such as presentations or role plays, you need to assess each individual's contribution towards the assessment requirements. Otherwise you could be passing the whole group when some learners may not have contributed much at all. If you are related to, or know personally, the learners you will assess, you should notify your organisation of any conflict of interest. They may also need to notify the relevant AO in case you are not allowed to assess a learner if they are a partner, a relative or a direct member of your family or your spouse's family.

Whatever subject you are going to assess, you need to ensure your learners have acquired and mastered the skills, attitudes, knowledge and/or understanding required at the right level for achievement. There is no point teaching your learners to repeat expected answers or to demonstrate a task if they don't really understand what they are doing and why.

Example

Isla had a group of learners working towards a qualification in desktop publishing. She had demonstrated how to carry out various functions on the computer and then asked them to work through past exam papers. The learners were soon able to pass all the papers, therefore they knew what they were doing, but did not understand why they were doing it that way. Consequently, when one of the learners got a job in desktop publishing, they were unable to perform it fully as they had only been taught to pass test papers.

Devising assessment materials

When you are devising assessment materials, for example assignments, essays or questions, you need to pitch these at the correct level for your learners. If you are assessing an accredited qualification, it will already be assigned a level, for example *Level 3 Certificate in Hospitality and Catering*. If it is not accredited, you will need to pitch your assessment materials at the level which is appropriate for your learners, for example beginners, intermediate or advanced, or level 1, 2 or 3. Knowing which level you are assessing will help you use the correct level of objectives when writing assessment materials.

Objectives

Objectives are verbs, i.e. what you expect your learners to do, such *as analyse, describe* or *list.* To *list* would be at a lower level than to *analyse.*

Table 3.3 gives examples of objectives you could use when devising assessment activities at different levels. If you are assessing an accredited qualification, you will need to follow the objectives stated in the assessment criteria, which might be different to those in Table 3.3.

Bloom (1956) believed that education should focus on the mastery of subjects and the promotion of higher forms of thinking, rather than an approach which simply transfers facts. His *taxonomy model* of classification places learning into three overlapping *domains.* These are:

1. the cognitive domain (intellectual capability, i.e. knowledge or thinking)

2. the affective domain (feelings, emotions and behaviour, i.e. attitudes or beliefs)

3. the psychomotor domain (manual and physical skills, i.e. actions or skills).

Table 3.3 Examples of objectives at different levels (note: some might occur or be repeated at different levels on the Qualifications and Credit Framework)

Level	Skills		Knowledge and understanding		Attitudes	
Foundation	Attempt Carry out Learn Listen Read		Answer Match Recall Repeat Show		Adopt Assume Contribute Listen	
I	Arrange Help Imitate Obtain	Switch Use View Watch	Access Know List Locate	Name Recap Recognise State	Adapt Co-operate Familiarise	
2	Assist Change Choose Connect Demonstrate Draw	Perform Practise Prepare Present Rearrange	Compare Describe Identify Reorder Select Write		Accept Consider Develop Express Question Understand	
3	Apply Assemble Assess Build Create Construct Design	Devise Estimate Facilitate Illustrate Make Measure Produce	Compose Explain Paraphrase Test		Apply Appreciate Challenge Defend Determine Discriminate Enable	Participate Predict Relate Review Study Visualise
4	Calculate Complete Convert Diagnose Explore Generate Maintain	Modify Plan Quality assure Research Search Solve	Analyse Invent Contextualise Outline Revise Summarise Verify		Appraise Command Criticise Debate Define Discuss Influence	Judge Justify Persuade Rationalise Reflect
5	Accept responsibility Encapsulate Establish	Interview Manage Organise Teach	Categorise Classify Contrast Evaluate Interpret		Argue Critically appraise Define	Differentiate Dispute Formulate Suggest
6	Operate Utilise		Extrapolate Synthesise Translate		Conclude Hypothesise Justifiably argue	
7	Modify		Strategise		Critically differentiate	
8	Lead		Redefine		Critically discriminate	

The three domains are summarised as *knowledge, attitudes* and *skills,* or *think, feel, do.* Your learners should benefit from the development of knowledge and intellect (cognitive domain); attitudes and beliefs (affective domain); and the ability to put physical skills into practice (psychomotor domain). You would therefore assess your learners at the right level for their learning, at the appropriate time, using the relevant domain.

Each domain contains objectives at different levels, such as *analyse, describe, explain* and *list.* You will see these objectives in the qualification handbook for your subject; they are often referred to as *assessment criteria.* If the qualification you are assessing is on the Qualifications and Credit Framework (QCF), it will be at a particular level (from foundation level to level 8) depending upon the subject and your learners.

Example

Pierre has a group of Level 1 learners working towards a Certificate in Engineering. He carries out formative assessment of his learners using objectives such as state (to test knowledge), familiarise (to test attitudes), and use (to test skills). When he is sure his learners have mastered the topics, he will give them a summative test which will assess the required knowledge, attitudes and skills needed to achieve the Certificate.

If Pierre used objectives such as *justify* and *facilitate,* these would be too high a level for his learners to achieve. If his learners progress to level 2, Pierre could then use objectives relevant to that level such as *describe* and *demonstrate.*

If you are assessing a qualification which is on the QCF, there will be specific *learning outcomes* to help you plan what you will teach, and *assessment criteria* for your learners to achieve. If a qualification is offered at different levels, often the learning outcomes are the same but the assessment criteria are different. The latter might use objectives such as *describe* for a lower level, *explain* for an intermediate level and *analyse* for a higher level. The content of the qualification remains the same; the difference is in the amount of work the learners will do to achieve a higher level. However, learners will often feel they are capable of achieving a higher level, even though that might not be the case.

Example

Elaine is assessing Equality and Diversity. She has a mixed group of Level 3 and Level 4 learners. All of the learners opt to take the Level 4 assessments. However, once Elaine assesses their responses, she realises most of them only meet the criteria for Level 3. When she informs them of this, they don't take the feedback well.

In this example, all the learners felt they were capable of a higher level of achievement and were therefore demoralised when told they did not meet the requirements. If an initial assessment had been carried out, the learners would have been aware of their abilities and which level to work towards.

If you have a mixed group of learners, to aid differentiation you could adapt your formative assessment activities to reflect what *everyone* should achieve, what *most* will achieve and what *some* will achieve. For example, everyone will *describe*, most will *explain* and some will *analyse*. This is a useful way of challenging more able learners while those less able can still achieve something.

Activity

Design four different assessment activities that you could use with your learners. They should be based around the criteria you are going to assess and be at the correct level for your learners. You should create example responses for any questions that you are asking. This will help when marking and will ensure consistent and reliable assessment decisions. If possible, carry out the activities with learners and evaluate their strengths and limitations.

Peer and self-assessment

Peer assessment involves a learner assessing another learner's progress. Self-assessment involves a learner assessing their own progress. Both methods encourage learners to make decisions about what has been learnt so far and to reflect on aspects for further development. Your learners will need to fully understand the assessment criteria and how to be analytical and objective with their judgements. Throughout the process of peer and self-assessment, learners can develop other skills such as listening, observing and questioning.

Peer assessment can also be useful to develop and motivate learners. However, this should be managed carefully, as you may have some learners who don't get along and might use the opportunity to demoralise one another. You would need to give advice to your learners regarding how to make a decision and how to give feedback. If learner feedback is given skilfully, other learners may consider more what their peers have said than what you have said. If you consider peer assessment to have a valuable contribution towards the assessment process, ensure you plan for it to enable your learners to become accustomed to and more proficient at giving it. The final decision as to the achievement of your learner will lie with you. Table 3.4 gives some advantages and limitations of peer and self-assessment.

Boud (1995) suggested that learning and development will not occur without self-assessment and reflection. However, this must be done honestly and realistically if it is going to aid improvement. This process can promote learner involvement and personal responsibility. All learners should be fully aware of the requirements of the qualification and therefore ensure their work is focused towards the assessment criteria.

Peer feedback could be written rather than given verbally and therefore be anonymous. This would encourage objective opinions as learners will not feel they are betraying their peers. Ground rules, such as the way feedback will be structured, should be established to ensure the process is valid and fair.

Table 3.4 Advantages and limitations of peer and self-assessment

Peer assessment advantages	Peer assessment limitations
<ul><li>helps develop communication skills</li><li>leads to discussions which everyone can benefit from</li><li>learners are focused upon the assessment requirements or can use a checklist</li><li>learners may accept comments from peers more readily than those from the assessor</li><li>peers might notice something the teacher has not</li><li>promotes attention as learners have to focus on what is happening</li><li>increases attention for activities such as peer presentations if feedback has to be given</li><li>promotes learner and peer interaction and involvement</li></ul>	<ul><li>all peers should be involved therefore planning needs to take place as to who will give feedback and to whom</li><li>appropriate conditions and environment are needed</li><li>assessor needs to confirm each learner's progress and achievements as it might be different from their peers' judgements</li><li>everyone needs to understand the assessment requirements</li><li>learners might be subjective and friendly rather than objective with their decisions</li><li>needs to be carefully managed to ensure no personality conflicts or unjustified comments</li><li>should be supported with other assessment methods</li><li>some peers may be anxious, nervous or lack confidence to give feedback</li></ul>
Self-assessment advantages	**Self-assessment limitations**
<ul><li>encourages learners to check their own progress</li><li>encourages reflection</li><li>mistakes can be seen as opportunities</li><li>promotes learner involvement and personal responsibility</li><li>learners are focused upon the assessment requirements</li><li>learners identify when they are ready for a formal assessment</li><li>learners take ownership of the process, i.e. identifying areas for improvement</li></ul>	<ul><li>assessor needs to discuss and confirm progress and achievement</li><li>difficult to be objective when making a decision</li><li>learners may feel they have achieved more than they actually have</li><li>learners must fully understand the assessment requirements</li><li>learners need to be specific about what they have achieved and what they need to do to complete any gaps</li><li>some learners may lack confidence in their ability to make decisions about their own progress</li></ul>

Examples of peer assessment activities include:

- assessing each other's work anonymously and giving written or verbal feedback

- giving grades and/or written or verbal feedback regarding peer presentations

- holding group discussions before collectively agreeing a grade and giving feedback, perhaps for a presentation

- suggesting improvements to their peers' work

- writing a written statement of how their peers could improve.

Examples of self-assessment activities include:

- awarding a grade for a presentation they have delivered

- suggesting improvements regarding their skills and knowledge

- compiling a written statement of how they could improve their work.

Communicating with others

You will need to communicate with other people if they are involved in the assessment process of your learners. These people might be internal to your organisation, i.e. adminis- trative staff, or external, i.e. employers. You should remain professional at all times as you are representing your organisation. People might not always remember your name; you might be known as *that person from XYZ organisation*. You therefore need to create a good and lasting impression of yourself and your organisation. In some organisations, you may be required to wear a name badge, carry identification, and sign in and out for security reasons.

You might need to liaise with support staff within your organisation, perhaps to arrange help with preparing and copying assessment materials and resources, or to make modifi- cations or adaptations to equipment and materials. You might also need to get in touch with others who have an involvement with your learners, for example parents, probation officers or social workers. If this is the case, remember aspects of confidentiality and data protection and keep notes of all discussions in case you need to refer to them again. You might teach a particular subject, but not assess it; for example, your learners may take an exam which is marked by AO personnel or a test which is marked by a colleague. You might have to plan for examinations to be taken, in which case you will need to ensure the administration staff are aware of what will take place and when, as invigilators may be needed, secure storage will be required for papers, and specific rooms will need to be timetabled accordingly.

If you are not the only assessor for your subject, you will need to standardise your prac- tice with other assessors. If you are assessing an academic qualification, you might use the term *double marking* rather than standardisation. This enables different assessors to mark one another's assessed work to ensure the correct grade has been given. This could take place blindly, i.e. you don't get to see the original grade. Having a marking scheme or expected answers will help you reach a fair decision. If standardisation is not carried out, assessment activities and decisions might not be fair to all learners.

People you may need to communicate with, besides your learners, are given in Table 3.5.

You will not have a second chance to make a first impression; it is therefore important to portray yourself in a professional way. That includes not only what you say but the way you say it, your attitude, body language and dress. A warm and confident smile, positive attitude, self-assurance and the use of eye contact will all help when communicating, particularly if you are meeting someone for the first time.

Table 3.5 Examples of internal and external contacts

Internal	External
• administrators • assessors • colleagues • exam officers • internal quality assurers (IQAs) • invigilators • managers • mentors • teachers • trainers • support staff	• careers advisers • employers • external quality assurers (EQAs) • inspectors and regulators • parents, guardians or carers • probation officers • social workers • staff from other organisations and agencies • witnesses and others involved in the assessment of your learners

You might act differently depending upon the circumstances and who you are with, for example informally with colleagues or formally with external quality assurers. Communication can be verbal, non-verbal or written. Whichever method you use, communication is a means of passing on information from one person to another.

Skills of communicating effectively include the way you speak, listen and express yourself, for example with body language and written information. You need to be confident and organised with what you wish to convey; the way you do this will give an impression of yourself for better or worse. You may have to attend meetings or video conferences, and wherever you are with other people, they will make assumptions about you based on what they see and hear. You may have to write reports, memos or e-mails, and the way you express yourself when writing is as important as when speaking.

If you feel it is difficult to make an objective decision with the current assessment activities used, you will need to discuss your concerns with other staff or with a contact from the AO. You may need to redesign some activities to make them more specific and/or unambiguous. If all your learners are achieving everything with ease, perhaps you need to be more challenging with the tasks you set.

If your subject or qualification is quality assured, IQAs and EQAs will sample your work to ensure your judgements and decisions are correct and fair. Some learners might have a mentor, someone who is supporting and encouraging them while they go through the learning and assessment process. They may also have other teachers who will assess them. However, do be aware of any sensitive or confidential issues relating to your learners which they may not wish you to pass on. Conversely, you may need to inform others of any particular learner requirements to ensure consistency of support.

If you have learners who are attending a programme in conjunction with a school or other organisation, you may need to liaise with their staff, i.e. to give reports of progress and attendance. You may need to communicate with employers, managers or supervisors whose staff you are assessing in the work environment. If this is the case, make sure you are aware of any protocols involved, and follow your organisation's procedures for dealing with external clients.

Activity

Find out whom you need to communicate with, either internally or externally, regarding the subjects you are assessing. How can you contact them and why would you? Make a note of telephone numbers, addresses, websites, e-mail addresses, etc. which could come in useful.

Types of communication

When communicating verbally, your tone, pace and inflections are all important factors in getting your message across. If you speak too quickly or softly, others may not hear everything you say; always try to speak clearly. It is useful to consider what reactions you want to achieve from the information you are communicating, and if others react differently, you will need to amend your methods. You might be communicating via the telephone and therefore be unable to see any reactions to what you say, which could lead to a misunderstanding. Always ask questions to check that the person you are communicating with has understood what you have said. Non-verbal communication includes your body language and posture, for example gestures and the way you stand or sit. Be conscious of your mannerisms, for example folded arms, hands in pockets or the gestures you make, and use eye contact with the person you are communicating with. The things you don't say are just as important as those you do say.

Written communication, for example in the form of feedback for assessed work or an e-mail, is also an expression of you as a person. The way you convey your words and phrases, and your intention, may not be how it is read or understood by the other person. There are always different ways of interpreting the same event. If you are working with learners via an online programme, you may never see them, but will probably build up a visual image; they may therefore be doing the same of you. Information can be easily misinterpreted; therefore the sender has to be sure the receiver will interpret any communication in the way that it was intended. You need to get your message across effectively; otherwise what you are conveying may not necessarily reflect your own thoughts and may cause a breakdown in communication. Any written text cannot be taken back, so there is less room for errors or mistakes and you need to be clear about the exact meaning you wish to convey. Your writing should be checked for spelling, grammar and punctuation. Don't rely on a computer to check these, as it will not always realise the context in which you are writing. This is particularly the case when writing feedback to learners; if you make a spelling mistake, they will think it is correct as you are deemed to be the more knowledgeable person.

You might give feedback to your learners via the internet, for example by using e-mail or a web-based system. If you use this type of medium for communication and/or assessment purposes, try not to get into the habit of abbreviating words or cutting out vowels. It is important to express yourself in a professional way; otherwise misunderstanding and confusion may arise. Just imagine you are talking to the other person and type your message appropriately and professionally.

Example

Aasif has a good professional working relationship with his group. He needs to e-mail his learners to remind them that the room they will be in next week is to be changed due to examinations taking place in their usual room. He keeps his e-mail brief and to the point by stating: 'Hi all, just a quick reminder that we will be in room G3 next week instead of G5, Aasif.' A poor alternative could have been: 'Hey, I told u last week we wld be in a different room cos of exams, so don't forget where u have to go, and dont get lost, A.'

The latter is unprofessional, is rather negative, contains errors and does not convey where the learners should go. This would not give a good impression, and the learners may lose respect for their assessor.

If your organisation takes on new assessors, you might be asked to mentor and support them. If they are unqualified and you are already a qualified assessor, you might also be asked to countersign their decisions to ensure they are valid and fair. New staff should be given an induction to the assessment policy and procedures, all relevant paperwork, systems and organisational requirements. If an assessor is leaving, there should be a system of succession planning to allow time for an appropriate handover and any relevant training to take place. Usually, the AO will need to be informed of any new staff to ensure that they are suitably qualified and experienced.

You could have learners who have excelled in some way, and your organisation or AO might have an award or medal for which they could be nominated. Your own organisation or department might hold a celebration event to present certificates to successful learners. This is a way of obtaining positive publicity for your organisation and of valuing and celebrating the success of your learners.

Knowing whom you need to deal with, how you should proceed, and what is involved in the communication process should make your role as an assessor more rewarding and professional.

Extension Activity

Consider the action planning or assessment planning process for your particular subject and, if possible, agree a vocational action plan or assessment plan with a group of learners or an individual. What might affect the dates you have planned and how would you overcome this?

Reviewing learner progress

It is important to review the progress of your learners so you know not only how they are progressing and what they have achieved, but also what they may need to do to improve. It is also an opportunity to discuss any concerns they may have. Reviews of progress with learners can form part of the assessment process and could provide the opportunity to carry out formative assessments in an informal way. They also give your learner the opportunity to discuss any concerns or ask questions they might have been self-conscious about asking in a group situation.

The review should be carried out at a suitable time during the learning and assessment process and records should always be maintained. Informal reviews and discussions can take place at any opportune time. Reviewing progress enables you to differentiate effectively, ensuring that the needs of your learners are met and that they are being challenged to develop to their full potential. If learners are taking a higher level qualification, you should be giving them more autonomy towards their achievement, i.e. not giving them the same amount of support as a learner taking a lower level qualification. The review process also helps ascertain if learners are experiencing any difficulties, enabling you to arrange for any necessary support or further training.

Reviewing learner progress enables you to:

- confirm progress and achievements
- plan areas for further development
- check skills and knowledge gained from a previous session, before commencing the current session
- discuss any confidential or sensitive issues
- give constructive and developmental feedback
- keep a record of what was discussed
- involve your learners, formally or informally
- motivate your learners
- plan for differentiation
- plan future learning and assessments
- plan more challenging or creative assessment opportunities
- provide opportunities for further learning, development and/or support
- review your own contribution to the learning and assessment process
- revise your scheme of work and session plans
- revise your strategies for assessment
- update your learner's action plan or assessment plan.

If possible, a formal one-to-one review should take place at some point during every programme as it is a key element of the assessment process.

Example

Richard has a group of 12 learners who are attending a weekly evening class in Pottery Skills from 7 to 9 pm for three terms. He has decided to dedicate one session every term for individual tutorials and reviews of progress. While he is carrying these out, the rest of the group will work on projects or use the organisation's library or computer facilities. This enables Richard to discuss individual progress, concerns and actions with each learner. It also helps him plan and evaluate the teaching, learning and assessment process.

If there is no set review procedure, or you are not required to review your learners' progress, it would still be a useful activity if you have the time. The review process should be ongoing until your learner has completed their qualification, even if it is on an informal basis. Regular reviews can help to keep your learners motivated, and make them feel less isolated and appreciate how they are progressing. It is also an opportunity for your learners to contribute to the assessment process by voicing their views and discussing any concerns they may have.

The review process should involve:

- arranging a suitable date, time and location, and confirming these with your learner

- communicating with anyone else involved in the assessment process

- obtaining in advance all relevant records relating to your learner, the subject and the assessments carried out

- discussing any issues or concerns, progress and achievements so far

- updating the action plan or assessment plan with achievements and dates

- identifying any training needs

- planning future assessment activities and targets, along with the next review date

- signing and dating the review record and giving a copy to your learner.

Always listen to what your learners have to say without interrupting them; they may not have the opportunity elsewhere to talk to someone about sensitive issues. Ensure the confidentiality of any information your learners disclose to you; otherwise you could lose their trust and respect. However, you need to know where your boundaries as an assessor are, and not get involved personally. There are exceptions, i.e. if you have any cause for concern as to your learner's safety. For example, if you suspect bullying, you must pass this information on to whoever is responsible in your organisation for safeguarding.

You could also review the progress of your learners as a group. At an appropriate time during the programme, you could hold a discussion regarding how they feel the sessions are progressing. This is particularly useful when you need to assess group activities. It could be that some activities don't suit the learning preferences of a few learners, therefore not enabling them to fully contribute. Using several different activities could alleviate this problem and make the process more interesting. Feedback from group reviews can inform the assessment planning process and also be a valuable tool to evaluate the programme as a whole.

When assessing and reviewing progress, always try to ensure that the environment meets your learners' basic needs, such as feeling safe and comfortable. This will enable them to feel secure enough to progress further. Maslow (1987) introduced the concept of a *Hierarchy of Needs* in 1954 after rejecting the idea that human behaviour was determined by childhood events. He argued that there are five needs which represent different levels of motivation which must be met. The highest level is *self-actualising*, meaning people are fully functional, possess a healthy personality, and take responsibility for themselves and their actions. In educational terms this can mean they are achieving what they wanted to. Maslow also believed that people should be able to move through these needs to the highest level, providing they are given an education that promotes growth. Figure 3.1 shows the needs expressed in educational terms in relation to learning.

Figure 3.1 Maslow's (1954) hierarchy of needs expressed in educational terms

Ensuring the assessment environment meets your learners' first-level needs will enable them to feel comfortable and secure enough to learn and progress to the higher levels. You will need to appreciate that some learners may not have these lower needs met in their home lives, making it difficult for them to move on to the higher levels in their learning. Therefore, if you can ensure the environment is suitable, not too hot or cold, and that learners can have a break for refreshments, this should help the learning process.

Supporting learners

At some point, you might have a learner who requires specialist support. Some learners will have barriers, challenges or needs that may affect their attendance and/or achievement. Hopefully, you can ascertain these prior to your learners commencing, perhaps from their application form or through the initial assessment process. However, you may become aware of some needs during the programme and you would need to plan a suitable course of action to help your learner, or refer them to an appropriate specialist or agency. If you can be proactive and notice potential needs before they become issues, you might be able to alleviate your learner's concerns. Otherwise, you will need to be reactive to the situation and deal with it professionally and sensitively.

Examples of potential barriers, challenges or needs might include:

- lack of access to or fear of technology
- age
- culture and language differences
- emotional or psychological problems
- faith and religion

- finance

- hearing or visual impairment

- hyperactivity

- lack of confidence, motivation or social skills

- lack of resources

- learning difficulties and disabilities

- limited basic skills such as English, maths or information and communication technology (ICT)

- peer pressure

- personal/work/home circumstances

- physical, medical, mental or health problems.

You may feel you can deal with some of these yourself. However, you should always refer your learners to an appropriate specialist or agency if you cannot. Never feel you have to solve any learner problems yourself and don't get personally involved; always remain professional.

When planning assessments, you need to consider any particular requirements of your learners to ensure they can all participate. Initial assessment would ensure your learners are able to take the subject. However, you (or the organisation) may need to make reasonable adjustments to adapt resources, equipment or the environment to support them (as stated in the Equality Act 2010). If anything is adapted, make sure both you and your learners are familiar with the changes prior to carrying out the assessment activity. You cannot change the assessment criteria issued by the AO, but you can change the way you implement the assessment process. If you need to make any changes, you must consult the relevant AO to discuss these. Most will have an *Access to Assessment* policy which will inform you of what you can and cannot do. You cannot change a set examination date and time without approval, and you may need consent in writing for other changes or amendments to assessments.

Activity

Think about your learners and the environment in which you will be assessing. Do you need to ask your learners if any adaptations or changes are required? Will the timing of the assessments impact on your learners in any way, for example during an evening session when they may not have had time to eat? Find out what you are allowed to amend in accordance with the qualification requirements. Check what documentation and guidance your AO provides to support learner needs.

All learners should have equality of opportunity and appropriate support to enable them to access assessment. It could be that you don't need to make any special arrangements just yet, but knowing what to do, and who to go to, will make things easier for you when such circumstances do occur.

Some learners may lack self-confidence, or have previous experiences of assessment that were not very positive. Many factors can affect a learner's motivation; therefore you need to ensure you treat all your learners as individuals, using their names and making the assessment experience interesting and meaningful to them. Some learners may need more attention than others. Just because one learner is progressing well does not mean you can focus on those who are not; all your learners need encouragement and feedback. You may not be able to change the environment or the resources you are using, but remaining professional and making the best use of what you have will help encourage your learners' development.

Example

Frank has a group of learners working towards a GCSE in Geography. One of his learners, Joan, seems to be losing motivation and is not paying attention during sessions. As Frank knows she enjoys working with computers, he arranges for the class to move to the computer room to use a specialist website which has GCSE online activities for learners to complete. These give immediate scores, which will help Frank monitor his learners' progress and retain the motivation of Joan and the group.

You need to encourage your learners to reach their full potential. If you use assessment activities that are too difficult, learners may struggle and become frustrated and anxious. If assessments are too easy, learners may become bored. Knowing your learners and differentiating for their needs should address the balance.

If you have learners who are quite motivated already, keep this motivation alive with regular challenges and constructive and positive feedback. A lack of motivation can lead to disruption and apathy. If you are teaching as well as assessing, ensure you are reaching all learning preferences as everyone learns differently. This will help you plan suitable assessment activities or modify the methods of assessment if appropriate. You might not be able to change the formal assessments required, but you could devise informal assessments which will help motivate and suit your learners' needs.

Example

Adele had always assessed her learners by assignments and tests. After encouraging them to complete a learning preference questionnaire, she realised several of her learners prefer a kinaesthetic approach. She has therefore changed some of her informal assessments to include role play and practical activities, which will meet their learning preferences.

Using the correct type of assessment to suit your learners, carrying out careful and appropriate assessment planning and reviewing progress will ensure you are meeting the needs of your learners. You will also make sure your learners are on the right pathway to achieving a successful result and that you are differentiating for any individual requirements.

Barriers to assessment

Some learners may have barriers to assessment, for example health problems, a lack of access to a particular room or transport issues. You may also have to challenge your own values and beliefs if you don't agree with those of your learners to ensure you remain professional at all times. Other learners may have a support assistant who will be present during the assessment process. They will be there to help your learner in case they have any difficulties. Make sure you address your learner, not their assistant, to ensure you are including them fully in the process. If you have a learner with a speech impediment, give them time to finish speaking before continuing.

Your organisation should have support mechanisms to meet any special assessment requirements or individual needs of learners, for example a learner services department. If this is not the case, you will need to find out who can provide advice and guidance when needed.

Examples of support for learners include:

- Dyspraxia – allow additional time and space if necessary for learners who have poor motor co-ordination.

- Dysgraphia – allow the use of a computer or other suitable media for learners who have difficulty with handwriting.

- Dyscalculia – allow additional time if necessary and the use of calculators or other equipment for learners who have difficulty with calculations or maths.

- Dyslexia – allow additional time or resources if necessary for learners who have difficulty processing language. Present written questions in a more simplified format, for example bullet points. Ask questions verbally and make an audio or visual recording of your learner's responses. Allow the use of a laptop for typing responses rather than expecting handwritten responses.

- A disability – learners could be assessed in a more comfortable environment where appropriate access and support systems are available. Learners could be given extra time to complete the assessment tasks or to take medication privately. Dates could be rearranged to fit around doctor or hospital appointments.

- A hearing impairment – an induction loop could be used where all or part of an assessment is presented orally. Instructions and questions could be conveyed using sign language. Specialist computer software could be used.

- A visual impairment – use large print or Braille, and specialist computer software if available. Ask questions verbally and make an audio recording of your learner's responses.

- Varying work patterns – try to schedule the assessment at a time and place to suit.

- English as a second or other language – if allowed, try to arrange assessments in your learner's first language, for example in Welsh. Many AOs can translate assessment materials if requested. Bilingual assessments should also be offered if required.

Example

If you have a learner who has dyslexia, it may be appropriate to ask questions rather than give a written test, or to have someone to scribe their responses. For a learner who is partially sighted, you could provide papers in a larger font or use a magnified reading lamp. For a learner who is deaf, you could give a written test instead of an oral test. For a learner with Asperger's syndrome, you could use written questions rather than oral questions. For some learners who might struggle with spelling and grammar, the use of a computer could help. An adapted keyboard or a pen grip could help a learner with arthritis.

If you have a learner requiring support for any reason, there is a difference between *learning support* and *learner support*. Learning support relates to the subject, or help with English, maths or ICT skills. Learner support relates to any help your learner might need with personal issues and/or general advice and guidance regarding their health, safety and welfare.

Always ask your learners how you can support them, but try to avoid making them feel different or uncomfortable. If you are unsure of what you can do to help your learners, ask your manager or internal quality assurer (IQA) at your organisation. The Equality Act (2010) requires organisations to make reasonable adjustments where necessary. Don't assume you are on your own when carrying out any amendment to provision; there should be specialist staff to help.

Extension Activity

Find out what is involved with the learner review process at your organisation. Is there a particular form you need to complete? Do you have to review all your learners regularly, for example monthly or termly? How can you support your learners should you identify any challenges or barriers to assessment, or any particular learning needs?

Questioning techniques

Questions are a really useful method of formative assessment to ensure your learners are acquiring the necessary skills, knowledge and understanding before moving on to a new topic. They can also be useful as a type of summative assessment at the end of a programme.

There are a variety of questioning techniques that you can use with groups or individuals. Questions can be oral (verbal) or written, for example open questions requiring a full answer or closed questions requiring a *yes* or *no* answer. If you are asking questions verbally to a group of learners, ensure you include all learners. Don't just let the keen learners answer first as this gives the ones who don't know the answers the chance to stay quiet. Tell your learners you are going to use a particular method when you ask questions. For example, pose a question, pause for a second and then pick a learner to answer the question. In this way, all learners are thinking about the answer as soon as you have posed the question and are ready to speak if their name is picked. This is sometimes referred to as pose, pause, pick (PPP). If you use this process, make sure you have enough questions for everyone in the group so that no one is left out. If your nominated learner does not know the answer, ask them to guess. That way they still have to think and cannot opt out. If they still don't know, say they made a good attempt and then move on to another learner.

To ensure you include everyone throughout your session, you could have a list of their names handy and tick each one off after you have asked them a question. This is fine if you don't have a large group. If you do, make sure you ask different learners each time you are in contact with them. When asking questions, only use one question in a sentence, as more than one may confuse your learners. Try not to ask *Does anyone have any questions?* as often only those who are keen or confident will ask, and this does not tell you what your learners have learnt. Try not to use questions such as *Does that make sense?* or *Do you understand?*, as your learners will often say yes as they feel that is what you expect to hear or they don't want to embarrass themselves.

Whenever possible, try to use open questions which require an answer to demonstrate understanding, rather than closed questions which only require a *yes/no* answer. The latter does not show you if your learner has the required knowledge as they could make a correct guess by accident. Open questions usually begin with *who, what, when, where, why* and *how* (WWWWWH).

If you are having a conversation with your learner, there are some other questioning techniques you can use such as probing, prompting, clarifying, leading, and asking hypothetical as well as open and closed questions.

Example

Open: How would you ...?

Closed: Would you ...?

Probing: Why exactly was that?

Prompting: What about ...?

Clarifying: Can you go over that again?

Leading: So what you are saying is ...

Hypothetical: What would you do if ...?

It takes practice to use these question techniques effectively. However, they are a much better way of finding out information from your learners than asking a question that will only give a *yes* or *no* response.

If there are no clear guidelines or assessment criteria for you to base your questions on, you might find yourself being *subjective* rather than *objective*. That is, you make your own decision without any guidance and therefore base it on your opinion rather than fact. It is harder to remain objective when learners are responding to open questions which don't have any clear assessment criteria to follow or any expected response as a guide.

If you have to produce written questions for your learners, think about the type of question you will use, for example short questions, essay-style questions with word counts, open, closed or multiple-choice questions, etc. If you are giving grades, for example A/B/C or pass/merit/distinction, you must have clear grading criteria to follow to make sure your decisions are objective; otherwise your learners may challenge your decisions.

Example

Haedish has a group of learners who need to achieve at least 8 out of 10 to pass. The questions have been written by a team of staff within the organisation, but no expected responses have been provided. Haedish has been told to use her professional judgement to make a decision, but finds this difficult. She knows her learners are very capable of achieving, but they don't always express themselves clearly when writing. She therefore devised a checklist of points to help her reach a decision. She also decided that any learner who achieves a lower mark will not be referred, but will be given the opportunity to respond verbally to the questions.

In this example, Haedish has made a decision to differentiate for her learners. However, she must first check with the other staff that this is acceptable, and if so, they must be able to offer the same option to their learners. This will ensure that all assessors are being fair to all learners. She should also share her checklist with the other staff to ensure they are all being fair when making decisions.

If you are writing multiple-choice questions, there should be a clear question and three or four possible answers. The question is known as the *stem*, the answer is called the *key* and the wrong answers are called *distracters*. Answers and distracters should always be similar in length and complexity (words or diagrams/pictures). They should not be confusing, and there should only be one definite key.

Example

Formative assessment is always:

   (a) before the programme commences

   (b) at the beginning of the programme

   (c) ongoing throughout the programme

   (d) when the programme ends.

You will see that all the answers contain a similar number and type of words. None of the answers contains a clue from the question. A, B and D are the distracters and C is the correct answer (the key).

If you issue any assessment activities as homework, you need to plan your own time accordingly to ensure you are able to assess all the work that will be submitted by a certain date. It could be that your organisation expects you to assess and give feedback within a certain time period, for example seven days.

If you are using the same questions with different learners at different times, be careful as they may pass the answers to each other. You may need to rephrase some questions if your learners are struggling with an answer as poor answers are often the result of poor questions. For essay and short-answer tests you should create sample answers to have something with which to compare learners' answers. Be careful with the use of jargon – just because you understand it does not mean your learners will. You might want to grade the responses once all your learners' work has been submitted. Otherwise, if you assess the first one in, you having nothing to compare it with and might feel it is really good, therefore giving a high grade. However, when the others are submitted they might be better and it could be too late to amend the first one's grade.

Plagiarism

Plagiarism is the wrongful use of someone else's work. You need to be aware of learners colluding or plagiarising work, particularly now that so much information is available via the internet. Learners should take responsibility for referencing any sources in all work submitted and may be required to sign a declaration or an authenticity statement. If you suspect plagiarism, you could type a few of their words into an internet search engine or specialist program and see what appears. You would then have to challenge your learner as to whether it was intentional or not and follow your organisation's plagiarism procedure.

Activity

Find out what your organisation's policy is regarding cheating, copying and plagiarism. Ensure all your learners are aware of it and encourage them to sign an authenticity statement. This ensures they are taking ownership of their work.

If assessors and learners are completing and/or submitting documents electronically, there might not be an opportunity to add a real signature to confirm the authenticity of the document. However, many companies are now accepting a scanned signature or an e-mail address, providing the identity of the person has been confirmed.

If you are assessing the work of learners you might not have met, for example by e-assessment, it can be very difficult to ensure the authenticity of their work. Your organisation might require each learner to attend an interview at some point and bring along some form of photo identification such as a driving licence, passport or employee card.

Unfortunately, some learners do copy or plagiarise the work of others. Sometimes this is deliberate; at other times it is due to a lack of knowledge of exactly what was required or a misunderstanding when referencing quotes within work. If you feel the work that has been handed to you might not be the actual work of your learner, ask them some questions about it. This will confirm their knowledge, or otherwise. If you feel it is not their work, you will need to confront them and let them know you will take the matter further. At this point your learner may confess or they may have what they consider a legitimate excuse. However, you must be certain the work is their own; otherwise it could be classed as fraud.

Example

Marie and Leanne are sisters, both taking a Certificate in Information Technology, which is assessed by assignments completed in their own time. When their assessor marked their work, he discovered the answers from both, which had been word-processed, were almost the same. He confronted them individually. Marie insisted the work was her own and had no idea why it looked similar to Leanne's. Leanne became quite upset and admitted accessing Marie's files without her knowledge. She had been worried about completing the work within the deadline. In this instance, the assessor credited Marie with the original work and asked Leanne to complete a different assignment on her own.

It is easier to compare the work of your own learners as you are familiar with them. However, other assessors in your organisation might also assess the same programme with different learners. In this case, the IQA may pick up on issues when they are sampling learner work. It is difficult to check and compare the work of all learners. The importance of authenticity must therefore be stressed to everyone at the commencement of their programme and continually throughout. Asking learners to sign and date hard copies of work, or adding a statement to electronic work, is a useful way of getting them to accept responsibility.

Some ways of checking the authenticity of learners' work include:

- spelling, grammar and punctuation – you know your learner speaks in a certain way at a certain level, yet their written work does not reflect this

- work that includes quotes which have not been referenced – without a reference source, this is direct plagiarism and could be a breach of copyright

- word-processed work that contains different fonts and sizes of text – this shows it could have been copied from the internet or someone else's electronic file

- handwritten work that looks different to your learner's normal handwriting or is not in the style or language your learner would normally use, or word-processed work when they would normally write by hand

- work that refers to information you have not taught or is not relevant.

Electronic assessment systems often allow contact to take place between the learner and assessor through a website platform. You could communicate in this way, or via e-mail, and then compare the style of writing in the submitted work to that within the communications.

The Copyright, Designs and Patents Act (1988) is the current UK copyright law. Copying the work of others without their permission would infringe the Act. Copyright is where an individual or organisation creates something as an original and has the right to control the ways in which their work may be used by others. Normally the person who created the work will own the exclusive rights. However, if the work is produced as part of your employment, for example if you produced several handouts or a workbook for your learners, then normally the work will belong to your organisation. Learners may be in breach of this Act if they plagiarise or copy the work of others without making reference to the original author.

Extension Activity

Design a questioning activity to carry out with your learners. This could be some oral questions that you will ask an individual learner or a multiple-choice test for a group of learners. Make sure you create expected responses. Use the activity with your learners and evaluate how effective it was. What would you change and why?

The role of ICT in assessment

Technology is constantly evolving and new resources are frequently becoming available. It is crucial to keep up to date with new developments and you should try to incorporate these within the assessment process. It is not only about you using technology to help assess your learners, but also about your learners using it to complete their assessment activities. Encouraging your learners to use technology will help increase their skills in this area. Technology can be combined with traditional methods of assessment, for example learners can complete a written assignment by word-processing their response and submitting it by e-mail or uploading it to a virtual learning environment (VLE). You can then give feedback via e-mail or the VLE system. Combining methods also promotes differentiation and inclusivity, for example learners could access assessment materials via the VLE outside the normal learning environment to support their learning. See Table 3.6 for some advantages and limitations of using technology in assessment.

New and emerging technologies include using:

- blogs, chat rooms, social networking sites, webinars and online discussion forums to help learners communicate with each other
- computer facilities for learners to word-process their assignments, save and back up their work
- cloud storage facilities that learners and assessors can use to upload and access materials from various devices
- digital media for visual/audio recording and playback
- electronic portfolios for learners to store their work
- e-mail for electronic submission of assessments, communication and informal feedback on progress
- interactive whiteboards for learners to use for presentations and to display their work

- internet access for research to support assignments or presentations
- mobile phones and tablets for taking pictures, video and audio clips, and communicating with others
- networked systems to allow access to applications and documents from any computer linked to the system
- online and on-demand tests which can give instant results, for example diagnostic, learning preferences and multiple-choice tests
- online discussion forums which allow asynchronous (taking place at different times) and synchronous (taking place at the same time) discussions
- scanners for copying and transferring documents to a computer
- web cameras or video conferencing if you cannot be in the same place as your learners and you need to see and talk to them
- VLEs to access and upload learning materials and assessment activities.

E-learning and assessment is constantly advancing. Unfortunately, there is not room in this book to explain it in great detail; please refer to other appropriate texts such as those listed at the end of this chapter.

Table 3.6 Advantages and limitations of using technology

Advantages	Limitations
<ul><li>Accessible and inclusive</li><li>Addressing sustainability, i.e. no need for paper copies</li><li>An efficient use of time and cost effective</li><li>Auditable and reliable</li><li>Available, i.e. resources and materials can be accessed at a time and place to suit</li><li>Give immediate results from online tests</li><li>On demand, i.e. tests can be taken when a learner is ready</li></ul>	<ul><li>Finance required to purchase or upgrade</li><li>Can lead to plagiarism via the internet</li><li>Time consuming to initially set up</li><li>Might create barriers if learners cannot access or use technology</li><li>Power cuts could cause problems</li><li>Some learners might be afraid of using new technology</li><li>There might not be enough resources available for all learners to use at the same time</li></ul>

Activity

Design an assessment activity that you could use with your learners which incorporates ICT, for example an online quiz. If you have learners at the moment, use it with them and then evaluate how effective it was. What changes would you make and why?

Analysing learner achievement

If you have a group of learners whom you are assessing, for example using written questions to check their knowledge and understanding, the results should be marked to ascertain the correct responses. When issuing questions, you will need to produce expected responses to ensure you are being fair when marking. If you don't, you might find yourself subconsciously giving a higher mark to the best learners in your group. You should always remain objective when assessing, avoid having any favourite learners and follow the marking criteria correctly. Otherwise you may find your learners dispute your decision and appeal. All learners have the right of appeal and there will be a procedure in your organisation for your learners to follow. It could be that another assessor reassesses your work to agree or disagree with your decision.

Norm referencing

If you want to compare the achievements of learners in your group, you could use *norm referencing*, which is a form of grading in addition to marking. Grading is when you give an A, B or C, whereas marking is whether they pass or not. Grading and marking go together when required, for example a GCSE grade C is still a pass mark.

Norm referencing will proportion your grades accordingly, as there will always be those in your group who will achieve a high grade and those who will achieve a low grade, leaving the rest in the middle. You would allocate grades according to a quota, for example the top 20 per cent would achieve an A, the next 20 per cent a B and so on. Norm referencing uses the achievement of a group to set the standards for specific grades or for how many learners will pass or fail. This type of assessment is useful to maintain consistency of results over time; whether the test questions are easy or hard, there will always be those achieving a high grade or a lower grade.

Example

Petra has a group of 25 learners who have just taken a test consisting of 20 questions – she wants to allocate grades A–E to her group. She has worked out the top 20 per cent will achieve an A, the second 20 per cent a B and so on. When she marks the tests, she is surprised to see the lowest mark was 16 out of 20, meaning a grade E. Even though the learners had done well in the test, they were still given a low grade in comparison to the rest of the group.

A fairer method would have been to just set a pass mark, for example 15 out of 20, and not use grading at all. Learners achieving 14 or below could be referred and could retake a different test at a later date.

Criterion referencing

Criterion referencing enables learners to achieve based upon their own merit, as their achievements are not compared with those of other learners. All learners therefore have equality of opportunity. If grades are allocated, for example a distinction, credit or pass, there will be specific criteria which must have been met for each. These criteria are usually supplied by the AO.

Example

Pass – described the activity.

Credit – described and analysed the activity.

Distinction – described, analysed and critically reflected upon the activity.

Some qualifications may simply be achieved by a pass or a fail, for example a multiple-choice test where learners must achieve 7 out of 10 for a pass. You would have a list of the correct responses, thus enabling you to mark objectively. You will also have regulations to follow in the event of a fail as to whether your learner can retake the test, and if so, when.

Online testing often utilises multiple-choice questions, and instant results can be given. This is fine for summative assessments. However, it might not be a good idea to use language such as pass or fail for formative assessments. Formative assessments are designed to aid development and negative results could demoralise your learners. However, you could always use terms such as *pass* or *refer*: any learners with a *refer* result could have the opportunity to retake the same test, or an alternative one, at a later date.

If learners are retaking the same test, it is advisable to leave a period of time, for example seven days, before they take it again. If learners are taking a test that other learners have already attempted, you need to ensure they have not communicated their responses. If learners feel the urge to cheat, they are ultimately only cheating themselves. A bank of questions would be useful; you could choose a certain number of random questions that will always be different. Computer-generated question papers should automatically choose different questions for different learners. If you are giving any guidance to learners who have been referred, for example their assignment needs more work, make sure you don't give too much support to the extent that their response is based on your guidance, not their own knowledge.

Sometimes, negative marking can be used whereby a mark is deducted for every incorrect answer. You would need to seek advice when using this type of assessment.

Results analysis

If you assess a programme which requires grades to be given to learners in addition to marking, you will need to analyse the results regarding their achievements. The grades could be expressed as:

- 1, 2, 3, 4, 5
- A, B, C, D, E
- achieved/not achieved
- competent/not yet competent
- distinction, credit, pass, fail
- pass, refer, fail
- percentages, for example 80 per cent
- satisfactory, good, outstanding.

Analysing the results will help you see not only how well your learners have done, but whether there are any trends. For example, if all your learners received an average of C, but another assessor's group achieved an average of B, is there a fault on your part?

If you had a group of 30 learners who all achieved an A grade, was this due to your excellent teaching, the skills and knowledge of your learners or you being too lenient with your grades when marking?

If you had a group of 15 learners who all failed an assignment, you could ask yourself the same questions. However, it could be that the assignment questions were worded in a confusing way or you had given the assignment too early in the programme. If most of your group averaged a grade of 50 per cent, whereas a colleague's group averaged 80 per cent, was this because you had given your learners misleading or ambiguous information relating to that topic?

Asking yourself these questions will help you ascertain if you are producing assessments that are fit for purpose; if you are not, you will need to do something about it. For example, you may need to amend your teaching or assessment methods, reword your questions or redesign some assessment activities.

Making decisions and giving feedback

You may find, when assessing, that your learners have not achieved everything they should have. When making a decision, you need to base this on all the information or evidence available to you at the time. If your learner has not met all the criteria, you need to give constructive feedback, discuss any inconsistencies and give advice on what they should do next. If your learner disagrees with your decision, they are entitled to follow your organisation's appeals procedure. If you are having difficulty making a decision, discuss this with your manager or a colleague to obtain a second opinion. You need to be fully confident when making decisions. Never feel under pressure to pass learners who have not fully achieved, for example due to targets or funding. You are not doing yourself or your learners any favours by saying they have achieved something when they have not.

Feedback can be informal and given during a training session, a one-to-one review or by telephone, e-mail or another relevant method. Verbal feedback could be given when you next see your learner, or if there are time constraints you might just give them back their work with the feedback attached for them to read later. It is always good practice to point out any errors in spelling, grammar, punctuation and sentence construction to help your learners realise their mistakes. Always give your learner a copy of the feedback record and keep the original yourself for audit purposes. Encourage your learners to get in touch if they need to clarify any points in your feedback, particularly if you are not giving feedback in person.

Feedback should be formalised by using an assessment document such as the *feedback and action record* in Table 3.7. The form could be word-processed each time a different aspect has been assessed, allowing it to be added to over time.

Table 3.7 Example feedback and action record

Feedback and action record			
Learner: Marcia Indira		**Assessor:** Abbi Cross	
Qualification: Level 2 Business, Administration and Finance		**Date:** I August	
Aspects assessed	**Feedback**	**Action required**	**Target date**
Q1 – Generate a range of ideas for a business enterprise	I like the ideas you have generated for your business; you have come up with some very original concepts. I feel your idea could become a real business opportunity. Do be careful when you are word-processing your work as you have a few spelling errors, for example *where* for *were* and *been* for *being*. If you were putting a proposal together to talk to investors you must ensure it is correct and professional. You could consider looking at various enterprise websites and Business Link to help with your idea.	No action required	
Q2 – Compare the viability of the business enterprise ideas	You have looked at the viability of your business by researching what is available elsewhere and compared your ideas to them. I like the way you have presented this task using graphs and tables. You do seem to have a really good idea that would benefit a lot of people. I would recommend in future you use some colour rather than black and white to make your points stand out.	No action required	
Q3 – Select and develop a business idea	You selected your idea as proposed in Q1 and have now followed your ideas through to the development of a business plan. Your plan is very professional looking and has taken into consideration everything we have discussed during the sessions. I enjoyed watching your presentation to your peers regarding your idea and how it will progress to the investment stage. Peer feedback was positive and your own self-evaluation was fair and objective. You have now successfully achieved learning outcome 2 – well done! We will create a separate action plan for the next learning outcome.	No action required	
Achievements	**Learning outcomes**	**Assessment criteria**	
Unit 1: Business Enterprise	2: Be able to develop a business enterprise idea	2.1 Generate a range of ideas for a business enterprise 2.2 Compare the viability of the business enterprise ideas 2.3 Select and develop a business idea	

When giving feedback, you should always try to be:

- constructive – to help retain your learner's motivation
- specific – by being factual and stating exactly what was achieved or not achieved
- developmental – by encouraging further learning, for example reading and research.

You also need to make sure you are not being ambiguous or vague, therefore leaving your learner not really knowing what they have achieved. You need to be factual regarding what they have achieved in relation to the assessment criteria and not just give your opinion. It is important to keep your learners motivated, and what you say can help or hinder their progress and confidence.

Example

All Fatima's learners had passed the required assessment criteria for their first assignment. When assessing these, Fatima just wrote 'pass', along with 'good' on each piece of work. Although there were a few spelling and grammatical errors within them all, she did not correct any. She did not have time to make any comments about how each learner could develop further.

While the learners in the example were probably happy they had achieved a pass, they would not be aware of what they could improve upon, what was good about their work or that they had made some mistakes. They would therefore continue to make these mistakes, as they would not know any different. It could be that Fatima did not even notice the mistakes herself. However, you would not want to demoralise your learners by writing too much regarding their first assessment activity. A combination of written and oral feedback might be better to retain motivation (see Chapter 2 for more details regarding assessment decisions, how to give feedback and maintain records).

Activity

Read the response to the following question and make a decision as to whether the learner has passed or not, with your reasons why. Compare your answer to the one on page 121.

Question
Analyse how types of assessment are used in lifelong learning.

Learner's response
Types of assessments that I might use with learners are initial assessments, which are designed to assess what the students already have in terms of skills and knowledge

Formative assessment is continuous throughout the course.

Summative assessment is at the end of the programme.

Learnign preferences can also be assessed through the use of VARK, "The acronym VARK stands for Visual, Aural, Read/Write and Kinessthetic" these are used for learning information."

All types of assesment can be either informal or formal and can be used with learners as a means of knowing that leaning has taken place.

Formal assesments tend to have certain criteria and constraints such as time limits and target dates.

Evaluating the programme

You should evaluate the full assessment process for each programme or qualification you assess. This will help you improve in the future, for example you could evaluate the resources you used, such as handouts, to ensure they are inclusive and promote equality and diversity.

You should evaluate whether the assessment types and methods you used were successful or whether there were any trends which need addressing, such as all learners not passing a particular aspect. You will need to ensure the activities you used to assess skills, knowledge and understanding were valid and reliable, and that you only assessed the criteria you were meant to assess. You will need to ask yourself if you assessed fairly and ethically, or if you had a favourite learner to whom you gave more attention or were lenient with for any reason.

You could use questionnaires or surveys to gain feedback from learners and others, which will help you evaluate your programme (see Chapter 4 for information regarding surveys and questionnaires).

Extension Activity

Evaluate a recent assessment activity you have used with your learners. Did you need to differentiate it in any way? Were there any trends with the results and, if so, what will you do now?

Continuing professional development

Continuing professional development (CPD) should be carried out regularly to maintain your occupational competence not only as an assessor, but also regarding the subject you assess as well as developments in new technology. It is useful to add relevant CPD to your curriculum vitae, particularly if you are applying for a job or promotion.

As a professional, you need to continually update your skills and knowledge. This knowledge relates not only to your subject specialism, but also to assessment methods, the types of learners you will be assessing and relevant internal and external requirements.

CPD can be formal or informal, planned well in advance or opportunistic, but it should have a real impact upon your job role and lead to an improvement in your practice. CPD is about more than just attending events; it is also about using critical reflection regarding your experiences which results in your improvement and/or development as an assessor.

Activity

Look at the following list and decide which of the activities would be relevant to you. What other activities could you carry out which would contribute towards your CPD?

Opportunities for professional development include:

- attending events and training programmes
- attending meetings
- e-learning and online activities
- evaluating feedback from peers, learners and others
- formally reflecting on experiences and documenting how it has improved practice
- improving own skills such as English and maths
- keeping up to date with relevant legislation
- membership of professional associations or committees
- observing colleagues
- reading textbooks
- researching developments or changes to your subject
- secondments
- self-reflection
- shadowing colleagues
- standardisation activities
- studying for relevant qualifications
- subscribing to and reading relevant journals and websites
- visiting other organisations
- voluntary work
- work experience placements
- writing or reviewing books and articles.

You will need to maintain a record of all CPD undertaken to prove you are remaining current with your assessment role and your subject specialism. You could keep a manual record, such as the one shown in Table 3.8, or an electronic record, perhaps as a spreadsheet or by using a specialist computer program.

Using a reference number for each activity enables you to cross-reference the activities to your documentation. For example, number 1 could be minutes of meetings, number 2 could be a certificate, number 3 a record of achievement. Adding the reference number to the relevant documents also enables you to locate them when necessary. Besides keeping your CPD record up to date, you should write a more detailed reflection of what you learnt and how it impacted upon your job role.

You will probably participate in an appraisal or performance review system at some time in your organisation. This is a valuable opportunity to discuss your progress, development

Table 3.8 Example CPD record

Continuing professional development record					
Name: Abbi Cross			**Organisation:** Excellence Training College		
Date	**Activity and venue**	**Duration**	**Justification towards assessment role and subject specialism**	**Action required**	**Ref. no.**
06 Jan	Attendance at standardisation event. Four assessors, I myself and the IQA discussed how we interpreted the requirements of units 101, 102 and 103 and reassessed each other's decisions.	3 hrs	Standardised assessment practice to ensure I am assessing the Level 3 Certificate in Hospitality & Catering in the same way as the other assessors.	Units 104 and 105 to be standardised next.	1
10 Feb	Attendance at a First Aid training day.	6 hrs	To ensure I am current with First Aid in case someone has an accident.	–	2
20 Mar	Attendance at staff training event for assessors. All assessors were able to get together and discuss the types of records we use. We were also given updates regarding policies and procedures.	3 hrs	To ensure I am up to date with policies and procedures regarding assessment practice.	–	3

and any training or support you may need. It is also a chance to reflect upon your achievements and successes. Always keep a copy of any documentation relating to your training and CPD, as you may need to provide this to funding bodies, AOs or regulatory bodies if requested. Having the support of your organisation will help you decide what is relevant to your development as an assessor and to your job role.

The practice of assessment has been recognised as a professional activity by the granting of Chartered Status to the Institute of Educational Assessors (CIEA). Their aim is to improve the quality of assessment in schools and colleges by working with educational assessors to develop their knowledge, understanding and capability in all aspects of educational testing and assessment. You can access their standards by visiting their website (www.ciea.org.uk).

Reflecting upon your own assessment practice, taking account of feedback from learners and colleagues, evaluating your practice and maintaining your professional development will enable you to become a more effective assessor.

Extension Activity

Decide on a system for documenting your CPD. You could use a form as in Table 3.8, or you could design your own. Reflect upon each activity you have carried out and how it has impacted upon your role as an assessor.

Summary

In this chapter you have learnt about:

- vocational assessment planning
- reviewing learner progress
- questioning techniques
- the role of ICT in assessment
- continuing professional development.

Evidence

Evidence from the completed activities within this chapter, plus the following, could be used towards the *Assessing vocational skills, knowledge and understanding* unit, for example:

- four completed action plans/assessment plans with at least two learners (methods must include those used to assess skills, knowledge and understanding in an environment which is not a learner's place of work)
- four assessment activities you would use with your learners (for example, assignment, case study, multiple-choice test, written questions)

- four completed feedback records for the two learners
- schemes of work and session plans showing assessment activities
- minutes of assessor team meetings
- records of standardisation activities
- written statements cross-referenced to the unit's assessment criteria
- answers to questions issued by your assessor
- records of discussions with your assessor.

Cross-referencing grid

This chapter contributes towards the following assessment criteria, along with aspects of the National Occupational Standards for Learning and Development. Full details of the learning outcomes and assessment criteria for each unit can be found in the Appendices.

Unit	Assessment criteria
Understanding the principles and practices of assessment	2.1 3.1, 3.2 4.2, 4.3, 4.4 6.3 7.2 8.2, 8.3, 8.4
Assess occupational competence in the work environment	1.1 2.1 3.1, 3.2, 3.3 4.2, 4.3, 4.4
Assess vocational skills, knowledge and understanding	1.1, 1.2, 1.3 2.1, 2.2, 2.3, 2.4, 2.5, 2.6 3.1, 3.2, 3.3 4.1, 4.2, 4.3, 4.4
National Occupational Standards	**Reference**
9 – Assess learner achievement	KU3, KU4, KU5, KU6, KU7, KU10, KU11, KU12, KU14, KU18 9.1, 9.2, 9.3, 9.4, 9.5, 9.6, 9.7, 9.8
11 – Internally monitor and maintain the quality of assessment	KU1, KU4, KU6, KU7, KU8, KU10, KU18 11.4
12 – Externally monitor and maintain the quality of assessment	KU5 12.3

Theory focus

References and further information

Belbin, M (1993) *Team Roles At Work*. Oxford: Elsevier Science and Technology.

Berne, E (1973) *Games People Play: The Psychology of Human Relationships*. London: Penguin Books.

Bloom, BS (1956) *Taxonomy of Educational Objectives: The Classification of Educational Goals*. New York: McKay.

Boud, D (1995) *Enhancing Learning through Self-assessment*. London: Kogan Page.

Gravells, A (2013) *The Award in Education and Training*. London: Learning Matters SAGE.

Hill, C (2008) *Teaching with E-learning in the Lifelong Learning Sector* (2nd edition). London: Learning Matters SAGE.

JISC (2010) *Effective Assessment in a Digital Age: A Guide to Technology-enhanced Assessment and Feedback*. Bristol: JISC Innovation Group. Available at: www.jisc.ac.uk/media/documents/programmes/elearning/digiassass_eada.pdf (accessed 27.09.13).

Maslow, AH (1987) *Motivation and Personality* (3rd revised edition, ed. Frager, R). New York: Pearson Education.

Murphy, P (1999) *Learners, Learning and Assessment*. London: Paul Chapman Publishing.

Ofqual (2009) *Authenticity – a guide for teachers*. Coventry: Ofqual.

Pachler, N, Mellar, H, Daly, C, Mor, Y and Wiliam, D (2009) *Scoping a Vision for Formative E-assessment* (FEASST) JISC. London: Institute of Education.

Read, H (2011) *The Best Assessor's Guide*. Bideford: Read On Publications Ltd.

Reece, I and Walker, S (2007) *Teaching, Training and Learning: A Practical Guide* (6th edition). Sunderland: Business Education Publishers.

Tummons, J (2011) *Assessing Learning in the Lifelong Learning Sector* (3rd edition). London: Learning Matters SAGE.

Websites

Association for Achievement and Improvement through Assessment (AAIA): www.aaia.org.uk

Chartered Institute of Educational Assessors: www.ciea.org.uk

Copyright, Designs and Patents Act (1988): www.legislation.gov.uk/ukpga/1988/48/contents

Equality Act (2010): www.legislation.gov.uk/ukpga/2010/15/contents

Joint Information Systems Committee (JISC): www.jisc.ac.uk

Maslow: www.maslow.com

Oxford Learning Institute: Giving and receiving feedback: www.learning.ox.ac.uk/supervision/stages/feedback/

Peer and self-assessment: www.nclrc.org/essentials/assessing/peereval.htm

Plagiarism: www.plagiarism.org and www.plagiarismadvice.org

QCF shortcut: http://tinyurl.com/2944r8h

Support for adult learners: http://webarchive.nationalarchives.gov.uk/20121015000000/www.direct.gov.uk/en/EducationAndLearning/AdultLearning/index.htm

Answer to the question regarding marking and feedback (page 114)

The learner has not passed as they have not met the criteria i.e. the learner does not analyse how types of assessment are used; they only state what initial, formative and summative are.

There are several spelling errors, such as Learnign and Kinessthetic, and assessment is often spelt wrongly. There is no full stop after the first paragraph. There are quote marks around some text in the fourth paragraph, but no reference as to where it is from. The terms course and programme are not consistently used, neither are student and learner.

Learning preferences are not a type of assessment, although they do relate to initial assessment. This is not made clear. Informal and formal types of assessment are mentioned, but there is no differentiation between progress and achievement. Although constraints are stated regarding formal assessments, there is no analysis of how types of assessment are used in lifelong learning.

4 PRINCIPLES AND PRACTICES OF INTERNALLY ASSURING THE QUALITY OF ASSESSMENT

Introduction

In this chapter you will learn about:

- the role of internal quality assurance
- key concepts and principles of internal quality assurance
- sample planning and the collection of information
- maintaining and improving the quality of assessment
- evaluation.

Within the chapter there are activities and examples which will help you to reflect on the above and to develop and enhance your knowledge of the principles and practices of internally assuring the quality of assessment. Completing the activities will help you to gather evidence towards the *Principles and practices of internally assuring the quality of assessment* unit. At the end of each section is an extension activity to stretch and challenge your knowledge and understanding.

At the end of the chapter is a list of possible evidence which could be used towards the *Principles and practices of internally assuring the quality of assessment* unit.

A cross-referencing grid shows how the content of this chapter contributes towards the TAQA units' criteria, and the National Occupational Standards. There is also a theory focus with relevant references, further information and websites to which you might like to refer.

The role of internal quality assurance

Quality *assurance* can be defined as a system to monitor and evaluate a product or a service. It should identify and recommend measures to make improvements to standards and performance, or at least maintain the status quo if everything is working well. This is in contrast to quality *control* which seeks to find problems, whereas quality assurance seeks to avoid problems, stabilise and improve products and services.

What is internal quality assurance?

Internal quality assurance (IQA) relates to the monitoring of the learner journey throughout their time at your organisation. It also includes monitoring the training and assessment activities, which are a substantial part of the IQA process. Internal verification was the previous term used for monitoring assessment. However, IQA monitors the whole process from when a learner commences to when they finish, i.e. the full learner journey. The IQA process can relate to a product or a service.

Example

Aharon is being assessed for a qualification which is accredited by an awarding organisation (AO). The IQA process is therefore of a product. Carmel is being assessed performing her job role in her place of work to ensure she meets her role specification. The IQA process is therefore of a service which is being offered to support her.

Usually, internal quality assurers (IQAs) are also experienced assessors in the subject area they are quality assuring. For example, if the subject area is motor vehicle maintenance, they should not be internally quality assuring other subjects they are not experienced in, for example hairdressing. The process might be the same for each subject, but the IQA must be fully familiar with the assessment criteria to make a valid and reliable decision. If you have not already read the preceding chapters regarding assessment, you will find them useful to update your assessment knowledge. If you are quality assuring an accredited qualification, you will need to read the assessment strategy from the AO. This will state whether you must also be a qualified assessor in the same subject that you will internal quality assure.

Roles and responsibilities of an internal quality assurer

Your main role will be to carry out the IQA process according to the qualification require-ments, or those of the programme or job specification which is being assessed. Your roles and responsibilities will include far more than those stated in the IQA cycle in Figure 4.1 (see page 130). However, there might be a quality assurance manager in your organisation who will be responsible for some of the duties.

Your role might include:

- advising, supporting and providing developmental feedback to assessors

- documenting the quality assurance strategy, process and decisions

- ensuring assessors interpret, understand and consistently apply the correct standards and requirements

- identifying issues and trends, for example several learners misinterpreting the same thing

- interviewing learners, assessors and other relevant staff

- leading standardisation activities to ensure the accuracy and consistency of assessment decisions between assessors

- monitoring and observing the full learner journey from commencement to completion

- planning and carrying out the sampling of assessed work

- taking part in continuing professional development (CPD)

- working towards relevant IQA qualifications.

The IQA units are at level 4 on the Qualifications and Credit Framework (QCF), whereas the Assessor units are at level 3. This demonstrates the importance of the role. Often IQAs are supervisors or managers and are naturally responsible for staff, systems and procedures. Some are still working as assessors and performing both roles. That is absolutely fine as long as they don't IQA their own assessment decisions, as that would be a conflict of interest. Some smaller organisations might only have one assessor and one IQA, which again is fine providing they remain fully objective when carrying out their role. Some small teams, i.e. one assessor and one IQA, can swap roles and IQA each other's assessment decisions. Again, it is not a problem unless the organisation deems it is. It could be considered a good way of standardising practice as they will be monitoring each other regularly to ensure consistency.

Activity

Have a look at the units in Appendices 4 and 5. Look at the learning outcomes and assessment criteria to see what an IQA should know and do. Appendix 4 relates to knowledge and Appendix 5 to performance.

IQAs might also be required to:

- analyse enrolment, retention, achievement and progression data

- carry out a training needs analysis with assessors

- compile self-assessment reports

- countersign other IQAs' judgements

- deal with appeals and complaints

- design advertising and marketing materials

- design, issue and analyse questionnaires and surveys, and set action plans based on the findings

- ensure qualifications are fit for purpose and validated by the organisation

- ensure strategies, policies and procedures are regularly reviewed

- facilitate appropriate staff development, training and CPD

- induct and mentor new staff, support existing staff and carry out staff appraisals

- interview new staff

- liaise with others involved in the IQA process, for example trainers, witnesses and external quality assurers (EQAs)

- prepare agendas and chair meetings

- prepare for external inspections and visits from AO personnel, or liaise with administrative staff who will carry out the preparations

- implement any action points

- provide statistics and reports to line managers

- register and certificate learners with an AO

- set targets and/or performance indicators.

Regulations

You should always follow any organisational and regulatory requirements such as the *Regulatory Arrangements for the Qualifications and Credit Framework* (2008) for England, Wales and Northern Ireland.

> *The regulatory arrangements are designed to reflect the qualifications regulators' policy commitment to a strategic, risk-based approach to safeguarding the interests of learners.*

(Ofqual, 2008, p3)

National Vocational Qualifications (NVQs) are qualifications predominantly assessed in the work environment which were on the previous national qualifications framework (NQF). However, the term NVQ is still used with certain qualifications which are now on the QCF. The NVQ Code of Practice (2006) will apply if you are involved with these types of qualifications. This means you must hold or be working towards relevant assessor or IQA units.

If you are internally quality assuring an accredited qualification, there should be an EQA from the AO who will monitor your practice. You will need to find out who this is and maintain regular contact with them. At some point they will sample the assessment and IQA systems used at your organisation (see Chapters 6 and 7 for more information regarding the EQA process).

There will be other requirements you may need to follow such as those imposed by the AO if you are quality assuring an accredited qualification. There will also be subject-specific guidance and legislation such as the Health and Safety at Work etc Act (1974) and the Equality Act (2010) (see Chapter 1 for further details regarding legislation).

Extension Activity

Find out what policies, procedures and regulations you need to follow to support the IQA process at your organisation. Are they available in hard copy format, or can you access and use them electronically? How will they impact upon your role?

Key concepts and principles of internal quality assurance

Key concepts of IQA relate to ideas, whereas principles are how the ideas are put into practice. For the purpose of this chapter, they have been separated for clarity. However, some concepts could also be classed as principles depending upon your interpretation.

Key concepts

Concepts are the aspects involved throughout the IQA process. They include the following (which are then explained in detail):

- accountability
- achievement
- assessment strategies
- confidentiality
- risk factors
- evaluation
- interim and summative sampling
- transparency.

Accountability
You need to be *accountable* to your organisation to ensure you are carrying out your role correctly. Your assessors should know why they are being monitored and why their decisions are being sampled. You will also be accountable to the AO if you assess an accredited programme. For example, if you or an assessor does something wrong the credibility of your reputation could be questioned.

Achievement
You may be required to analyse *achievement* data and compare this to national or organisational targets. The funding your organisation receives might also be related to achievements. It is always a useful evaluation method to keep a record of how many learners your assessors have and how many successfully achieve. If one assessor has a high number of learners who are not achieving, is it because of the assessor or some other factor?

Assessment strategies
Following the *assessment strategy* for your subject will ensure you are carrying out your role correctly, are holding or working towards the required qualifications and are supporting your assessors. You might also need to recruit and interview new assessors and ensure they meet the assessment strategy (if applicable). It would also be useful to have a succession plan in place in case an assessor leaves at short notice. You cannot have learners without an assessor, and you will need to inform the AO of any changes in staff.

Confidentiality

Confidentiality will ensure you maintain records in accordance with organisational and statutory guidelines such as the Data Protection Act (1998) and Freedom of Information Act (2000).

Risk factors

There are many *risk factors* to take into consideration when planning IQA activities, for example:

- assessor expertise, confidence and competence; whether new, experienced, inexperienced, qualified or working towards assessor units

- assessors (or teachers/trainers) who assess the same subject but with different groups of learners

- whether the learners have been registered with an AO (if applicable), as assessment decisions might not be valid otherwise

- workload and caseload of assessors

- locations of learners and assessors

- type of qualification or programme being assessed, problem areas or units

- changes to standards and qualifications

- assessment methods and types of evidence provided by learners

- whether evidence and records are stored manually or electronically

- reliability of witnesses

- authenticity of learners' work.

All the above can impact upon the amount of IQA activities which need to be carried out, with whom and when.

Evaluation

Evaluation of the assessment and IQA process should always take place to inform current and future practice. All aspects of the IQA cycle should be evaluated on a continuous basis.

Interim and summative sampling

Sampling should also take place on an ongoing basis and not be left until the end of the programme. It should be *interim,* i.e. part-way through, and *summative,* i.e. at the completion stage. If a problem is identified at the interim stage, there is a chance to put it right. Sampling at the summative stage can check the full assessment process has been successfully completed and that all documents are signed and dated correctly.

Transparency

To assist *transparency,* you need to ensure that everyone who is involved in the assessment and IQA process clearly understands what is expected and can see there is nothing untoward taking place. That includes your own interpretation and understanding of the assessment criteria as well as that of your assessors. There should be no ambiguity, i.e. everyone should know what is expected of them.

Auditable records must always be maintained throughout the IQA process. If your organisation is claiming funding, full and accurate records must be maintained to show what was claimed and why. Transparency is also about having nothing to hide and being open to scrutiny.

Key principles

Principles are based upon the concepts and relate to *how* the IQA process is put into practice.

One important principle is known by the acronym VACSR and applies to assessment as well as IQA. You need to ensure all assessed work is:

- **v**alid – relevant to the assessment criteria

- **a**uthentic – has been produced solely by the learner

- **c**urrent – still relevant at the time of assessment

- **s**ufficient – covers all the assessment criteria

- **r**eliable – consistent across all learners, over time and at the required level.

If the above are not checked, you will not be supporting your assessors correctly. This could lead them to think their practice is acceptable when in reality it might not be.

Key principles of IQA include:

- assessor competence – ensuring assessors are experienced and competent in their role, meeting the requirements of the assessment strategy (if applicable) and maintaining their CPD

- communication – ensuring this takes place regularly with learners, assessors, other IQAs, employers, witnesses, anyone else involved

- CPD – maintaining currency of knowledge and performance to ensure your practice is up to date

- equality and diversity – ensuring all assessment activities embrace equality, inclusivity and diversity, represent all aspects of society and meet the requirements of the Equality Act 2010 (see Chapter 1 for further details)

- ethics – ensuring the assessment and IQA process is honest and moral, and takes into account confidentiality and integrity

- fairness – ensuring assessment and IQA activities are fit for purpose, and planning, decisions and feedback are justifiable

- health and safety – ensuring these are taken into account throughout the full assessment and IQA process, carrying out risk assessments as necessary

- motivation – encouraging and supporting your assessors to reach their maximum potential

- record keeping – ensuring accurate records are maintained throughout the learning, assessment and IQA process

- SMART – ensuring all assessment activities are **s**pecific, **m**easurable, **a**chievable, **r**elevant and **t**ime bound

- standardisation – ensuring the assessment and IQA requirements are interpreted accurately and that all assessors and IQAs are making comparable and consistent decisions

- strategies – ensuring a written strategy is in place which clearly explains the full process of what will be internally quality assured, when and how.

Following the key concepts and principles of IQA will ensure you are performing your role according to all relevant regulations and requirements.

Internal quality assurance rationale

A good IQA system will start with a written rationale: this is the reason *why* IQA should take place. This could be due to the qualification being accredited and the requirements for assessors and IQAs to hold a recognised qualification (whether the assessment strategy for the subject requires it or not).

Example

The IQA rationale is to comply with internal and external organisations' requirements to assure the quality of assessment for all learners. All assessment decisions will be carried out by qualified assessors in each subject area and sampled by qualified IQAs. This will ensure the safety, fairness, validity and reliability of assessment methods and decisions. It will also uphold the credibility of the qualification and reputation of the organisation.

Having a rationale will help ensure all assessment and IQA activities are robust, and that they are safe, valid, fair and reliable.

- Robust: the activities are strong and will endure the test of time.

- Safe: the activities used are ethical, there is little chance of plagiarism by learners, the work can be confirmed as authentic, confidentiality is taken into account, learning and assessment are not compromised, nor is the learner's experience or potential to achieve. (Safe in this context does not relate to health and safety but to the assessment methods used.)

- Valid: the activities used are based on the requirements of the qualification, programme or job specification.

- Fair: the activities used are appropriate to all learners at the required level, taking into account any particular learner needs. Activities are fit for purpose, and planning, decisions and feedback are justifiable and equitable.

- Reliable: the activities used would lead to a similar outcome with similar learners.

Internal quality assurance process

IQA should be carried out from the commencement to the completion of the product or service. If there is no external formal examination taken by learners, there has to be a system of monitoring the performance of assessors. If not, assessors might make incorrect judgements or pass a learner who has not met the requirements, perhaps because they were biased towards them or had made a mistake. Assessment and IQA systems should be monitored and evaluated continuously to identify any actions for improvement, which should then be implemented. This also includes the CPD of assessors and IQAs.

An IQA must be appointed to carry out the quality assurance role within an organisation where there are assessment activities taking place. As a minimum, the IQA should:

- plan what will be monitored, from whom and when

- observe trainer and assessor performance and provide developmental feedback

- sample assessment records, learners' work and assessor decisions

- meet with learners and others, for example witnesses

- facilitate the standardisation of assessor practice

- support assessors.

Activity

Obtain a copy of the qualification handbook or other criteria that will be assessed and internally quality assured. Familiarise yourself with the requirements and decide what aspects of the assessment process you will monitor and why.

If there is more than one IQA for a particular subject area, one person should take the lead role and co-ordinate the others (see Chapter 8 for further details as this is a management role). All IQAs should standardise their practice with each other to ensure they interpret the requirements in the same way.

Figure 4.1 IQA cycle

If IQA does not take place, there are risks to the accuracy, consistency and fairness of assessment practice. This could lead to incorrect decisions and ultimately disadvantage the learners.

Depending upon the subject, you will usually follow the IQA cycle as in Figure 4.1. The cycle will ensure the assessment process is constantly monitored and improved. Records of all activities must be maintained throughout to satisfy your organisation, the regulatory authorities and AOs.

The IQA cycle involves the following aspects.

- Identify the product or service – ascertain what is to be assessed and internally quality assured and why, for example learners working towards a qualification, a programme of learning, or staff being observed performing their job roles. The criteria will need to be clear, i.e. units from a qualification or aspects of a job specification. Learners should be allocated to assessors in a fair way, for example according to location or workload.

- Planning – devise a sample plan to arrange what will be monitored, by whom and when. Plan the dates to observe assessor performance, hold team meetings and standardisation activities. Information will need to be obtained from assessors to assist the planning process and risks taken into account, such as assessor knowledge, qualifications and experience.

- Activity – carry out the activities such as sampling learners' work, observing trainer and assessor performance, and sampling assessment records and decisions. This also includes holding meetings and standardisation activities, supporting and training assessors and communicating with others involved in the assessment and IQA process.

- Decision and feedback – make a judgement as to whether the assessor has performed satisfactorily and made valid and reliable decisions. Provide developmental feedback as to what was good or what could be improved. Agree action points if necessary and follow them up (see Chapter 5 for further information regarding providing feedback to assessors).

- Evaluation – review the whole process of assessment and IQA to determine what could be improved or done differently. Agree action plans if necessary, implement them and follow them up. Follow any action plans from EQAs or others involved in the IQA process. Write self-assessment reports as necessary.

The cycle will then begin again with an identification of what needs to be monitored and when. Throughout the cycle, standardisation of practice between IQAs should take place; this will help ensure the consistency and fairness of decisions. Records must be maintained of all activities for audit requirements. All staff should maintain their CPD and follow legal and organisational requirements. If the qualification is accredited by an AO, EQA will also take place to ensure IQA is effective.

Extension Activity

Look at the bulleted lists of key concepts and principles on page 126 and 128 and describe how each will impact upon your role as an IQA. You may need to research some aspects further or speak to relevant staff at your organisation.

Sample planning and the collection of information

To perform your role fully, you need to create sample plans, monitor assessment activities and collect information. You might have several plans for different activities, for example a plan to observe your assessors, a plan to sample their assessed work and a plan for meetings and standardisation activities. You might be able to combine the plans if there is only a small number of assessors. To help you plan effectively, you need to have an IQA strategy on which to base your activities.

Internal quality assurance strategy

Think of the IQA strategy as the starting point for all the activities, monitoring and sampling which you will carry out. It should be a written statement of what will be carried out and is based on the IQA rationale and any identified risk factors. Having a strategy will help you plan what will be monitored and ensure that your systems are fit for purpose. If you are quality assuring an accredited qualification, it will be a requirement of the AO that you have a written strategy.

Systems should be in place to ensure all key concepts and principles are met, and that monitoring and sampling are effective. The strategy might be produced by your organisation or it might be your responsibility to write it.

Example

The following is an IQA strategy for Level 2 Customer Service (one IQA, four assessors, 100 learners).

The IQA will:

- *observe each assessor every six months*
- *talk to a sample of learners and witnesses*
- *sample at least five assessed units from each assessor across a mix of learners (new assessors will have a higher sample rate)*
- *chair a bi-monthly team meeting*
- *facilitate regular standardisation activities to cover all units over a period of time*
- *maintain full records of all IQA activities*
- *implement EQA action points.*

The IQA strategy should take into account factors such as:

- assessment methods – are they safe, valid, fair and reliable; are they complex and varied; do they include online assessments; are witnesses used?

- availability of assessors for observations and meetings – some assessors could be located at a distance – can activities take place remotely via the internet?

- experience, workload and caseload of assessors – experienced assessors can be sampled less than new assessors; some assessors might work part time or have other work commitments; some assessors might have more learners than others

- holistic assessment – if aspects from more than one unit are assessed simultaneously, can the achievement of each unit be separately tracked?

- learners with specific needs – do assessors need to adapt any assessment methods?

- number of learners to assessors – allocating learners to assessors should be fair, assessors should not be overloaded

- problem areas or units – assessors might interpret them differently, or learners might have problems achieving them

- qualification or criteria to be assessed – are assessors familiar with these; have assessors standardised their interpretation of them; are standards due to be revised?

- types of records to be completed – manual or electronic.

Activity

Write a strategy for the subject you will internally quality assure. Consider what you will need to do and how you will do it. If you are not currently quality assuring, create a hypothetical strategy. Are there any implications for your job role because of the particular subject you will internally quality assure?

Internal quality assurance sampling

Once you have your strategy, you will need to use your organisation's documents to create your sampling plans. The plans will show the activities and sampling that you will carry out over a period of time. If plans are not available, you will need to design your own, perhaps based on those in this chapter.

As a minimum, you will need:

- an observation plan

- a meeting and standardisation plan

- a sample plan and tracking sheet.

You could have separate plans for each activity if there are a lot of assessors and learners, or combine them if numbers are small. Your plans should show continual activity over the period of assessment. If IQA is carried out near or at the end of the assessment process, there is little opportunity to rectify any concerns or issues. There are lots of variables to take into consideration when creating your plans, for example the experience and location of your assessors, the number of learners they have, the complexity of what is being assessed and the use of witnesses. You need to consider all of this in your strategy before planning your activities.

Observation plan

You should observe each assessor over a period of time to ensure they are carrying out their role effectively, supporting their learners adequately, making correct decisions and giving developmental feedback. When planning to observe, you will need to take into consideration their experience, the number of learners they have and the different locations where they assess. When you have built up confidence in an assessor's performance, you could carry out fewer observations. If you have inexperienced or newly qualified assessors, you might want to observe them more. If you plan well in advance and liaise with your assessor as to what they will be assessing, you can ensure you cover a variety of aspects being assessed.

Observing the same unit across different assessors will aid the standardisation process. You might find your assessors do things quite differently and in this way you will be able to discuss ways of ensuring consistency of practice. It is the ideal time after an observation to talk to learners and witnesses and you should maintain records of these discussions. A visual planner, as in Table 4.1, helps everyone see when the various activities will take place. Specific dates can then be added according to the assessor activities, and an observation report completed. If learners and witnesses are interviewed after the observation, a report should also be completed. Completed examples of these reports can be found in Chapter 5.

Table 4.1 shows a plan for observing four assessors, two of whom have already been observed. The dates of these observations have been added to the plan. As J Smith is unqualified and S Hans is newly qualified, they will be observed more often until the IQA has confidence in their work. Unit 101 will be sampled from every assessor to ensure a standardised approach.

Meeting and standardisation plan

Regular team meetings between all assessors and IQAs should take place to discuss general issues regarding progress. A plan will reflect when these will take place and ensure staff are available to attend. An agenda should be issued in advance and minutes taken and distributed after the meeting. If someone cannot attend, they should be given access to a copy of the minutes and be given the opportunity to discuss the content with you at some point. Meetings could take place virtually via teleconferencing or be visually recorded and viewed later.

Part of the IQA process is to ensure assessors are standardising their practice. Standardisation activities can be timetabled to take place as part of the meeting or as a separate event. Besides the standardisation of assessment practice, if there is more than one IQA for a subject, they should all meet to ensure the consistency of their own practice, systems and records. They can also meet separately from their assessors for their own standardisation activities. A visual planner, as in Table 4.2, will help everyone see when the various activities will take place.

Table 4.1 Example observation plan

Observation plan

Qualification: Level 2 Customer Service   **IQA:** H Rahl

Assessor	Jan	Feb	Mar	Apr	May	Jun	Jul	Aug	Sep	Oct	Nov	Dec
P Jones qualified	Unit 101 31.01.16						Unit 102					
M Singh qualified		Unit 101 18.02.16						Unit 103				
J Smith unqualified			Unit 101		Unit 102			Unit 103	Unit 104			
S Hans newly qualified				Unit 101				Unit 103		Unit 105		

135

Table 4.2 Example meeting and standardisation plan

Meeting and standardisation plan

Qualification: Level 2 Customer Service   **IQA:** H Rahl

Activity	Jan	Feb	Mar	Apr	May	Jun	Jul	Aug	Sep	Oct	Nov	Dec
Assessor team meeting	4th		9th		7th		6th		8th		10th	
Assessor standardisation activity		16th Unit 101		13th Unit 102		15th Unit 103		17th Unit 104		12th Unit 105		
IQA team meeting			18th			29th			17th			3rd
IQA standardisation activity				22nd				30th				15th

If there is only one assessor, they will not have the opportunity to standardise with other assessors. You could double assess one of their units, enabling a discussion to take place to ensure you are both interpreting it in the same way. However, if you have double assessed a unit, you cannot then internally quality assure it. Alternatively, your assessor could link up with assessors from other organisations to help standardise their practice, perhaps as part of a consortium.

If your qualification is externally quality assured, the AO will need you to maintain thorough records of meetings and standardisation activities (see Chapter 2 for further details of assessment standardisation and an example template which could be used).

Sample plan and tracking sheet

A sample plan and tracking sheet will identify what you will sample, from whom and when. It should then track the dates when interim and summative sampling have actually taken place. This allows an audit trail to be followed by any EQAs or inspectors. The plan should cover all assessors, what they are assessing and the assessment methods used. You should look at all areas of the qualification or criteria being assessed on a continuous basis over time. You should not sample everything from every assessor. Imagine if you were a baker sampling the cupcakes which have been made by several of your cooks. You might only taste one cupcake from one batch made each day by each cook, as tasting them all would render them unsaleable.

Some areas of learners' work that you sample might be incomplete and other areas will be complete. This will enable you to see how the learners are progressing and monitor how long they are taking to achieve the required outcomes. There is no need to sample something from every learner unless there is a reason to do so, for example a concern about a particular assessor's decisions.

You will need to sample a cross-section of work from assessors, learners, methods and decisions. To decide on what to sample and from whom, you should consider factors such as:

- assessors – qualifications, experience, workload, caseload, locations
- learners – particular requirements, ethnic origin, age, gender, locations
- methods – observation, questions, witness statements, tests, prior learning, work products
- decisions – assessment records, feedback given, VACSR.

Once you are familiar with the above, you can plan your sample using an appropriate method. There are various sampling methods you could use; some are more effective than others. The following terminology relates to how they are viewed on a sample plan, for example:

- diagonal – one area from all learners
- horizontal – something from all areas over time
- percentage – for example, ten per cent from each assessor or learner
- random – unsystematic method
- theme based – relating to a particular activity such as work products, witness statements, etc.
- vertical – the same area from each learner.

Table 4.3 Example sample plan and tracking sheet

Sample plan and tracking sheet						
Level 2 Customer Service **IQA:** H RAHL						
Assessor: P Jones						
Learner and location	**Unit 101**	**Unit 102**	**Unit 103**	**Unit 104**	**Unit 105**	**Summative**
Ann Bex X Company	Jan *Sampled on 12 Jan*	Feb *Sampled on 18 Feb*	Aug	Sep	Oct	Nov
Eve Holler X Company	Jan *Sampled on 12 Jan*	Feb *Sampled on 18 Feb*				
Terri Frame Y Company	Mar		July			
Jon Vanquis Z Company	April			Aug		
Naomi Black Z Company	July				Sep	Oct

Table 4.3 shows a mixture of diagonal, horizontal and vertical sampling for five units of a quali-fication from one assessor and their learners. Two of the units have already been sampled. The IQA will sample all the evidence provided for each unit. The summative sample ensures all doc-umentation has been correctly completed when the learner finishes their programme.

It is the IQA's choice what they sample and when, according to their strategy: for exam-ple theme-based sampling for witness statements from Unit 101, assessment plans and feedback records from Unit 102, observation reports from Unit 103 and everything from Unit 104. The dates for sampling should tie in with the learners' progress. There is no point planning to sample Unit 101 in January if no one is working towards it. Regular commu-nication with your assessors will help you keep track of what is taking place and the plan can be updated or amended at any time. Team meetings are also a good opportunity for assessors to give you an update of their learners' progress. It is your choice what to sam-ple, not an assessor's.

Whichever methods you choose, they should be fit for purpose and ensure that some-thing from each assessor is sampled over time. You are looking for quality, not quantity. A mixture of diagonal, horizontal and vertical sampling is best as it ensures everything will be monitored over time. Percentage and random sampling are not good practice as aspects can easily be missed. However, they can be used in addition to other methods, such as theme-based sampling, if a problem is found and you need to sample further. If an assessor covers several locations, work from learners at each location must be sampled to ensure a standardised approach and fair practice.

Sampling everything from everyone (i.e. 100 per cent sampling) is time consuming and is not good practice. It becomes double assessment rather than quality assurance and does not improve or enhance the assessment process.

Once the sample has taken place, a report must be completed and the findings shared with the assessor. An example report can be found in Chapter 5. The actual date of the sample can then be added to the plan to show an audit trail from planning to completion.

Extension Activity

State the advantages and limitations of each of the following sampling methods in respect of the subject you will be internally quality assuring:

- diagonal
- horizontal
- percentage
- random
- theme based
- vertical.

Which methods will you use and why?

Maintaining and improving the quality of assessment

If you have a robust quality system, you will sustain the reputation of your subject or qualification as well as that of the AO (if applicable). Carrying out observations of your assessors and sampling their learners' work, the assessment decisions and records will all help ensure IQA is an effective, valid and reliable process. However, it needs to remain effective and cannot be allowed to decline in any way. You therefore need to ensure you maintain and improve assessment and IQA systems on an ongoing basis.

You must maintain an audit trail of everything you do. If you plan to IQA something in March and don't sample it until April, that is absolutely fine. However, the actual date you carried out the activity must be added to the plan. Having *March* on the sample plan but *12 April* as the actual sampled date is reflecting reality. Not everything will occur when you planned it, perhaps due to holidays, the late submission of learner work, absence or illness, etc. If you do change any dates, don't be tempted to alter them or use correction fluid. Just cross out one date and write in another so that the original can still be seen. If you save your plans electronically, resave the changes as a different version so that you can access the previous versions if required. You might need to justify your reasons to auditors as to why there have been changes.

To help improve the quality of assessment, you need to ensure your assessors are maintaining their occupational competence for the subject area they are assessing. You also need to make sure they are fully competent using your organisation's systems and procedures, and in their assessment practice in general. If your assessors are qualified, they should be operating at the required standard to support their learners. If you have assessors who are currently working towards an assessor qualification, their decisions may need to be counter-signed by another qualified assessor in the same subject area. As the IQA, you cannot do this as you will then be sampling their assessed work, which is a conflict of interest. However, you will need to ensure all countersigning has correctly taken place when sampling the work of unqualified assessors. Your AO will be able to give you further guidance on this.

When a new assessor commences at your organisation, you will need to induct them to ensure they understand their job role and the requirements of what will be assessed. The following checklist of points is useful to cover with new staff, as well as with existing staff from time to time:

IQA checklist

☑ tour of the organisation and training/assessment locations

☑ introductions to other assessors/IQAs and relevant staff

☑ organisation's policies and procedures, vision and mission statement

☑ assessment strategy and assessment documentation

☑ internal and external quality assurance procedures

☑ the standards or qualification criteria to be assessed

☑ details of learners they will be responsible for

☑ curriculum vitae, CPD and qualifications to be checked

☑ sample signature and identification checked

☑ target date agreed for achieving the assessor qualification (if applicable)

☑ countersignatory identified if the assessor is unqualified

☑ other aspects such as access to resources, photocopying, administrative support, travel expense claims/pay claims, etc.

You should also discuss the training and development needs of your assessors to ensure they are keeping up to date with their knowledge and practice. This process will identify any requirements they have, which can then be met through CPD. Improving your assessors' performance should lead to an improvement in the quality of assessment.

Example

Philip had been assessing the same qualification for a number of years, but had missed the latest team meeting where the recently revised standards had been discussed. Kim, the IQA, assumed Philip would be fine and had forgotten to send him a copy of the minutes. However, during a chance meeting with Philip she quickly realised he was not aware of a lot of the changes. As a consequence, his learners were not meeting the required standard for one of the units. Kim quickly arranged for Philip to meet with another assessor to update his knowledge and standardise his practice.

Other aspects which might need improving include the records which are used for the IQA and assessment process. It might be that two forms are currently being used which could be merged into one form, or some questions on a document are no longer relevant. A standardisation activity could be arranged to review and update all the documentation and records used. It is useful to include the date or a version number on each document as a footer and keep a separate list of these details for tracking purposes. In this way, you can quickly see if your assessors are using the most up-to-date version.

Example

Magda sampled the assessment documents used for Unit 104 from each of her four assessors. She found one of the assessors had used completely different documentation to the other three. Magda random sampled further units from this assessor and found the same. She was then able to give feedback to the assessor as to where the current versions could be located and how they should be used.

Encouraging staff to access documents electronically from a central system when they need them, rather than keeping a stack of hard copies, will help ensure they are using the most up-to-date version.

The role of ICT in internal quality assurance

Information and communication technology (ICT) can be used to support and enhance the IQA process. This is particularly useful when the IQA is located in a different area from the assessors. A virtual learning environment (VLE) or electronic portfolio could be used to upload learners' work and assessors' records. This would enable the IQA to sample various aspects remotely at a time to suit. Reports could then be completed electronically, uploaded to the VLE or e-mailed to the assessor.

Communication through e-mail or web-based forums can simplify the contact process between the IQA and their assessors. There will be times when people are not available at the same time, either for a meeting or a telephone call. Using ICT enables messages to be left which can be responded to when convenient.

Meetings and standardisation activities could also take place remotely, for example through video/teleconferencing or webinars. Everyone does not need to be in the same room at the same time for activities to be effective. Materials could be produced and circulated electronically prior to the remote meeting and then discussed when everyone is accessible.

Never assume that staff are familiar with how to use the various aspects of ICT. Training sessions may need to be carried out and resources might need to be updated.

Other aspects for performing IQA activities include:

- using a mobile phone/smart phone, tablet or digital camera to record an assessor activity; this is useful if the IQA cannot be present at the time – the assessor could make a recording and forward it on

- using web conferencing to talk to learners and witnesses if they are quite a distance away

- using e-mails with integrated video facilities to send visual messages

- using webinars to view presentations or software packages, enabling participants to remain in their own locations rather than travel to a central location

- recording verbal information and making podcasts or visual recordings of conversations, meetings and/or information regarding updates and changes

- observing live assessment activities via an online visual communication program

- making digital recordings or videos of role-play activities or case studies, for example assessor decisions and developmental feedback – assessors could view them remotely to comment on strengths and limitations of a particular feedback method

- making visual recordings of how to complete documents and reports – if an assessor is unsure how to complete a document they could access a video to see an example.

See Chapter 3 for the role of ICT in the assessment process.

Activity

Consider how you could use ICT for your IQA role. What resources could you use and how would you use them to effectively support the IQA process?

Appeals and complaints

An appeal is usually about an assessment decision, whereas a complaint is more likely to be about a situation or a person. Learners who appeal or complain should be able to do so without fear of recrimination. Confidentiality should be maintained where possible to ensure an impartial outcome, and the learner should feel protected throughout the full process. If anyone does make an appeal or complaint, this should not affect the way they are treated and the outcome should not jeopardise their current or future achievements.

At some point during the assessment process, a learner may wish to appeal against one of your assessor's decisions. There should be an appeals procedure with which learners and assessors are familiar. Information could also be displayed on notice boards, in a learner handbook, or be available via your organisation's intranet or VLE. Learners will need to know who they can go to and that their issue will be followed up. This process will involve various stages and have deadlines, such as seven days to lodge an appeal, seven days for a response, etc., and all stages should be documented. Usually, an appeals process is made up of four stages: assessor, IQA, manager and EQA (if applicable). It might be your role to monitor appeals from learners and it could be that at the second stage in the appeals pro-cess you will need to make a decision whether to uphold the learner's appeal. If you don't uphold it, it will then escalate to the next stage, i.e. your manager. The manager's decision could be final, or if the qualification is externally quality assured, it might then escalate to the EQA, whose decision should be final. The nature of the appeal can be used to inform future practice to prevent further appeals.

Example

Cheng had lodged a formal appeal to the IQA, Julia, regarding his assessor's decision for Unit 301. He felt he should have passed as he had supplied all the required evidence. Julia spoke to the assessor and reviewed Cheng's evidence. It transpired that the assessor was correct in asking for a further piece of evidence. Julia spoke to Cheng and explained that four pieces of evidence were required and he had only submitted three. He accepted Julia's decision and agreed to supply a further piece of evidence. Cheng then retracted his appeal.

If Cheng had used the first stage of the process and discussed his concern with the assessor, there would have been no need to involve the IQA. Some organisations will provide an appeals pro-forma for learners to complete, which ensures all the required details are obtained, or encourage an informal discussion with the assessor first. Statistics should be maintained regarding all appeals and complaints; these will help your organisation when reviewing its policies and procedures, and should be provided to relevant external auditors if requested.

A complaint could also be made by one of your assessors against something you have or have not done as part of your role. An assessor might appeal against a decision you have made, for example if you disagreed with one of their judgements. There should be a formal appeals procedure for assessors, similar to that for learners. However, if possible, try to discuss it with your assessor first to reach an amicable outcome.

Having a climate of respect and honesty can lead to issues being dealt with informally, rather than procedures having to be followed which can be upsetting for both parties concerned.

Extension Activity

Locate, read and summarise your organisation's policies and procedures for appeals and complaints in your particular subject area. Are any templates of documents supplied, and what are the time limits for submission and follow up? If your qualification is accredited, find out what role the AO plays regarding appeals and complaints.

Evaluation

Evaluation is not another term for assessment. Evaluation relates to the programme, whereas assessment relates to the learners. Assessment is specific towards a learner's progress and achievement and how they can improve and develop. Evaluation obtains feedback from your learners and others to help you improve and develop your own practice and the overall learner experience on the programme.

Evaluation includes surveys or questionnaires, reviews, appraisals, and informal and formal discussions, telephone calls and meetings. Feedback can come from learners, assessors, IQAs, EQAs and others such as witnesses and employers. Information gained from evaluations should lead to an improvement for the learners, your assessors, yourself and your organisation. Never assume everything is going well just because you think it is, or no one has appealed or made a complaint.

Information to help you evaluate assessment and IQA practice includes statistics such as enrolment, retention, success and progression data. This could affect the amount of funding received or future targets. Feedback from meetings and standardisation activities can also influence the way you evaluate the process. You might decide to redesign some of the assessment documentation or the way in which forms are completed, for example electronically rather than paper based.

Any issues or trends, and areas of good or poor practice you have identified throughout the IQA process, should be summarised and fed back to your assessors or used as a standardisation activity.

Evaluation of both practice and systems can improve the service everyone receives and contribute to future planning within the organisation.

Surveys and questionnaires

These are useful ways of formally obtaining feedback from everyone involved in the assessment and IQA process. If you use them, you need to consider what you want to find out, who you will ask and why. Don't just ask questions for the sake of issuing a questionnaire, and don't just give them to those you know will give a positive response. Everyone should be given the opportunity to be involved and left to decide if they wish to respond or not.

When writing questions, you need to gauge the language and level to suit your respondents. You might be able to use jargon or complex terms with assessors, but not with others. The type of question you choose will depend upon the amount of information you require. Using a *closed* question, i.e. a question only requiring a *yes* or *no* response, will not give you as much information as an *open* question, which enables the respondent to give a detailed answer.

Example

Did you receive a detailed assessment plan? YES/NO

Was the assessment activity as you expected? YES/NO

Did you receive feedback? YES/NO

Was your assessor supportive? YES/NO

These closed questions would not help you to understand what it was that your learner experienced, and they might just choose 'yes' to be polite. It would, however, be easy to add up the number of *yes* and *no* responses to gain *quantitative data*. Think of this as the *quantity* of something, i.e. in terms of the total number of *yes* and *no* responses. The questions would be better rephrased as open questions to encourage learners to answer in detail. This would give you *qualitative data*, therefore giving you more information to act on. Think of this as the *quality* of something which gives you information to work with rather than just data.

How detailed was your assessment plan?

What assessment activity was used and why?

How did you receive feedback?

How supportive was your assessor?

Using questions beginning with *who, what, when, where, why* and *how* (WWWWWH) will ensure you gain good quality answers. If you would rather use questions with *yes/no* responses, you could ask a further question to enable the learner to elaborate on why they answered *yes* or *no*.

Was the assessment activity as you expected? YES/NO

Why was this?

This enables the learner to expand on their response and gives you more information to act on. When designing questionnaires, use the KISS method: **K**eep **I**t **S**hort and **S**imple. Don't overcomplicate your questions, for example by asking two unrelated questions in one sentence, or make the questionnaire so long that learners will not want to complete it.

You could consider using the Likert (1932) scale, which gives respondents several answers to a question from which they need to choose one, such as:

1. Strongly disagree

2. Disagree

3. Neither agree nor disagree

4. Agree

5. Strongly agree

However, you might find respondents choose option 3 as a safe answer. Removing a middle response and giving four options forces a choice:

1. Strongly disagree

2. Disagree

3. Agree

4. Strongly agree

Anonymity should be given for any survey or questionnaire used. If the respondent works closely with you, this might not be possible; the same goes for telephone or face-to-face questioning. Electronic questionnaires that are e-mailed back will denote who the respondent is. However, postal ones will not. There are lots of online programs for surveys that will guarantee anonymity and will also analyse the results of quantitative data. Some of these, such as www.surveymonkey.com, offer a free basic service.

Activity

Design a short survey or questionnaire that could be used with learners. Consider the types of questions you will ask and how you will ask them, based upon the information you need to ascertain. Decide how the questionnaire will be implemented, for example paper based, online or in person. If possible, ask your assessors to use it with their learners by a set date, analyse the results and recommend improvements to be made based on these.

Always set a date for the return of any surveys and don't be disappointed if you don't get as many replies as you had hoped. Denscombe (2001) predicted a 30 per cent response rate, which is not very high. If you give learners time to complete a questionnaire, perhaps immediately after meeting them, they will hand it in straight away rather than take it away and forget about it. However, this will not ensure anonymity.

Always inform your respondents why you are asking them to complete the questionnaire and what the information will be used for. Make sure you analyse the results, create an action plan and follow this through; otherwise the process is meaningless. Informing the respondents of the results and subsequent action keeps them up to date with developments and shows that you take their feedback seriously.

Another way of obtaining feedback is through *focus groups* – a face-to-face group meeting and discussion. This could be carried out via teleconferencing if not everyone can attend a certain venue at the same time.

Focus groups show signs of taking over from questionnaires ... they share with postal questionnaires the advantages of being an efficient way of generating substantial amounts of data. However, as with questionnaires, these perceived advantages are offset by considerable disadvantages. For example, it is difficult or impossible to follow up the views of individuals and group dynamics or power hierarchies affecting who speaks and what they say.

(Robson, 2002, p284)

You could gain informal feedback from your assessors after you have observed them. This will help you realise how effective you were and what you could improve in the future. It may also help you identify any problem areas, enabling you to do things differently next time. You could also encourage your assessors to gain informal feedback from their learners after they carry out an assessment activity, for example during a one-to-one conversation or a group discussion.

Always make sure you do something with the feedback you receive to help improve the product or service offered to everyone involved in the assessment and IQA process.

Self-evaluation

Self-evaluation is a good way of continually reflecting upon your own practice to ensure you are carrying out your role effectively. When evaluating your own practice, you need to consider how your own behaviour has impacted upon others and what you could do to improve.

A straightforward method of reflection is to have an experience, then describe it, analyse it and revise it (EDAR). This method incorporates the WWWWWH approach and should help you consider ways of changing and/or improving.

Experience ⟶ Describe ⟶ Analyse ⟶ Revise (EDAR)

- **Experience** – a significant event or incident you would like to change or improve.

- **Describe** – aspects such as who was involved, what happened, when it happened and where it happened.

- **Analyse** – consider the experience deeper and ask yourself how it happened and why it happened.

- **Revise** – think about how you would do it differently if it happened again and then try this out if you have the opportunity.

As a result, you might find your own skills improving, for example giving more effective, constructive and developmental feedback to your assessors.

Reflection should become a habit, for example mentally running through the EDAR points after a significant event. As you become more experienced and analytical with reflective practice, you will progress from thoughts of *I did not do that very well*, to aspects of more significance such as *why* you did not do it very well and *how* you could change something as a result. You may realise you need further training or support in some areas, therefore partaking in relevant CPD should help.

There are various theories regarding reflection. Schön (1983) suggests two methods:

- reflection in action
- reflection on action.

Reflection *in action* happens at the time of the incident, is often unconscious and allows immediate changes to take place. It is about being *reactive* to a situation and dealing with it straight away.

Reflection *on action* takes place after the incident and is a more conscious process. This allows you time to think about the incident, consider a different approach, or talk to others about it before making changes. It is about being *proactive* and considering measures to prevent the situation happening again in the future.

Example

Aalia was observing Mark, an assessor, with a group of learners in a welding workshop. She noticed one of them was not wearing a visor correctly, which could lead to an accident. She immediately went over to the learner and showed him how to wear it the right way. This enabled her to deal with the situation at once. On reflection, she felt she should have asked Mark to deal with the situation with his learner. When giving Mark feedback after the observation, Aalia gave him additional advice on the importance of health and safety.

Part of reflection is about knowing what you need to change. If you are not aware of something that needs changing, you will continue as you are until something serious occurs. Maintaining your CPD and keeping up to date with developments in your subject area, changes in legislation, changes in qualifications or standards and developments with ICT will assist your knowledge and practice.

Extension Activity

Reflect upon a recent meeting you have chaired or attended. Evaluate how the meeting went, how you reacted to situations and what you could do differently next time. Consider what CPD you might need to help you with your IQA role.

Summary

In this chapter you have learnt about:

- the role of internal quality assurance

- key concepts and principles of internal quality assurance

- sample planning and the collection of information

- maintaining and improving the quality of assessment

- evaluation.

Evidence

Evidence from the completed activities within this chapter, plus the following, could be used towards the *Principles and practices of internally assuring the quality of assessment* unit, for example:

- written statements cross-referenced to the unit's assessment criteria

- answers to questions/assignments issued by your assessor

- records of discussions with your assessor.

Cross-referencing grid

This chapter contributes towards the following assessment criteria, along with aspects of the National Occupational Standards for Learning and Development. Full details of the learning outcomes and assessment criteria for each unit can be found in the Appendices.

Unit	Assessment criteria
Understanding the principles and practices of internally assuring the quality of assessment	1.1, 1.2, 1.3, 1.4 2.1, 2.2, 2.3 3.1, 3.2 4.1, 4.2, 4.3 5.1 6.1, 6.2, 6.3, 6.4
Internally assuring the quality of assessment	1.1, 1.2 2.3, 2.4 3.2 4.1, 4.2 5.1, 5.3, 5.4
Plan, allocate and monitor work	1.1, 1.2, 1.3, 1.4 3.1
National Occupational Standards	**Reference**
9 – Assess learner achievement	KU16, KU17, KU18 9.8
11 – Internally monitor and maintain the quality of assessment	KU1, KU2, KU5, KU6, KU7, KU11, KU13, KU14, KU15, KU16, KU17, KU18 11.1, 11.2, 11.3, 11.4, 11.5, 11.7, 11.8, 11.9, 11.10
12 – Externally monitor and maintain the quality of assessment	KU2, KU3, KU4, KU5, KU6, KU7, KU17 12.2, 12.3, 12.4, 12.5

Theory focus

References and further information

Boud, D (1995) *Enhancing Learning Through Self-assessment.* London: Kogan Page.

Denscombe, M (2001) *The Good Research Guide.* Buckingham: Open University Press.

Likert, R (1932) A Technique for the Measurement of Attitudes. *Archives of Psychology,* 140: 1–55.

Ofqual (2008) *Regulatory Arrangements for the Qualifications and Credit Framework.* Coventry: QCA.

QCA (2006 Revised) *NVQ Code of Practice.* London: QCA.

Robson, C (2002) *Real World Research* (2nd edition). Oxford: Blackwell Publishers.

Sallis, E (2002) *Total Quality Management in Education* (3rd edition). Abingdon: Routledge.

Schön, D (1983) *The Reflective Practitioner*. London: Temple Smith.

Wilson, L (2012) *Practical Teaching: A Guide to Assessment and Quality Assurance*. Andover: Cengage Learning.

Wood, J and Dickinson, J (2011) *Quality Assurance and Evaluation in the Lifelong Learning Sector*. London: Learning Matters SAGE.

Websites

Data Protection Act (1998): www.legislation.gov.uk/ukpga/1998/29/contents

Freedom of Information Act (2000): www.legislation.gov.uk/ukpga/2000/36/ contents

Health and Safety Executive: www.hse.gov.uk

Qualifications and Credit Framework: http://tinyurl.com/447bgy2

Skype online visual communication site (free): www.skype.com

Surveys and questionnaires (free): www.surveymonkey.com

Video e-mail (free): www.mailvu.com

5 INTERNALLY ASSURING THE QUALITY OF ASSESSMENT

Introduction

In this chapter you will learn about:

- internal quality assurance planning
- monitoring assessment activities
- decision making
- providing feedback to assessors
- record keeping – internal quality assurance.

Within the chapter there are activities and examples which will help you to reflect on the above and to develop and enhance your knowledge of how to internally assure the quality of assessment. Completing the activities will help you to gather evidence towards the *Internally assuring the quality of assessment* unit. At the end of each section is an extension activity to stretch and challenge your knowledge and understanding.

At the end of the chapter is a list of possible evidence which could be used towards the *Internally assuring the quality of assessment* unit.

A cross-referencing grid shows how the content of this chapter contributes towards the relevant TAQA units' criteria and the National Occupational Standards. There is also a theory focus with relevant references, further information and websites to which you might like to refer.

Internal quality assurance planning

As soon as you are appointed as an internal quality assurer (IQA), you should find out if there are any others in the same subject area as yourself, who can give you advice and guidance. If so, you can communicate with them to find out what you need to do. You will need to familiarise yourself with the internal quality assurance (IQA) policy, rationale, strategy and documentation.

You should then get in touch with your assessors to introduce yourself to them, for example at a team meeting. You should have a job description which will help you understand the requirements of your role and you should familiarise yourself with it. If you don't have a job description, following the requirements of the IQA units will ensure you are performing your role adequately (see Appendices 5 and 6). You will also need a copy of what is being assessed and internally quality assured, i.e. the syllabus, qualification handbook or job specification, along with copies of the assessment and IQA documentation.

Example

Vince has been employed as a Level 2 Motor Vehicle Maintenance assessor for five years. He has recently passed the IQA knowledge unit and has now been promoted to carry out some IQA activities. This will enable him to gather evidence towards the performance unit and support the five assessors in the team. As he has worked as part of the team, he is familiar with the assessors, the qualification and the assessment documentation. His first task is to familiarise himself with the IQA policy, rationale, strategy and documentation.

A large part of your role is about planning and monitoring assessor practice. However, before carrying this out, you could use a checklist like the one here to help you prepare.

☑ Do all assessors have an up-to-date copy of what they are assessing learners towards?

☑ Are there any areas which might cause concern, i.e. aspects which are difficult for learners to achieve or which involve complex activities?

☑ Are all assessors qualified and experienced? You may need to check that their curricula vitae (CVs) and certificates conform to any requirements.

☑ Do any assessors need to take an assessor qualification or gain any further experience? If so, you may need to arrange training and development activities for them. You may need to ensure unqualified assessors have their decisions countersigned by another qualified assessor in the same subject area.

☑ Are there adequate policies and procedures such as appeals and complaints? If not, you may need to produce or update them, and ensure assessors and learners are familiar with them.

☑ Is there a suitable IQA rationale and strategy? If not, you will need to create them or update the previous ones (see Chapter 4 for details).

☑ Have learners been allocated to assessors? If not, you need to do this fairly according to each assessor's location and workload.

☑ Are the assessment and IQA records and documents suitable or do they need updating? If there are not any, you will need to create them. Examples are given here and in Chapters 3 and 4.

Activity

Make a list of any other aspects you need to check to help you prepare for your role, in addition to those in the previous checklist. Find out who can give you support and guidance should you need it.

Once you have all the information and documentation you need, you can begin to plan and monitor assessor practice. You should have the support of the management within your organisation and have sufficient time and resources to perform your role effectively. If not, this could jeopardise the quality assurance process and disadvantage the learners.

If your qualification is externally quality assured, a member of the relevant awarding organisation (AO) will visit to ensure you are compliant with their requirements, assessment and quality assurance strategies. They will be known as an external quality assurer (EQA) or external quality consultant.

If there are not many learners and they have confidence in your systems, the EQA might carry out a remote sample rather than a visit. This means you will post learners' work, assessment and IQA records to them, or give them remote access to electronic portfolios and records.

The EQA is there to help ensure the qualification is assessed and internally quality assured in accordance with the AO's and other relevant requirements and regulations. They would not want you to do anything that contravenes any regulations. You should share all advice and support you receive with your assessors, other IQAs and managers.

Extension Activity

Make a list of the assessors you are responsible for and ensure you can get in touch with them. Check that learners have been allocated to assessors in a fair way. Obtain all the IQA documentation you will need to perform your role effectively and begin to create sample plans. See Tables 4.1, 4.2 and 4.3 in Chapter 4 for some examples of plans.

Monitoring assessment activities

You should plan to regularly monitor the activities that your assessors carry out, along with the decisions they make. This is to ensure they are performing their job role correctly and not disadvantaging their learners in any way. You will also need to satisfy the requirements of the AO if you are internally quality assuring an accredited qualification. If you are monitoring the work of assessors who are assessing employees in the workplace, you might also be required to report to their supervisor or manager.

When planning the activities you will carry out, you should base them on the risk factors you have identified in your strategy, for example the experience of your assessors or any problem units you have identified which could cause concern.

Activities that you should plan to carry out include:

- observing assessor practice
- talking to learners
- sampling assessed learners' work and assessment records
- arranging team meetings
- arranging standardisation activities.

Activity

Consider what IQA activities you will carry out with your assessors and the risk factors that would influence the frequency. Will you be required to do everything in the bullet list above, or more? It could be that there are other IQAs in the same subject area as yourself who might perform some of these activities. If so, you will need to liaise with them to ensure all aspects are co-ordinated and documented.

You should always keep records of any activity you carry out for audit purposes. When completing any records, if signatures are required, these should be obtained as soon as possible after the event if they cannot be signed on the day. Any signatures added later should have the date they were added, rather than the date the form was originally completed. If you are completing documents electronically, you will need to find out if an e-mail address or electronic signature is required or not.

Observing assessor practice
A good way of ensuring your assessors are performing adequately is to see them in action. Not only will this give you the opportunity to see them making assessment decisions, but you will also be able to talk to their learners afterwards. Documenting your observations using a checklist like the one in Table 5.1 will help to ensure you remain objective when making decisions regarding your assessor's competence.

When arranging to carry out an observation, you will need to make sure the learner is aware that you are observing not them but their assessor. Your assessor, and indeed their learner, might be nervous about being observed. You will need to try to put them at ease, and explain you are there to help and support, not to be critical of them. You need to ensure your assessor is performing their job role correctly and making valid and reliable assessment decisions. You also need to check that the area is safe and that any resources used are appropriate.

Table 5.1 Example assessor observation checklist

Assessor observation checklist				
Assessor: P Jones	**IQA:** H Rahl			
Units/aspects being assessed: Unit 101	**Location of assessment:** X Company **Date:** 31 January			
Checklist	**YES NO N/A**	**Comments/action required by assessor**	**Target date**	**Achieved**
Was the learner put at ease and aware of what would be assessed?	Y	You prepared the learner well by explaining what you would observe and how. This helped relax your learner.		
Was an appropriate assessment plan in place?	Y	You had a detailed assessment plan in place.		

Were the resources and environment healthy, safe and suitable for the activities being assessed?	Y	All resources were appropriate and suitable.		
Were questions appropriate and asked in an encouraging manner?	Y	You asked open questions to confirm knowledge.		
Were current and previous skills and knowledge used to make a decision?	Y	You took into account the fact that your learner had already achieved an aspect of the unit.		
Was constructive and developmental feedback given?	Y	Feedback was very positive and constructive.		
Was the assessor's decision correct?	Y	Your judgement was correct and accurate.		
Did the learner's evidence meet VACSR requirements? (valid, authentic, current, sufficient and reliable)	Y	You checked VACSR for all aspects assessed.		
Were all assessment records completed correctly?	N	Complete the observation report – copy to go to learner.	7 Feb	8 Feb
Did the assessor perform fairly and satisfactorily?	Y	Yes, apart from filling in all the feedback records due to time limits.		
Does the assessor have any training needs? If so, how can these be addressed?	Y	You hold the A1 Assessor Award. However, you need to produce evidence to show you are demonstrating the current TAQA assessor standards.	30 April	
Does the assessor have any questions?	Y	Q – Do I need to retake the assessor unit? A – No, just keep documents which prove you are meeting the standards.		
What assessment activities were used and why?	Observation and questioning to confirm performance and knowledge			

Feedback to assessor:

I liked the way you were unobtrusive during the observation, yet asked open questions to confirm knowledge as the learner carried out the activity. I appreciate you did not want to fully complete the observation report until you had asked a few more questions to confirm knowledge – this was due to time constraints. Once this is done, please ensure you give a copy to your learner.

Talking to learners

After observing your assessor, it is an ideal time to talk to their learner and gain feedback regarding the assessment process. A checklist can be used for this purpose, as in Table 5.2. Always give the learner the opportunity to ask you any questions and to discuss any aspects of the assessment and IQA process with you. If you are not able to answer any questions from the learner, make sure you find out and then get back to them. Thank the learner for their time and wish them well with their future progress. Don't be tempted to tell them anything about their assessor's performance or make excuses for any problems. You can then give feedback to your assessor away from their learner. This should take place as soon as possible after the observation and in an appropriate location. If you or the assessor has any other commitments at the time, a quick verbal account can be given and then a date and time arranged for formal feedback.

Table 5.2 Example learner discussion checklist

Learner discussion checklist				
Assessor: P Jones **Units/aspects assessed:** Unit 101 **Learner:** A Bex		**IQA:** H Rahl **Location of assessment:** XY Company **Date:** 31 January		
Checklist	**YES NO N/A**	**Comments/action required by assessor**	**Target date**	**Achieved**
Are you aware of your progress and achievements to date?	Y	Assessor explained these well to the learner.		
Did you discuss and agree an assessment plan in advance?	Y	Always done in advance.		
Do you have a copy of the standards and understand what you are being assessed towards?	Y	Has a full copy of the assessment requirements.		
Did you have an initial assessment and/or were your previous skills and knowledge taken into account?	Y	Had told assessor what had been achieved previously.		
Were you asked questions to test your knowledge and understanding?	Y	Assessor asks questions when appropriate.		
Did you receive helpful feedback?	Y	This was verbal but needs to be formally documented. Assessor to follow up.	7 Feb	8 Feb
Is your progress regularly reviewed?	Y	Once every 6–8 weeks during a one-year programme.		
If you disagreed with your assessor, would you know what to do?	N	Assessor to explain the appeals procedure to learner.	7 Feb	8 Feb
Do you have any learning needs or require further support?	N	Learner happy with support given.		
Do you have any questions?	Y	Q – When do I get my certificate? A – Three weeks after successful achievement.		
Feedback to assessor: Your learner was very pleased with the way the assessment was conducted. However, she is unsure of the appeals procedure. Please give her the handout which explains this.				

It could be that you identify some areas for development, in which case you will need to discuss this sensitively with your assessor and reach an agreement on how to proceed. You should always follow up any action points you set to ensure they have been met, and then update the observation checklist accordingly.

Sampling assessed learners' work and assessment records
An excellent way of monitoring assessor practice and decisions is to sample the learners' work they have assessed, along with the assessment records. You should have a plan to show what you will sample, from whom and when (see Table 4.3 in Chapter 4 for an example plan). This should be on an interim and summative basis; interim is part-way through each learner's progress and summative is at the completion stage. If a problem is identified at the interim stage, there is a chance to put it right. Interim sampling can look at aspects of assessment and learner evidence. Summative sampling can check that the full assessment process has been completed successfully and that all documents are complete.

The benefits of interim sampling are that it gives opportunities to monitor:

- all assessment types and methods, whether they are safe, valid, fair and reliable
- consistency of decisions between assessors
- consistency of assessor interpretation of what is being assessed
- good practice that can be shared between assessors
- how assessors are completing their records
- how effective assessment planning is
- how effective feedback to learners is
- how learners are progressing and what has been achieved
- if assessors need any support or further training
- if learners need any support or have any particular requirements
- if there are any problems that need addressing before the learner completes
- the views of others, for example learners, employers and witnesses
- whether the learner has been registered with the AO (if applicable, as any assessments prior to registration might be classed as invalid by an AO).

The benefits of summative sampling are that it gives opportunities to check:

- all documents are fully completed
- all requirements have been met, enabling certificates to be claimed (if applicable) or records of achievement to be printed
- assessors have implemented any action points
- the assessment decisions are correct
- the learner evidence is VACSR
- there are adequate assessment plans and feedback records.

Arranging team meetings

You should have a plan to reflect when you will hold meetings with your team of assessors (see Table 4.2 in Chapter 4 for an example plan). If you can plan the dates a year in advance, this will ensure everyone knows when they will take place and therefore will be able to attend. If you have a large team you could hold a meeting every month, or less often if your team is smaller. You could use an agenda, like the one in Table 5.3, to ensure all important aspects of the assessment and IQA process are covered.

The agenda could be circulated in advance by e-mail or be uploaded to your organisation's intranet. It might be your responsibility to chair the meeting and take minutes. If so, try to produce them as soon as possible after the meeting. Always ensure everyone who attends, or was absent, receives a copy or can access them electronically.

Table 5.3 Example agenda

AGENDA *Internal quality assurer and assessor team meeting* *(Date)*
1. Present
2. Apologies for absence
3. Minutes of last meeting
4. Matters arising
5. Programme: recruitment, new starters, changes/updates to standards and qualifications
6. Assessment: record keeping, methods used, current progress of learners, issues or concerns, continuing professional development activities
7. Internal quality assurance – observations and sampling dates, registrations and certifications, appeals and complaints, general feedback to assessors from monitoring activities
8. External quality assurance – feedback and reports, action points
9. Standardisation – feedback from recent activity, planning new activities
10. Equality and diversity
11. Health and safety
12. Any other business
13. Date and time of next meeting

Arranging standardisation activities

You will need to plan and manage standardisation activities with your assessors and any other IQAs (see Table 4.2 in Chapter 4 for an example plan). Standardisation of practice ensures the assessment and IQA requirements are interpreted accurately, and that everyone is making comparable, fair and consistent decisions. You could have separate events for assessors and for IQAs (if there is more than one for your subject). If the team is small, you could include a standardisation activity during the team meeting.

Aspects which can be standardised include:

- assessment activities – looking at safety and fairness, validity and reliability, deciding alternative methods for particular learner requirements or needs
- creating a bank of assessment materials, i.e. assignments, multiple-choice questions, oral questions, along with expected answers
- how assessors interpret the standards and assessment requirements and how they reach their decisions
- how learner evidence meets the requirements
- the way assessment plans and feedback records are completed
- the way feedback is given to learners
- the way learner reviews are carried out
- the way witness statements are used
- updating assessment and IQA documentation, i.e. checklists, records and templates.

One way to standardise practice between assessors is to ask them each to bring along a learner's evidence for a unit or aspect they have assessed, with their supporting assessment records. These can be swapped between assessors who can then reassess them. The activity could be anonymous if learner and assessor names are removed beforehand. A discussion can then take place to see if all assessors are interpreting the assessment requirements in the same way and are making the same decisions. This is also a chance to see how different assessors complete the records and the amount of detail they write. The activity can lead to an action plan for further training and development of assessor practice.

Assessment types and methods should also be standardised. If one assessor has produced a project or an assignment for their learners to carry out, they should share it with the other assessors. This will ensure all learners have access to the same assessment materials. It is also a chance to make sure any questions are pitched at the right level for the learners.

Example

Shane had produced an assignment for his learners which would holistically assess two units from a level 1 Numeracy qualification. Part of the assignment expected learners to reflect upon their progress. When the assignment was discussed by the assessor team at a standardisation meeting, it was felt that the learners might not be skilled enough to reflect adequately. It was also noticed that an aspect of one of the units had been missed. The team decided that reflection would not be used formally. Shane rewrote the assignment and e-mailed it to his colleagues for further feedback before use.

All assessment activities used must be fit for purpose. Formative assessments are often informal and don't usually count towards achievement. They can therefore be more flexible to cater for different learner needs and their progress at the time, for example using a quiz to check knowledge gained at a given point. Summative assessments are formal and are either produced by the AO or by the assessor, for example a test. If more than one assessor is involved for the same subject, they should get together to standardise all activities, resources and expected answers.

Records will need to be kept of all standardisation activities that show all units or aspects have been covered over a period of time. See Table 2.4 in Chapter 2 for an example of a standardisation record for assessed work.

Extension Activity

Plan an activity to standardise an aspect of practice between your assessors. Carry out the activity and evaluate how well it was received by your assessors, and what could be done differently next time.

Decision making

When sampling learner work, you are not reassessing or remarking it, but making a decision as to whether it meets the assessment requirements. You are ensuring the assessor's plans and feedback records are documenting all the activities, and that their decisions are valid and reliable. You might agree with your assessor, in which case you can give them feedback as to what they have done well. You might agree, but feel your assessor could have given more developmental feedback to their learner. You can then give your assessor appropriate feedback as to how they could develop and improve their feedback skills. Alternatively, you might disagree with an assessor's decision and refer the work back to them. If this is the case, you would need to be very explicit as to why the work had not met the requirements, and give your assessor advice on how they can support their learner's achievement. This should all be documented and a target date for completion agreed.

Assessors should never do any work for their learners, but help them see how they can achieve it for themselves. You might decide to sample more work from this assessor for the same aspect but with different learners, to see if it was a one-off. If you find that other assessors are having the same problems with a particular aspect, you can discuss it with them all to help standardise their interpretation of the requirements. Otherwise, the learners might be disadvantaged due to no fault of their own.

Another quality assurance term is *internal moderation*. If an area of a learner's work is sampled and there are problems, all the learner's work for that area will need to be referred back to the assessor. It could be that it was just an issue with one learner. However, it could be that the assessor had misinterpreted something which resulted in all the learners making the same mistake.

When sampling learners' work, you should always read the accompanying assessment plans and feedback records as well as any other assessment records such as observation reports and witness statements. Reviewing all the assessment documentation will help you gain a clear picture of learner progress and achievement. If witnesses are used, you should contact a sample of them to confirm their authenticity and that they understand what their role entails. If a qualification relies heavily on the use of witness statements as evidence, you might need to carry out adequate training and give support to them.

You should compare different assessors' records to ensure they are completing them in a standardised way. Some assessors might be very brief with their feedback and others quite comprehensive. If this is the case, the assessor who only writes brief comments might not be fully supporting their learner. You could take copies of some records, remove the assessors' names and use them during a standardisation meeting to agree a consistent approach.

When sampling work you must complete a report of what you have reviewed. Make sure you keep a note on your sample report of anything you have asked your assessor to do,

Table 5.4 Example IQA sample report

Internal quality assurance sample report		
Learner: A Bex	**Programme/Qualification:** Customer Service Level 2	
Assessor: P Jones	**IQA:** H Rahl	
Interim/Summative sample	**Date:** 12 January	
Unit/ aspect sampled	**Comments**	
Unit 101	I have observed the assessor performing satisfactorily today – see separate observation report for details. The evidence provided by the learner has also been sampled and fully meets the assessment criteria. Products of work, a witness statement and a learner statement were sampled. The feedback record completed by the assessor regarding the evidence which had already been assessed is detailed and constructive. The assessor just needs to fully complete the observation report, and document the questions and answers from today's observation.	
Is the evidence?	If no – action required and target dates	Date completed
Valid Yes/No		
Authentic Yes/No		
Current Yes/No		
Sufficient Yes/No		
Reliable Yes/No		
Have assessment plans and records been completed, signed and dated?		YES/NO
Is the assessor's decision correct?		YES/NO
Summative IQA – can the certificate now be claimed?		YES/NO
Feedback to assessor: Don't forget to complete and sign the observation report and give a copy to your learner by 7 February.	**Assessor's response:** I plan to complete this by next week.	

so that you can follow it up by the target date. Always update your records to reflect what was sampled and when, and what action has been met and when. A clear audit trail of all activities must be maintained to assist compliance and transparency. It also helps in the event of an appeal or complaint. Table 5.4 is an example of an IQA sample report.

When sampling work from different assessors, if you are sampling the same aspects, you can see how consistent the different assessors are. You can then note any inconsistencies to discuss at the next team meeting. For example, if one assessor is giving more support to learners, or expecting them to produce far more work than others, this is clearly unfair.

Sampling learners' work is also a good opportunity to check for aspects such as plagiarism and copying. It could be that two learners have submitted a piece of work which is almost identical. Hopefully your assessor will have noticed this. However, you would need to satisfy yourself that they had not worked together or copied one another's work. You and your assessors need to be aware of learners colluding or plagiarising work, particularly now that so much information is available via the internet. Learners should take responsibility for referencing any sources for all work submitted, and may be required to sign an authenticity statement to confirm the work is theirs. If you suspect plagiarism, you could type a few of their words into an internet search engine or specialist program and see what appears. You would then have to refer it back to your assessor to challenge their learner as to whether it was accidental or intentional.

Activity

Find out what your organisation's policy is regarding cheating, copying and plagiarism, and what your involvement would be. Ensure all your assessors are aware of the policy and discuss any issues at your next team meeting.

When sampling, you need to make sure all work is VACSR (see Chapter 4 for details). If you are in any doubt, you must refer it back to your assessor or have an informal discussion with them. It might be that the assessor has omitted to state something on their feedback record or it might be more serious. Never feel pressured to agree with your assessor if you feel something is not quite right. If there are other IQAs in the same subject area as yourself, you could discuss your findings with them first.

You will also be making decisions as to whether the assessment types and methods used are adequate, fair and appropriate. If one assessor is carrying out three observations with all their learners, but another is only carrying out one, that is clearly not fair. If one assessor is expecting some learners to write a 2,000-word essay, and others a 1,500-word essay, then again that is not fair. Your assessor might justify their actions by saying they are challenging the more able learners. However, unless the assessment requirements state this is acceptable, then it is not.

As you are only sampling aspects of the assessment process, there will be some areas that are missed. This is a risk as you cannot sample everything from everyone. You need to build up your confidence in your assessors to know they are performing adequately. If you find a problem when sampling, or have any concerns, you will need to increase your sample size. Conversely, you could reduce the sample size for your experienced assessors if you have confidence in them.

However, never assume everything is fine as experienced assessors could become complacent. If all your assessors know what you will be sampling and when, they might not be as thorough with the areas you are not due to sample. You can always carry out an additional random sample at any time and ask to see an aspect of assessor practice which is not on your original plans.

After a period of sampling, you should analyse your findings and give overall feedback to your assessors, perhaps at the next team meeting. You might have found patterns or trends, for example all assessors might be making the same mistake with a particular unit. You might see that one assessor is taking more time than others to pass their learners, or that several of their learners have left. Conversely, you might find another assessor whose learners are completing really quickly and you will need to find out why.

Communicating with assessors

People act differently depending upon the situation they are in and the people they are with at the time. You might find that on a one-to-one basis an assessor is quite mature but in a meeting can be rather disruptive and immature.

Berne's (1973) Transactional Analysis Theory is a method of analysing communications between people. Berne identified three personality states: the *child*, the *parent* and the *adult*. These states are called *ego states* and people behave and exist in a mixture of these states, due to their past experiences, gestures, vocal tones, expressions, attitudes, vocabulary and the situation they are in at the time.

Transactional Analysis assumes all past events, feelings and experiences are stored within, and can be re-experienced in current situations. You might see this with assessors who take on a different state depending upon who they are with, for example acting like a child and asking for help from a colleague, but acting like an adult with a manager.

Transactions are verbal exchanges between two people: one speaks and the other responds. If the conversation is complementary then the transactions enable the conversation to continue. If the transactions are *crossed*, i.e. child to adult, the conversation may change its nature or come to an end.

Berne recognised that people need *stroking*. Strokes are acts of recognition which one person gives to another and can be positive or negative, i.e. words of appreciation or otherwise. Giving or receiving positive strokes develops emotionally healthy people who are confident in themselves and have a feeling of being *okay*. Negative strokes can lead to a person being demoralised if not given in a skilful way.

Example

Ibrahim was working towards his Assessor Units and wanted to prove to his assessor how good he was. He kept saying to himself, I'll be okay if I produce all the required work to please my assessor and don't make any mistakes. By doing this, Ibrahim felt he would be looked upon more favourably and receive strokes of appreciation in the form of positive feedback, which he felt would encourage and motivate him.

Understanding a little about the different states of the child, parent and adult will help you see how your assessors take on different roles in different situations, particularly in meetings where some may be more vocal than others.

If you ever feel like a *child* at work, it may be because your manager is operating in their *parent* mode and you are responding in your *child* mode. Your *child* makes you feel small, afraid, undervalued, demotivated and rebellious. These feelings may make you undermine, withdraw, gossip, procrastinate, plot revenge or attempt to please in order to be rewarded. In this *child* mode, you will find it very hard to become a successful professional.

As you are in a managerial role, you may find yourself acting like a *parent*. You may have learnt this from your parents' responses to you years ago. The *parent* mode makes you feel superior, detached and impatient. Being in this state can make you harden your tone, not listen to people, shout, bribe others into complying and criticise them more than encourage them.

The best option is to remain in the *adult* state. As an *adult*, you feel good about yourself, respectful of the talents and lives of others, delighted with challenges, proud of accomplishments and expectant of success. These feelings make you respond to others by appreciating and listening to them, using respectful language, perceiving the facts, considering alternatives, and having a long-term view and enjoyment of work and life.

If you realise that you have moved into a *role*, it is possible to change if you need to. When you feel your *child mode* about to make you withdraw, gossip or undermine, you can choose instead to participate, find out the facts and resolve your differences in the *adult* state.

When you feel your *parent mode* about to make you criticise or take over, you can choose instead to speak warmly, be patient, listen and find enjoyment in the challenge.

However, it is very difficult to consistently be in the *adult* state. You may find yourself adapting to different situations and responding to the states other people have taken on. However, trying to remain in the adult state should help you gain confidence and respect from your assessors, as well as perform your job role satisfactorily.

Neuro Linguistic Programming

Neuro Linguistic Programming (NLP) is a model of interpersonal communication concerned with relationships and experiences. It can be useful when providing feedback to assessors to help influence their development. NLP is a way to increase self-awareness and to change patterns of mental and emotional behaviour. Richard Bandler and John Grinder, the co-founders of NLP in the 1970s, claimed it would be instrumental in finding ways to help people have better, fuller and richer lives. They created the title to reflect a connection between neurological processes (neuro), language (linguistic) and behavioural patterns (programming), which have been learnt through experience and can be used to achieve specific goals. The model was based on how some very effective communicators were habitually using language to influence other people.

NLP training should help turn negative thoughts into positive thoughts. It provides the skills to define and achieve outcomes, along with a heightened awareness of the five senses.

NLP is an attitude which is an insatiable curiosity about human beings with a methodology that leaves behind it a trail of techniques.

Richard Bandler (co-creator of NLP; www.inlpf.com/whatisnlp.htm, accessed 27.09.13)

The strategies, tools and techniques of NLP represent an opportunity unlike any other for the exploration of human functioning, or more precisely, that rare and valuable subset of human functioning known as genius.

John Grinder (co-creator of NLP; www.inlpf.com/whatisnlp.htm, accessed 27.09.13)

NLP techniques can be used to:

- coach assessors on how to gain greater satisfaction from their contributions
- enhance the skills of assessors
- improve own and others' performance
- improve an individual's effectiveness, productivity and thereby profitability
- set clear goals and define realistic strategies
- understand and reduce stress and conflict.

NLP provides questions and patterns to make communication more clearly understood, for example all thoughts and behaviours have a structure, and all structures can be reprogrammed. Do you use jargon, complex terms or clichés without thinking? Your assessors might not understand what you are talking about because you assume they already have the knowledge. To improve your own communication skills, you could observe others who are skilled and experienced to see how they perform.

Activity

Arrange to observe an experienced IQA, preferably in your subject area, to watch how they interact with their assessors. Are they using any NLP techniques to make communication easier? If you cannot carry out an observation, watch or listen to influential people on the television, radio or internet. Ask yourself what it is about them that makes them successful. Can you emulate this in yourself? If so, how?

Emotional intelligence

Emotional intelligence (EI) is a behavioural model, given prominence in Daniel Goleman's book *Emotional Intelligence* (1995). However, work originally began on the model in the 1970s and 1980s by Howard Gardiner.

Goleman identified five domains of emotional intelligence:

- knowing your emotions
- managing your emotions

- motivating yourself

- recognising and understanding other people's emotions

- managing relationships, i.e. the emotions of others.

The principles of EI provide a new way to understand and assess people's behaviour, attitudes, interpersonal skills, management styles and potential. This could be useful if you have a large team of assessors who are not always working in a consistent manner. By developing EI, Goleman suggested that people can become more productive and successful at what they do, and can help others to be more productive and successful too. He also suggested that the process and outcomes of developing EI contain aspects which are known to reduce stress for individuals and organisations. This can help improve relationships, decrease conflict, and increase stability, continuity and harmony.

EI has been described as:

> The ability to perceive emotions, to access and generate emotions so as to assist thought, to understand emotions and emotional knowledge, and to reflectively regulate emotions so as to promote emotional and intellectual growth.
>
> (Salovey and Sluyter, 1997, p197)

Becoming aware of your own emotions and how they can affect your activities will help you develop more fulfilling and professional relationships with your assessors.

The EI concept argues that Intelligence Quotient (IQ), or conventional intelligence, is too narrow as there are wider areas of emotional intelligence that dictate and enable how successful people are. Possessing a high IQ rating does not mean that success automatically follows.

Demonstrating and evaluating your interpersonal and intrapersonal skills should help you deal effectively with situations which might occur with your assessors.

Belbin's (2010) team roles

Belbin defined team roles as: *A tendency to behave, contribute and interrelate with others in a particular way.* Belbin's research identified nine clusters of behaviour, each of which is termed a *team role*. Each team role has a combination of strengths they contribute to the team and allowable weaknesses. It is important to accept that people have weaknesses; if you can focus on their strengths, you will be able to help manage their weaknesses. See Table 5.5 Team Role Summary Descriptions for the contributions and allowable weaknesses of each team role.

The team roles are grouped into *action, people* and *cerebral* roles:

- action-oriented roles: Shaper, Implementer and Completer Finisher

- people-oriented roles: Co-ordinator, Team worker and Resource Investigator

- cerebral roles: Plant, Monitor Evaluator and Specialist.

Sometimes groups or teams become problematic, not because their members don't know their subject, but because they have problems accepting, adjusting and communicating with each other as they take on different roles. Knowing that individuals within teams take on these different roles will help you manage group work more effectively, for example by grouping a mixture of the *action*, *people* and *cerebral* roles within each group.

Table 5.5 Team Role Summary Descriptions

Team Role	Contribution	Allowable Weaknesses
Plant	Creative, imaginative, free-thinking. Generates ideas and solves difficult problems.	Ignores incidentals. Too preoccupied to communicate effectively.
Resource Investigator	Outgoing, enthusiastic, communicative. Explores opportunities and develops contacts.	Over-optimistic. Loses interest once initial enthusiasm has passed.
Co-ordinator	Mature, confident, identifies talent. Clarifies goals. Delegates effectively.	Can be seen as manipulative. Offloads own share of the work.
Shaper	Challenging, dynamic, thrives on pressure. Has the drive and courage to overcome obstacles.	Prone to provocation. Offends people's feelings.
Monitor Evaluator	Sober, strategic and discerning. Sees all options and judges accurately.	Lacks drive and ability to inspire others. Can be overly critical.
Teamworker	Co-operative, perceptive and diplomatic. Listens and averts friction.	Indecisive in crunch situations. Avoids confrontation.
Implementer	Practical, reliable, efficient. Turns ideas into actions and organises work that needs to be done.	Somewhat inflexible. Slow to respond to new possibilities.
Completer Finisher	Painstaking, conscientious, anxious. Searches out errors. Polishes and perfects.	Inclined to worry unduly. Reluctant to delegate.
Specialist	Single-minded, self-starting, dedicated. Provides knowledge and skills in rare supply.	Contributes only on a narrow front. Dwells on technicalities.

Providing feedback to assessors

You should provide feedback to your assessors whenever you get the opportunity. Formal feedback could be given verbally after an observation of their practice, after sampling their assessed work, or during an appraisal or meeting. This should always be followed up with written feedback. Informal feedback can be given at any time to help confirm assessors' practice and development. It can enable your assessors to see what they are doing right and what they can do to improve. Formal feedback should be given at an appropriate date, time and place, and in a constructive and developmental manner. Always remember that it is unprofessional to give feedback to an assessor in front of their learners. You should also give your assessor a copy of any report you have completed. This acts as a formal record of feedback and any action required, which should always be followed up.

Feedback should be concentrating on the assessment process and not be critical of the assessor as a person. It should be used to confirm competence, and to motivate and encourage rather than apportion blame for any reason. Above all, it should be to help your assessor develop their assessment practice, and to maintain and improve the quality of the assessment process for their learners.

If you find something that the assessor has done wrong, or that they could improve upon, don't be critical but state the facts. You could ask your assessor to reflect upon their performance before you give feedback. That way, they might realise any mistakes before you have to point them out. You can then suggest ways of working together to put things right. It could be that your assessor was unaware of something they should or should not have done. Communicating regularly with them and identifying any training needs should prevent problems from occurring.

You might not find anything wrong, in which case you still need to give feedback, which will confirm that what they are doing is right. If you have an assessor who is performing really well, you could ask them to mentor an underperforming or new assessor, providing they have the time.

Always allow your assessor time to clarify anything you have said and to ask any questions. Don't interrupt them when they are speaking and avoid jumping to any conclusions. Use eye contact and listen carefully to what they are saying. Show that you are a good listener by nodding your head and repeating key points. Your assessor should leave knowing exactly what needs to be done and by when.

Example

Sarah sampled six assignments that John had marked from his group of 30 learners. She found his handwritten records difficult to read and his feedback to his learners was very sparse. However, all the learners had met the criteria and produced some really good work. When Sarah gave feedback to John, she began with something positive and then moved on to the developmental points: John, I enjoyed reading your learners' assignments and I felt they had all put in a lot of effort. However, I do feel that your feedback to them is not as detailed as it could be, and I found your writing hard to read. Could you word-process your feedback and take the opportunity to state something specific regarding each learner's achievement?

This example shows how John could improve his feedback skills to help his learners. It was also given in an encouraging manner. The use of the word *however* to link the points is much better than the word *but*, which can sound negative.

Feedback should always be:

- based on facts and not opinions, and aimed at assessors not learners

- clear, genuine and unambiguous

- developmental – giving examples for improvement or what could be changed

- documented – records must be maintained

- focused on the activity, not the person

- helpful and supportive – guiding the assessor to useful resources and CPD activities

- honest and detailed regarding what was or was not carried out

- positive and constructive – focusing on what was good and how assessment practice can be improved or changed

- specific and detailed regarding what was sampled and what was found

- strategic – seeking to improve the assessor's performance.

See Chapter 2 for information on different feedback methods, such as evaluative or descriptive, constructive or destructive, and objective or subjective.

Carry out an activity such as sampling some learner's work which has been assessed. Did you agree with your assessor's decision? How detailed was their feedback to their learner? What feedback would you give to your assessor and why?

Record keeping – internal quality assurance

It is important to keep records to satisfy company, quality assurance, AO and regulatory authorities' audit requirements. This will usually be for a set period, for example three years. See Table 5.6 for examples of records you might keep as part of your role.

There might be a standardised approach to completing the records, for example the amount of detail which must be written or whether the records should be completed manually, i.e. hard copies, or electronically. You will need to find out what your organisation expects you to do. If hard copies are required as opposed to electronic ones, the original records should be kept, not photocopies or carbon copies, to guarantee authenticity.

Table 5.6 Examples of IQA records

Types of IQA records you might maintain	Other records you might maintain
• Assessor observation checklists • IQA sample reports (interim and summative) • IQA rationale and strategy for your subject area • Learner discussion checklists • Minutes of meetings • Observation plan, meeting and standardisation plan, sample plan and tracking sheet • Questionnaire or survey results with evaluations and actions • Standardisation activities • Witness discussion records	• Details of assessors and IQAs, e.g. their CVs, CPD records and copies of certificates • Enrolment, retention, achievement and progression data • Equal opportunities data • EQA reports, inspection reports and actions taken • Records of appeals and complaints • Records of learner registration and certification details with an awarding organisation (if applicable) • Self-assessment reports

Find out what records you need to maintain for your role, how they should be completed and how long they should be kept.

Records should always be accurate, dated and legible. If you are sampling hard copies of learners' work and assessment records, you could use a coloured pen to date and initial what you have sampled. This would create a visual audit trail which is easily identifiable if an EQA wishes to see what you have sampled. The dates you use should agree with the dates on your reports.

You must ensure your assessors are keeping the required records for their role (see Chapter 2 for details). All records should be kept secure and should only be accessible by relevant staff. You also need to ensure you comply with organisational and statutory guidelines such as the Data Protection Act (1998) and the Freedom of Information Act (2000) as detailed in Chapter 2.

Extension Activity

What internal organisational or external regulatory requirements must you follow regarding record keeping and why? What impact will they have on your role, and that of your assessors?

Summary

In this chapter you have learnt about:

- internal quality assurance planning

- monitoring assessment activities

- decision making

- providing feedback to assessors

- record keeping – internal quality assurance.

Evidence

Evidence from the completed activities within this chapter, plus the following, could be used towards the *Internally assuring the quality of assessment* unit, for example:

- IQA rationale and strategy for your subject area

- observation plan, meeting and standardisation plan, sample plan and tracking sheet

- two completed assessor observation checklists

- two completed learner discussion checklists

- four completed IQA sample reports

- minutes of two meetings

- records of two standardisation activities

- external reports and actions taken (if applicable)

- CPD record

- critical reflections of own practice

- written statements cross-referenced to the unit's assessment criteria

- answers to questions issued by your assessor

- records of discussions with your assessor.

Cross-referencing grid

This chapter contributes to the following assessment criteria, along with aspects of the National Occupational Standards for Learning and Development. Full details of the learning outcomes and assessment criteria for each unit can be found in the Appendices.

Unit	Assessment criteria
Understanding the principles and practices of internally assuring the quality of assessment	1.1, 1.2, 1.3, 1.4 2.1, 2.2, 2.3 3.1, 3.2 4.1, 4.2, 4.3 5.1 6.1, 6.2, 6.3, 6.4
Internally assuring the quality of assessment	1.1, 1.2 2.1, 2.2, 2.3, 2.4, 2.5, 2.6 3.1, 3.2 4.1, 4.2 5.1, 5.2, 5.3, 5.4
Plan, allocate and monitor work	1.1, 1.2, 1.3, 1.4 3.1, 3.2 4.1, 4.2
National Occupational Standards	**Reference**
9 – Assess learner achievement	KU16 9.8
11 – Internally monitor and maintain the quality of assessment	KU1, KU4, KU5, KU7, KU8, KU11, KU13, KU14, KU16, KU17, KU18 11.1, 11.2, 11.3, 11.4, 11.5, 11.6, 11.7, 11.8, 11.9, 11.10, 11.11
12 – Externally monitor and maintain the quality of assessment	KU2, KU3, KU4, KU5, KU6, KU7 12.2, 12.3, 12.4, 12.5

Theory focus

References and further information

Belbin, M (2010) *Team Roles At Work* (2nd edition). Oxford: Elsevier Science & Technology.

Berne, E (2010) *Games People Play: The Psychology of Human Relationships*. London: Penguin.

Goleman, D (1995) *Emotional Intelligence*. London: Bloomsbury.

Salovey, P and Sluyter, D (1997) *Emotional Development and Emotional Intelligence: Educational Implications*. New York: Basic Books.

Wood, J and Dickinson, J (2011) *Quality Assurance and Evaluation in the Lifelong Learning Sector*. London: Learning Matters SAGE.

Websites

Association for Neuro Linguistic Programming: www.anlp.org

Belbin Team Roles: www.belbin.com

Data Protection Act (1998): www.legislation.gov.uk/ukpga/1998/29/contents

Emotional Intelligence: www.unh.edu/emotional_intelligence/index.html

Freedom of Information Act (2000): www.legislation.gov.uk/ukpga/2000/36/ contents

Ofqual: www.ofqual.gov.uk

Ofsted: www.ofsted.gov.uk

Plagiarism: www.plagiarism.org and www.plagiarismadvice.org

6 PRINCIPLES AND PRACTICES OF EXTERNALLY ASSURING THE QUALITY OF ASSESSMENT

Introduction

In this chapter you will learn about:

- the role of external quality assurance
- functions of external quality assurance
- planning external quality assurance activities
- aspects to perform when planning a visit or a remote monitoring activity
- evaluating the quality of assessment and internal quality assurance.

Within the chapter there are activities and examples which will help you to reflect on the above and to develop and enhance your knowledge of the principles and practices of externally assuring the quality of assessment. Completing the activities will help you to gather evidence towards the *Principles and practices of externally assuring the quality of assessment* unit. At the end of each section is an extension activity to stretch and challenge your knowledge and understanding.

At the end of the chapter is a list of possible evidence which could be used towards the *Principles and practices of externally assuring the quality of assessment* unit.

A cross-referencing grid shows how the content of this chapter contributes to the relevant TAQA units' criteria and the National Occupational Standards. There is also a theory focus with relevant references, further information and websites to which you might like to refer.

The role of external quality assurance

External quality assurance (EQA) relates to the monitoring of assessment and internal quality assurance (IQA) processes within a *centre* which has been approved by an awarding organisation (AO) to deliver and assess their qualifications. Any organisation can become an approved centre, for example colleges, charities, public, private and voluntary organisations and training providers, providing they meet the qualification and the AO's requirements. However, the external quality assurer (EQA) role is not just about monitoring: it is also about supporting the centre staff, and giving advice and guidance to help them get things right. If a positive working relationship is developed and maintained, the centre should be able to meet the requirements.

Why carry out external quality assurance?

EQA must take place on behalf of an AO to ensure the learners who have been registered with them have received a quality service. It also seeks to ensure that assessment and IQA in this context have been conducted in a consistent, safe and fair manner.

- Consistent: all staff are using similar assessment methods and making similar decisions across all learners. All learners have an equal chance of receiving an accurate decision.

- Safe: the methods used to assess and internally quality assure are ethical, there is little chance of plagiarism by learners, the work can be confirmed as authentic, confidentiality was taken into account, learning was not compromised, nor was the learner's experience or potential to achieve. (Safe in this context does not relate to health and safety but to the assessment and IQA methods used.)

- Fair: the methods used are appropriate to all learners at the required level and take into account any particular learner needs. Activities are fit for purpose, and planning, decisions and feedback are justifiable and equitable.

To become an external quality assurer (EQA), you need to work for an AO. This could be part time or on a freelance or self-employed basis. They will often advertise any vacancies on their websites. AOs often prefer their EQAs to remain current with their practice in the areas they are quality assuring, therefore not many are employed full time. You should have considerable experience in the subjects you will externally quality assure, and either hold or be working towards a recognised EQA qualification. You might also be working in a centre as an assessor or an internal quality assurer (IQA). This is not a conflict of interest, providing you declare the centre name to the AO. It is actually a benefit, as it means you are current with your knowledge and practice. Other terms for the role include external verifier, quality consultant and qualification consultant (see Introduction for details of the EQA qualification units). If you have not already done so, reading the preceding chapters in this book regarding assessment and IQA will help inform your knowledge of these aspects.

Example

Liang is considering becoming an EQA. He is currently working as an assessor and IQA of Carpentry and Joinery qualifications. He has been looking at vacancies on several AOs' websites and notices there is a position available to cover the north of England, which is where he lives. He will complete the online application form and, in the meantime, he will read up on all the regulations and requirements which are relevant to the role.

You will need to follow the AO's guidelines as well as relevant regulations such as those issued by Ofqual. Ofqual is the regulator of qualifications, examinations and assessments in England, and vocational qualifications in Northern Ireland. Ofqual approves and regulates

AOs and you will need to comply with their *General Conditions of Recognition* (2012). This document sets out certain conditions which AOs must ensure their centres adhere to. Examples include managing conflicts of interest, identifying and managing risk, and dealing with malpractice.

Activity

Obtain a copy of the 2015 General Conditions of Recognition (just type those words in an internet search engine if you cannot obtain a hard copy) and have a look at the conditions. Make a note of how they will impact upon your role as an EQA.

You will probably be externally quality assuring qualifications which are on the Qualifications and Credit Framework (QCF). You will therefore be required to adhere to the *Regulatory Arrangements for the Qualifications and Credit Framework* (2008) for England, Wales and Northern Ireland. This will ensure the learners within the centres are not being disadvantaged in any way.

The regulatory arrangements are designed to reflect the qualifications regulators' policy commitment to a strategic, risk-based approach to safeguarding the interests of learners.

(Ofqual, 2008, p3)

Role and responsibilities of an external quality assurer

Your main role will be to carry out the EQA process according to the AO's requirements and to follow all regulatory and qualification guidelines. You should also ensure your centres are complying with all the requirements. The *General Conditions of Recognition* (2012) put the onus upon AOs to ensure centres are carrying out their requirements. You should advise and support your centres to ensure they maintain and improve the assessment and IQA processes. This should ensure the learners receive a good service, as they will ultimately receive a certificate with the AO's name on when they successfully complete.

A sound knowledge and understanding of the subject area, as well as of assessment and IQA systems, is important for the role, particularly when making decisions regarding compliance. For example, if the subject area is motor vehicle maintenance, the EQA should not be externally quality assuring hairdressing. The process might be the same for each subject, but the EQA must be fully familiar with the qualification content to make a valid and reliable decision. You will find it useful to read the current assessment and IQA guidance from your AO. This should be available on their website and will help you ensure your centres are meeting the requirements. Some qualifications and subjects state that you must also be a qualified assessor and/or IQA as well as a qualified EQA. This information will be in the qualification handbook supplied by the AO.

You will be representing the AO when communicating with centres. You should therefore act professionally and with integrity, uphold the standards of the qualification, remain impartial and objective, and maintain confidentiality where necessary.

Aspects of the EQA role include:

- advising and supporting centre staff on an ongoing basis (not just during visits)

- communicating with centre staff and the AO on an ongoing basis

- completing a report of what was sampled, highlighting any action and improvement points, and judging whether the centre has a low, medium or high risk rating (see *risk ratings* later in this chapter)

- ensuring a centre's policies, procedures, systems and resources meet AO and qualification requirements

- ensuring centre staff interpret, understand and consistently apply the correct standards and requirements

- ensuring learners are registered with the AO within the required timescale (learners who are not registered should not be sampled)

- ensuring quality throughout the learner journey within a centre

- ensuring centre staff meet any requirements and regulations, and standardise their practice

- ensuring the accuracy and consistency of assessor and IQA decisions

- evaluating and approving centres to offer qualifications, releasing certification (known as *direct claims status*) when they are performing satisfactorily or recommending removal of direct claims status if necessary

- giving guidance to centre staff regarding the qualification criteria and requirements

- identifying issues and trends, for example if all assessors are misinterpreting the same aspect of something

- keeping full and confidential accurate records

- monitoring and auditing the full learner journey from commencement to completion, for example information, advice and guidance (IAG), recruitment, initial assessment, induction, training, formative and summative assessment, decision making, feedback, support for progression opportunities

- monitoring risk within a centre, i.e. when new standards are introduced, if there is a high staff turnover

- observing assessment, feedback and IQA practice

- planning what will be monitored and communicating this to all concerned within the AO's timescales

- sampling assessed and internally quality assured learners' work (and records) according to a planned strategy and making decisions based on facts

- updating own continuing professional development (CPD) regarding subject knowledge and EQA practice.

As you become more experienced, you might be asked to mentor and support new EQAs. This might involve shadowing them during a centre visit and giving advice and guidance as necessary. Hopefully, this type of support will be given to you when you first start, as the role can often feel quite isolated. While you are working towards your EQA qualification, you might also be shadowed and supported by another qualified EQA.

Activity

Have a look at the units in Appendices 6 and 7. Look at the learning outcomes and assessment criteria to see what an EQA should know and do. Appendix 6 relates to knowledge and Appendix 7 to performance.

Regulations, policies and procedures

You will need to follow your AO's policies and procedures, which should include:

- access arrangements
- fair assessment
- appeals and complaints
- confidentiality of information
- copyright and data protection
- equality and diversity
- health, safety and welfare (including safeguarding)
- malpractice.

There is also legislation such as The Data Protection Act (1998), The Freedom of Information Act (2000), The Health and Safety at Work etc Act (1974), Safeguarding Vulnerable Groups Act (2006) and The Equality Act (2010), which may impact upon your role (see Chapters 1 and 2 for further information).

There may be other AO requirements such as:

- behaviour code
- dress code
- acceptable use of information and communication technology (ICT)
- management of information and records
- use of languages and bilingualism.

You might be required to interview young and/or vulnerable learners when visiting a centre and your AO should give you guidance regarding this. You could be required to undertake a criminal records check through the Disclosure and Barring Service (DBS).

Useful information to support the qualifications being externally quality assured can be obtained from the specific Sector Skills Council (SSC) or Standards Setting Body (SSB) for your subject area. There are 18 SSCs and five SSBs which work with over 550,000 employers to define the skills needs and set the standards on which qualifications are based.

Extension Activity

Locate the SSC or SSB for the subject you will externally quality assure. Most can be found at www.sscalliance.org. Have a look at the information which relates to your particular subject and identify how it will impact upon your role.

Functions of external quality assurance

There needs to be a system of monitoring the performance and decisions of assessors and IQAs within a centre. If not, staff might make incorrect judgements or pass a learner who has not met all the requirements, perhaps because they were biased towards them or had made a mistake. As an EQA, you should remain objective and not become personally involved with the centre staff.

An effective external monitoring system will:

- ensure accuracy and consistency of assessment and IQA decisions

- uphold credibility (of the qualification and AO) by ensuring compliance with all regulations and standards.

The external quality assurance cycle

Depending upon the subject you will externally quality assure, you will usually follow the EQA cycle. The cycle will ensure the assessment and IQA process is constantly monitored. Records of all activities and decisions must be maintained throughout to satisfy the AO and the regulatory authorities, for example Ofqual.

Figure 6.1 The external quality assurance cycle

- **Identify the product or service** – ascertaining what is to be externally quality assured and why. The criteria will need to be clear, i.e. units from a qualification (product) or aspects of the learner journey such as induction, initial assessment, tutorial reviews (service). EQAs might also carry out approval and advisory visits, as well as a monitoring visit or a remote monitoring activity to sample learner work and staff records.

- **Planning** – devising a sample plan to arrange what will be monitored, from whom and when. Planning the dates to observe staff and talk to learners and others involved such as witnesses. Information will need to be obtained from the centre staff to assist the planning process, and risks taken into account such as staff knowledge and experience.

- **Activity** – carrying out the activities such as sampling assessment and IQA decisions and practice, sampling records and talking to learners and others. Centre staff should comply with the required assessment strategy for the qualification and be consistent in their role. Concerns, issues, trends, complaints and appeals should always be monitored. The activities could be carried out during a visit to the centre or remotely (where documents are posted to the EQA), and should ensure quality and compliance of all aspects. Activities might also include approving centres to offer qualifications and making decisions to release certification (known as *direct claims status*). AOs will give advice regarding the activities that should be performed.

- **Decision and feedback** – making a judgement as to whether the centre staff have performed satisfactorily, made valid and reliable decisions, and followed all required policies and procedures. Giving developmental feedback as to what was good or what could be improved. Agreeing action points if necessary with appropriate target dates. Completing the AO's report and identifying a risk rating of low, medium or high.

- **Evaluation** – reviewing the whole process to determine what is good practice, what could be improved or what could be done differently. Partaking in the AO's review, appraisal and standardisation processes.

The cycle will then begin again with an identification of what needs to be monitored and when. Throughout the cycle, standardisation of practice between EQAs should take place; this will help ensure the consistency and fairness of decisions and the support given to centres. This might be at formal meetings, or via online webinars or another appropriate method. Records must be maintained of all activities. All EQAs should maintain their CPD to ensure their own practice is current, and should follow all relevant legal and organisational requirements.

Activity

Obtain a copy of the qualification handbook or other criteria that you will externally quality assure. Familiarise yourself with the content and requirements. See if any aspects of the cycle will impact upon how you will monitor activities at a centre.

Key concepts and principles of external quality assurance

Key concepts of EQA relate to ideas, whereas principles are how the ideas are put into practice. For the purpose of this chapter, they have been separated for clarity. However, some concepts could also be classed as principles depending upon your interpretation.

Key concepts
Concepts are the aspects involved throughout the EQA process. They include:

* competence – ensuring your own competence, skills and knowledge are up to date, not only regarding the job role, but also regarding subject knowledge of the qualification and standards being quality assured

* communication – ensuring this takes place regularly with centre staff and AO staff

* equality and diversity – ensuring all activities embrace equality, inclusivity and diversity, represent all aspects of society and meet the requirements of the Equality Act (2010) (see Chapter 1 for further details)

* ethics – ensuring all activities are honest and moral, and take into account confidentiality, integrity and transparency

* health and safety – ensuring these are taken into account throughout the full monitoring process, carrying out risk assessments as necessary and ensuring appropriate safeguarding procedures are in place

* record keeping – ensuring accurate records are safely maintained throughout the monitoring process; records should also remain secure and confidential, and only be shown to those with a legitimate interest

* risk ratings – identifying whether a centre is low, medium or high risk; the AO will give guidance on this and it is covered later in this chapter

* standardisation – ensuring the qualification requirements are interpreted accurately by all EQAs, that they are making comparable and standardised decisions, and giving consistent support to centres

* strategy – ensuring a written strategy is in place which clearly explains the full process of what will be externally quality assured, when and how.

Key principles
Key principles include the acronyms SMART and VACSR:

* SMART – ensuring all activities are **s**pecific, **m**easurable, **a**chievable, **r**elevant and **t**ime bound

* VACSR – ensuring all work sampled is **v**alid, **a**uthentic, **c**urrent, **s**ufficient and **r**eliable.

Activity

Look at the bulleted lists of concepts and principles and describe how each will impact upon your role as an EQA. You may need to research some aspects further or speak to relevant staff at your organisation.

Following the key concepts and principles of EQA will ensure you are performing your role according to all relevant regulations and requirements.

External quality assurance rationale
A good EQA system will start with a *rationale*. This is the reason *why* EQA takes place and ensures the activities used are valid and reliable.

- Valid: the methods used are based on the requirements of the qualification or standards being sampled.

- Reliable: a similar decision would be made with similar centres.

A rationale will help maintain the credibility of the service given on behalf of the AO.

Example

All EQA activities will be carried out by qualified and experienced staff. This is to support centres, maintain compliance and uphold the credibility of the qualification and the reputation of the AO. EQAs will monitor centre activity to ensure the safety, fairness, validity and reliability of assessment and IQA decisions throughout the learner journey.

An EQA *strategy* will then be produced based upon the rationale, to formalise what activities will be carried out and when.

External quality assurance strategy
An EQA strategy should take into account all aspects of the assessment and IQA process from learners commencing to when they leave a centre, i.e. the full learner journey. You should follow all your AO's requirements, which will include having a strategy for each centre you support and monitor. Your strategy will give a structure to your planning and sampling activities. It should be a written statement based on any possible risk factors within the centre. Having a strategy will help ensure that each centre's assessment and quality assurance systems are fit for purpose.

Example

Sample strategy for a visit to a centre which offers the Level 2 Customer Service qualification (one IQA, four assessors, 100 learners)

The EQA will:

- *follow up previous EQA action points*
- *observe feedback from the IQA to at least one assessor*
- *observe the practice of at least one assessor with one learner*

- *interview a sample of learners and witnesses from different locations*

- *sample assessed and internally quality assured learners' work (at all levels) along with supporting documents from all units and all methods of assessment*

- *sample the planning, decisions and feedback records from all assessors and IQAs*

- *sample supporting materials such as initial assessment, induction, tutorial reviews, minutes of meetings, standardisation records, policies and procedures, evaluations with supporting data analysis and action points*

- *maintain full records of all EQA activities and communications with the centre.*

Factors to consider when creating a strategy

When planning your strategy, use the five W and one H model (WWWWWH) of *who, what, when, where, why* and *how.* This will help you consider the following factors that you need to take into account when planning your activities with a centre.

- **W**ho will you need to meet, observe or interview?

- **W**hat activities will be carried out and what records will you need to complete?

- **W**hen will the activities take place?

- **W**here will the activities take place?

- **W**hy are you doing certain activities?

- **H**ow will you carry out the activities, and how will you make your decisions, complete your report and give feedback to centre staff?

Example

Andrea has just been allocated a centre, as the previous EQA has now retired. She has obtained the centre details and introduced herself by telephone. She has read the last three reports which did not contain any action points. As this is a small, low-risk centre, she has agreed with the AO that she will visit in four months' time. Prior to the visit, she will obtain details of all relevant staff and learners to help her decide on her strategy of what to sample, and from whom.

The strategy should take into account factors such as:

- assessment methods – are they safe, valid, fair and reliable; are they complex and varied; do they include initial assessments, online assessments, witnesses statements, recognition of prior learning (RPL)?

- what has been assessed i.e. the qualification or programme – are IQAs/assessors familiar with these; are standards about to be revised?

- availability of staff for observation – some could be located at a distance; can activities take place remotely via the internet?

- experience, workload and caseload of staff – consider staff turnover

- number of learners to assessors – allocating learners to assessors should be fair; assessors should not be overloaded

- number of assessors to IQAs – should also be fair

- units – staff might interpret them differently or learners might have problems achieving them.

Extension Activity

Write a strategy for the subject you will externally quality assure. Consider what you will need to do and how you will do it. If you are not currently quality assuring, create a hypothetical strategy for a fictitious centre. Are there any likely implications of the particular subject area which you will externally quality assure?

Planning external quality assurance activities

To perform your role fully, you will need to carry out certain administrative tasks. Once appointed, the AO will allocate centres to you and they should give you any necessary advice, support and training to successfully carry out the requirements of your role.

You will need to obtain information about your centres and the qualifications they offer to help you formulate a plan of what you will sample. This might include:

- communication details: phone numbers and e-mail addresses of key contacts

- details of centre policies and procedures, for example appeals, complaints, assessment, IQA, etc.

- details of each centre: location and address, named contact, AO centre number

- details of qualifications offered, dates approved, dates certification was released, and final dates for registration and certification

- details of staff: names, curricula vitae (CVs), qualifications and experience

- details of learners: names, registration numbers, qualifications working towards, locations, allocated assessors and IQAs.

Some of this information might be given to you by the AO. However, you will need to contact the centre directly to obtain further details. The key contact person might be an administrator and not the person who is able to give you all the specific information you need. You will therefore need to find out who at the centre can give you all the details you require.

Activity

What other information, besides that in the previous bulleted list, might you need to obtain to help perform your role?

Table 6.1 Example sample plan for a visit to a centre

Centre name:	XYZ Company	Centre number:	0123456
Centre contact:	Jean Haverham (IQA)	Location/s to be visited	Manor Building Main Road MillerVille
External quality assurer:	Paulo Hancock	Contact details:	01234 234567
Date of visit:	5 September	Time of arrival and duration of visit:	9.00 am Approx 6–7 hours
Qualification/s to be sampled:	Level 2 Customer Service Certificate	Performance and knowledge units	
Staff to meet:	Jean Haverham Phil Scholey Terri Mandalay	IQA and centre co-ordinator Tutor/Assessor Tutor and Trainee Assessor	
Learners to meet:	Marie Maine		
Activities to be carried out with approximate timings:	9.00 9.30 10.00 11.00 12.00 12.30 3.00 3.30	Arrival, meet team and discuss progress since approval. Answer any questions. Check IQA systems and procedures. Observation of Phil delivering a training session in the centre to a group. (I will just observe the first half hour, then talk to a few learners.) Travel to workplace then carry out an observation of Jean observing Terri with Marie Maine. Talk to Terri and Marie, then return to centre. Interview with Jean and Phil. Commence sampling learners' work and associated assessment and IQA records, while having a working lunch. Sample minutes of meetings, standardisation records, staff CPD records and updated policies and procedures. Complete report and provide feedback to staff, answer any questions and discuss action and improvement points. Depart.	
Learners' work to be sampled, along with associated assessment and IQA records	Pierre Smithson Jeremy Globe Jo Trotter Melanie Green Frank Glass Jeremiah Marsh	Unit 1 Units 1 and 2 Units 1 and 3 All units completed to date All units completed to date Units 1, 2 and 3	
Additional comments:	Please check the last report and ensure all action points have been met. I may carry out an additional sample on the day.		
Date form sent to the centre:	5 August		

You should obtain and read any previous EQA reports and action plans regarding the centre to familiarise yourself with how they operate. You should also obtain and read copies of the AO guidelines, the qualification handbook for the subject you will externally quality assure and any other relevant guidelines and regulations, if you have not already done so.

Based on the information you obtain, any action points and risks associated with the centre, you will be able to plan what you need to sample. The AO will supply you with a sample plan template, which might look like the one in Table 6.1 when completed. The sample plan gives a focus to your activities and informs the centre what you wish to carry out.

Resources

You will need to have appropriate resources to carry out your role. Not all AOs supply these; therefore you might need to provide some yourself.

Resources include:

- access to appropriate transport
- appropriate clothing and name badge
- briefcase, pens, paper
- computer/laptop/tablet or other device with internet access
- copies of AO guidelines, qualification handbook, regulations and other relevant documents (manual or electronic)
- insurance such as professional indemnity, business car insurance
- money for expenses, for example bridge tolls, meals, transport costs (some of which you might be able to reclaim)
- telephone: landline or mobile.

Example

Aadi is a new EQA who has just been allocated five centres on a self-employed contract. This means he will only be paid when he carries out a monitoring activity, and he must declare his income to the Inland Revenue. However, he will be able to claim travel expenses. He has received training from the AO and has been given electronic access to all the guidelines and documentation he needs to carry out his role. He has also been given a name badge and a pen with the AO logo. He was shocked to find that he needed to provide everything else himself. This included having insurance for business use of his car and using his own laptop, printer and phone.

New technology

ICT can be used to support and enhance the EQA process. Technology is constantly evolving and new resources are frequently becoming available. It is crucial to keep up to date with new developments and you should try to incorporate these whenever possible. Communication through e-mail or web-based platforms can simplify the contact process between yourself and the centre staff and the AO staff.

If you are monitoring the decisions of centre staff which have been made based on electronic learner evidence, you need to be sure the work does belong to them. The assessor should have confirmed the identity of the learner, and the learner should sign an authenticity statement to confirm the work is theirs.

Examples of using ICT include:

- communicating via e-mail, Skype, or particular website platforms, forums or networking sites

- accessing an electronic sample remotely online rather than visiting the centre

- accessing the AO's website to find documentation

- completing a report online

- partaking in video conferencing and webinars, for example AO updating and standardisation activities

- electronic record keeping.

Extension Activity

What communication methods can you use with your centres during a visit and in between visits? How can you use technology to make the process easier?

Tasks to perform when planning a visit or a remote monitoring activity

When you have agreed a date to monitor a centre's activity, you can prepare a sampling strategy based on any identified risks. A remote monitoring activity is where the centre posts learner work and supporting records to you (or gives you electronic access to them) rather than you visiting in person.

You will need to perform the following.

- Confirm to the centre contact when the visit/remote monitoring activity will take place, at what time and where.

- Obtain learner details, either via the AO's website or from the centre, i.e. names, start dates, registration dates, unit completion dates, assessment and IQA dates, completion dates and certification dates (if relevant). You should be able to check this information with the AO records to ensure the centre has not missed anyone off their list for any reason.

- Decide what will be sampled along with what other documents you need to see, for example policies, procedures, records of appeals and complaints, assessor and IQA records and tracking, evidence of completed actions, minutes of meetings and standardisation.

- Devise a plan of what you wish to sample and monitor (the AO will probably supply you with a template for this) and send it to the centre; this should be within the AO's timescales. It should also include a list of your activities with suggested timings for, for example, interviewing staff and learners, observing practice, sampling learners' work and the supporting records of assessment, and IQA decisions and feedback. Remember to allow time for conversations, questions from staff, additional random sampling (in case you identify a trend), report writing and feedback. If you need anything specific, such as an internet connection, make sure you ask well in advance. A remote monitoring activity might include speaking to staff via the telephone and/or observing live activities via the internet.

- Ensure the centre has received your plan and can meet the requirements.

Nearer the date, you need to:

- reconfirm the date and time

- if you are visiting, ascertain information such as access to the centre (transport and timings, car parking arrangements, sites to be visited) and whether you will need to provide your own refreshments and meals

- find out the named person you will meet on arrival: this might be a manager rather than an IQA or assessor

- ensure you have personal identification such as a badge or AO identification card

- have all necessary documents and forms, either manual or electronic.

Always ensure you have read a copy of the last report and any action and improvement points, as this will form the basis of your activity. Improvement points are for guidance, whereas action points are monitored and can affect a centre's risk rating if they are not met by an agreed date.

If the centre is new, there will be a report based on the approval process which may still contain action points which must be followed up. Ideally, if you keep in touch with your centres between monitoring activities, you will have been kept up to date with their progress regarding any action points.

When planning what to sample, you should take into account learners' work that has been assessed but has not been internally quality assured as well as work that has been internally quality assured, along with work from current and previous learners. You might need to adapt your plan based on the needs of your centre or anything that occurs during the monitoring process. This might include challenging a decision an assessor has made or carrying out a random sample if you have found plagiarism in a learner's work. Whatever happens, you should never compromise quality or take anything personally; you should always remain objective with your decisions. More information regarding monitoring activities will be covered in Chapter 7.

Managing risk

Whenever possible, it is best to be proactive regarding any risks a centre might pose rather than being reactive to a situation after the event. If you are in contact with your centres on a regular basis, you should encourage them to inform you of any concerns they might have, in order that you can give relevant advice and support. For example, a learner might have been caught plagiarising another learner's work. In this situation you would need to check that the centre had an adequate plagiarism policy and that it had been followed correctly. If you are not aware of any situations which might pose a risk, the situation could become quite serious when you visit the centre.

It is important to monitor and manage the risks a centre might pose to ensure adequate support can be given and that the learners are not disadvantaged in any way.

Example

Angela has been notified by the IQA from one of her centres that two assessors have left. This only leaves one assessor, which is not enough for the number of learners registered. Angela identifies this as a risk and notifies the AO, which places the centre on a high risk rating until the issue is resolved. Angela asks the centre to keep in touch with her to update her on the situation. She also makes a note to sample more of the new assessors' decisions at her next visit, the date of which will be brought forward.

There are many *risk factors* to take into consideration when planning EQA activities, for example:

- achievement of previous action points

- assessment methods used and types of evidence provided by learners

- assessor expertise, knowledge and competence, whether new, experienced, qualified or working towards an Assessor/IQA qualification; staff should have appropriate job descriptions and development plans

- assessors (or teachers/trainers) who assess the same subject but with different groups of learners

- authenticity of learners' work

- caseloads and pressures of work placed upon staff, for example expected targets to be met, funding based on achievements, staff having unclear roles

- changes to qualifications, standards, documents, policies and procedures, and records

- language barriers

- locations of learners, assessors and IQAs

- numbers of learners and how long they take to complete

- possible plagiarism by learners

- previous risk rating of the centre

- reliability of witnesses, if used

- type of qualification or programme being assessed, problem areas or units

- use of appropriate holistic assessments and RPL

- use of technology and its reliability in assessment and IQA

- whether evidence and records are manual or electronic

- whether the learners have been registered with the AO (an EQA should not sample from a learner who is not registered).

You should also consider any risks regarding your own role, for example making an invalid decision or giving inappropriate feedback because you are not up to date with the qualification or AO's requirements. You need to make sure your own practice is current and that your judgements are valid and reliable.

Risk ratings

Most AOs grade their centres on a risk rating of low, medium or high. The more serious a risk a centre poses, the more serious a sanction they are given. A sanction can mean a centre losing its direct claims status to apply for certificates unless an external sample takes place. More serious sanctions include a centre losing both registration and certification rights until it puts right all the problems. It is best to talk to the AO before completing your report and giving feedback to the centre. If you need to talk to an AO during a visit, you could do this discreetly by leaving the room to make a phone call. The final decision rests with the AO. You must therefore contact them before informing the centre of any serious sanctions.

Table 6.2 Examples of risk ratings

Risk rating	Meaning	Sanction
Low	The centre is complying with all AO and qualification requirements. There might be some minor issues that need addressing and an appropriate action plan can be agreed with the centre.	The centre is not sanctioned and can register and certificate their learners.
Medium	There is some non-compliance, for example insufficient record keeping.	The centre can register their learners, but cannot claim certificates unless the EQA carries out a sample.
High	There are serious non-compliance issues, for example insufficient staff, no IQA system in place, inaccurate data is maintained.	The centre cannot register any more learners or claim certificates for existing learners. High risk can also mean a centre having their approval withdrawn from offering a particular qualification if aspects are very serious.

Placing a centre on sanctions or changing their status to a high risk rating can affect their operation and any funding they might receive. You might feel pressured by staff during a centre visit not to place them on a higher risk rating because of this. You must always remain objective and ensure you do everything *by the book* in accordance with Ofqual and the AO. If you are in doubt about anything, give your AO contact a call.

AOs will give guidance as to how to make a decision which results in a low, medium or high risk rating being attributed to a centre (see Table 6.2). Although you can recommend sanctions, it is the AO that makes the final decision.

You might be alerted to a risk within a centre due to:

- a long period of no communication from the centre

- changes of staff or resources not communicated to you until you visit

- documents from the centre being unclear or showing serious anomalies

- inconsistencies between the information the AO holds and that supplied by the centre

- the AO alerting you to an issue

- requested information from the centre not received by the due date, or incomplete.

You might also like to view the centre's most recent Ofsted report, if applicable, to get a feel for how it operates. These are freely available online and can be accessed by anyone (the web address is at the end of this chapter).

You must make a decision as to whether the centre could potentially damage the credibility, integrity and validity of the qualification and of the AO. However, learners should not be disadvantaged due to the centre's errors. Therefore you should support the centre to put things right through clear action points, or the AO might place the centre on further sanctions.

Malpractice
Malpractice can include learners plagiarising each other's work, assessors signing off units which are incomplete and IQAs completing records for aspects they have not sampled. It could be intentional or accidental and you would tactfully need to find out which.

Activity

If you are currently working as an assessor, an IQA or an EQA, obtain a copy of the AO's quality manual or qualification handbook. Find out what their risk ratings mean, what sanctions can be imposed and what their malpractice procedure is.

If you suspect malpractice, don't bring this to the attention of the centre staff; contact your AO immediately and discuss how to approach it with them first. They might ask you to sample the current learners who have completed the qualification to allow certificates to be claimed, but future certificates cannot be claimed until the required action points have been met.

Other areas where malpractice could occur are:

- an IQA overruling an assessor (due to pressures to meet targets) when the assessor did not pass the learner

- assessment records being signed off when assessments did not take place

- certificates being claimed for learners who don't exist

- dates of commencement and achievement not agreeing with those that the learners tell you

- dates on records not matching the ones when the activities took place

- learners' work and supporting records you have requested not being available

- minutes of meetings being produced when they did not actually take place

- signatures on documents not matching those of the people

- standardisation records being completed for activities that did not take place.

It will not be your responsibility but the responsibility of the AO to follow up any serious issues. You should not inform your centre an investigation is taking place as this information should remain confidential. If an investigation is carried out, you may be asked to give a statement.

Extension Activity

What will you need to do when your AO allocates a centre to you? Make a list of the information you will need to obtain from both the AO and the centre. Consider how you will use this information to plan your first visit to a centre.

Evaluating the quality of assessment and internal quality assurance

Evaluation is not another term for assessment; evaluation is a review and judgement of the *learning process*, whereas assessment is a decision regarding the *learner's achievement*. Your AO might ask for feedback from your centres regarding how you have performed your role, which might be used during their appraisal or review process. You can also ask for feedback from your centres to help you evaluate the service you are giving them. Obtaining the views of others will greatly assist you when reflecting upon your role.

Feedback from staff in centres might impact upon your role by making you aware of other aspects, for example how you gave advice, guidance and feedback. Don't always think that the feedback you receive will be negative; often centres are happy with the service they receive from EQAs as it often confirms they are doing things right.

Always make sure you do something with the feedback you receive which will lead to an improvement in your practice.

Alex was partaking in the annual review of all EQAs. His manager, Jon, had received feedback from all six of the centres Alex has been monitoring and used this as a basis for the meeting. Feedback was very positive regarding the advice and support Alex had been giving, both during visits and in between. All centres were impressed with his knowledge and professionalism, and one centre in particular had commented on how helpful Alex was when they had a particular problem. However, one centre felt he had not spent enough time answering their questions. Alex accepted this and agreed he would allow more time for centre staff to ask questions, perhaps at the beginning of the visit as well as at the end.

Whether you take part in an appraisal or a review or not, you should self-evaluate aspects to help you improve by asking yourself the following questions.

- How effective was my communication with the centre staff?

- Do I keep adequate and accessible records?

- Did I carry out everything I had planned to do during a visit or a remote monitoring activity?

- Did I deal with any awkward situations effectively?

- Did I give constructive and developmental feedback?

- Did I complete the report correctly and agree relevant action and improvement points?

- Did I ask for feedback from the centre regarding my performance?

- Do I standardise my practice with other EQAs?

- Do I keep up to date with changes and developments?

Standardisation of practice

The support you give to one centre should be similar to that you give to another.

You therefore need to ensure a standardised quality service is given to all your centres, which also equals that given by other EQAs. You must not show any favouritism, nor do things which are not *by the book*, i.e. you must follow all written guidelines and regulations. You must not ask a centre to do something which is not a requirement just because you want them to. You need to be fully aware of your AO's policies, procedures and practices and follow all relevant legal and other requirements. The AO should provide you with written guidance and you should ensure you are familiar with it.

How can you standardise the way you perform your role with that of other EQAs?

You could standardise your practice by:

- communicating with other EQAs as to how they carry out their role and support their centres

- comparing decisions from other EQAs, i.e. by looking at anonymised documents and reports as part of an AO's standardisation event

- carrying out peer observations (with the approval of the AO and centres)

- requesting an accompanied visit by another EQA

- keeping up to date with changes to qualification criteria to ensure you interpret them in the same way as others.

Example

Bronia has been working as an EQA for several years. A new EQA, Helga, has just commenced and Bronia has been asked if Helga could accompany her on a visit. Bronia is happy for Helga to do this as it will help Helga standardise her practice for her own visits in the future.

Why evaluate external quality assurance practice?

You should evaluate the full EQA process for each centre you are responsible for. This includes communication before, during and after a visit or a remote monitoring activity.

This will ensure:

- a professional service is given to centres

- the process is fair to all

- you are meeting AO and regulatory requirements

- you can learn from any incidents

- you can improve your practice.

It is important to give a good service to your centres, and to maintain and improve on this where possible. However, the credibility of the AO and the quality of the service you provide must never be compromised. A compromise might occur due to being too friendly with centre staff rather than remaining objective and professional.

Reflective practice

Reflective practice is an analysis of your actions which should lead to an improvement in practice. The analysis can be written down, or just thought through. It is useful to reflect on your own practice, as well as the feedback you receive from centres and the AO, to help you improve.

Part of reflection is about knowing what you need to change. If you are not aware of something that needs changing, you will continue as you are until something serious occurs. You may realise you need further training or support in some areas and partaking in relevant CPD should help.

As a professional, you need to continually update your skills and knowledge. This knowledge relates not only to your subject specialism, but also to your practice as an EQA and your knowledge of assessment and IQA.

CPD can be formal or informal, planned well in advance or opportunistic, but it should have a real impact upon your role and lead to an improvement in your practice. CPD is about more than just attending events; it is also about using critical reflection regarding your experiences, which results in your development and leads to a positive improvement in your practice.

Planning and maintaining continuing professional development

In education and training changes often occur, and you will need to keep up to date with these. They include qualification revisions, standards updates, changes to Ofsted and AO regulations, and relevant assessment and quality assurance policies and procedures. Keeping up to date is all part of your CPD.

Feedback from others and your own reflections will help you realise what CPD you need to undertake. You could shadow colleagues to observe how they carry out their EQA role, join professional associations, and carry out internet research regarding your specialist subject, assessment and IQA practice.

CPD activities could include:

- attending events, meetings, standardisation activities and training programmes (some of which might be a mandatory requirement of the AO)
- e-learning activities
- evaluating feedback from centres, peers and others
- improving skills such as English, maths and ICT
- joining professional associations or committees
- observing and shadowing colleagues
- researching developments or changes to your subject and/or relevant legislation
- self-reflection
- studying for relevant qualifications
- subscribing to and reading relevant journals and websites
- voluntary work
- writing or reviewing relevant books and articles.

Records must always be kept of any CPD activities undertaken to be shown to your AO or regulatory bodies if requested.

Reflecting upon your practice, taking account of feedback and maintaining your CPD will all help you to become a more effective EQA.

Extension Activity

Consider what CPD activities you could carry out to improve your role as an EQA. This relates not only to your role, but also to the subject you will externally quality assure, and any guidelines and regulations you need to be familiar with. If you are currently carrying out an EQA role, reflect upon your last visit to a centre to consider what you would change or improve.

Summary

In this chapter you have learnt about:

- the role of external quality assurance

- functions of external quality assurance

- planning external quality assurance activities

- aspects to perform when planning a visit or a remote monitoring activity

- evaluating the quality of assessment and internal quality assurance.

Evidence

Evidence from the completed activities within this chapter, plus the following, could be used towards the *Principles and practices of externally assuring the quality of assessment* unit, for example:

- written statements cross-referenced to the unit's assessment criteria;

- answers to questions/assignments issued by your assessor;

- records of discussions with your assessor.

Cross-referencing grid

This chapter contributes to the following assessment criteria, along with aspects of the National Occupational Standards for Learning and Development. Full details of the learning outcomes and assessment criteria for each unit can be found in the Appendices.

Unit	Assessment criteria
Understanding the principles and practices of externally assuring the quality of assessment	1.1, 1.2, 1.3, 1.4 2.1, 2.2, 2.3, 2.4 3.1, 3.2, 3.3 4.2 6.1, 6.2, 6.3, 6.4
Externally assuring the quality of assessment	1.1, 1.2, 1.3 5.1, 5.3, 5.4
Plan, allocate and monitor work	1.1, 1.2, 1.3, 1.4 3.1
National Occupational Standards	**Reference**
9 – Assess learner achievement	KU16, KU17, KU18 9.8
11 – Internally monitor and maintain the quality of assessment	KU1, KU2, KU5, KU6, KU7, KU11, KU13, KU14, KU15, KU16, KU17, KU18 11.1, 11.2, 11.3, 11.4, 11.5, 11.7, 11.8, 11.9, 11.10
12 – Externally monitor and maintain the quality of assessment	KU2, KU3, KU4, KU5, KU6, KU7, KU8, KU11, KU16, KU17 12.2, 12.3, 12.4, 12.5

Theory focus

References and further information

Ofqual (2008) *Regulatory Arrangements for the Qualifications and Credit Framework.* Coventry: QCA.

Ofqual (2015) *General Conditions of Recognition.* Coventry: Ofqual.

Pontin, K (2012) *Practical Guide to Quality Assurance.* London: City & Guilds.

Read, H (2012) *The Best Quality Assurer's Guide.* Bideford: Read On Publications Ltd.

Roffey-Barentsen, J and Malthouse, R (2009) *Reflective Practice in Education and Training* (2nd edition). London: Learning Matters SAGE.

Scales, P, Pickering, J, Senior, L, Headley, K, Garner, P and Boulton, H (2011) *Continuing Professional Development in the Lifelong Learning Sector.* Maidenhead: McGraw Hill.

Wilson, L (2012) *Practical Teaching: A Guide to Assessment and Quality Assurance.* Andover: Cengage Learning.

Wood, J and Dickinson, J (2011) *Quality Assurance and Evaluation in the Lifelong Learning Sector.* London: Learning Matters SAGE.

Websites

Confidentiality of information: www.yourrights.org.uk/yourrights/privacy/confidential-information.html

Continuing Professional Development: www.ifl.ac.uk/cpd

Data Protection Act: www.legislation.gov.uk/ukpga/1998/29/contents

Disclosure and Barring Service: www.gov.uk/government/organisations/disclosure-and-barring-service

Equality Act: www.homeoffice.gov.uk/equalities/equality-act/

Evaluation: www.businessballs.com/kirkpatricklearningevaluationmodel.htm

Health and Safety At Work etc Act: www.hse.gov.uk/legislation/hswa.htm

Ofqual General Conditions of Recognition: www.ofqual.gov.uk/for-awarding-organisations/96-articles/611-the-general-conditions-of-recognition

Ofsted inspection reports: www.ofsted.gov.uk/inspection-reports/find-inspection-report

Plagiarism: www.plagiarism.org and www.plagiarismadvice.org

Reflective practice: www.learningandteaching.info/learning/reflecti.htm

Sector Skills Councils and Standard Setting Bodies: www.sscalliance.org/

7 EXTERNALLY ASSSURING THE QUALITY OF ASSESSMENT

Introduction

In this chapter you will learn about:

- external quality assurance planning
- external quality assurance activities
- making decisions
- providing feedback to centre staff
- record keeping – external quality assurance.

Within the chapter there are activities and examples which will help you to reflect on the above and to develop and enhance your knowledge of how to externally assure the quality of assessment. Completing the activities will help you to gather evidence towards the *Externally assuring the quality of assessment* unit. At the end of each section is an extension activity to stretch and challenge your knowledge and understanding.

At the end of the chapter is a list of possible evidence which could be used towards the *Externally assuring the quality of assessment* unit.

A cross-referencing grid shows how the content of this chapter contributes towards the TAQA units' criteria and the National Occupational Standards. There is also a theory focus with relevant references, further information and websites to which you might like to refer.

External quality assurance planning

External quality assurers (EQAs) are appointed by an awarding organisation (AO) and should be given a job description and/or a contract which outlines the requirements of the role. If you are working for more than one AO, you might find they differ. However, you should familiarise yourself with the job description and/or contract of each AO. If you don't have a job description, following the requirements of the units in Appendices 6 and 7 will ensure you are performing your role adequately. The word *quality* is in your job title, and it is therefore important that you monitor quality within a centre as well as giving a quality service to the centre staff.

If you have been externally quality assuring for a while, you may find your AO will reallocate your centres after a period of time. This is to ensure you, and other EQAs, are not becoming too complacent or too familiar with how a centre operates. Another EQA could see things that you might not.

Karina had been an EQA for two centres for over three years. She knew the centre staff very well and was familiar with their policies and procedures. Her reports were very favourable and there were no action points or sanctions. Although Karina had done nothing wrong, the AO now felt it was time for a change. This would enable someone else to see things differently and support the centres in new ways. Karina was therefore allocated two different centres.

The AO will inform you when you can plan and monitor centre practice. You will need to obtain certain information from the centre to enable you to choose an appropriate sample based on risk (see Chapter 6 for details). When communicating with centres, it is useful to keep a record of contact to enable you to keep track of your activities with each centre. You could do this manually or electronically and an example is given in Table 7.1. It can be more than a record of contact, as you can add details of the staff you have met, when you have checked their curricula vitae (CVs), and when you have authorised the release of certification for particular qualifications.

Activity

Create a contact log for each of the centres you have been allocated, similar to the one in Table 7.1. Start completing them with information regarding your centres and their staff.

Sample plans

A sample plan gives a focus to the activities you wish to carry out with a centre. It is sent to the centre in advance of the visit or remote monitoring activity and informs the centre staff who you want to meet, what you will do and when. It should be based on your EQA strategy, which will be different for each centre (see Chapter 6 for details of a strategy).

Having a sample plan ensures you can monitor a good cross section of:

- staff: qualifications, experience, workload, caseload, locations

- learners: any particular requirements, ethnic origin, age, gender, locations

- qualification units: any problem areas

- assessment methods: observation, questions, witness statements, tests, recognition of prior learning (RPL), products of work, etc.

(Continued)

Table 7.1 Example centre record of contact

Centre details				
Centre name	XYZ Company	**Centre number**	0123456	
Contact name	Jean Haverham	**Contact's position**	Internal quality assurer	
Address	Manor Building, Main Road, MillerVille			
E-mail address of contact	j.haverham@xyzcompany			
Tel numbers Landline	01112 345678	**Mobile**	07123 456789	

Qualification details				
Qualifications	**Levels**	**Code no.**	**Date approved**	**Date certification released**
Customer Service – Certificate	1, 2	0123 01 and 02	03.04	05.09
Customer Service – Diploma	3, 4	0123 03 and 04	03.04	15.03
Customer Service – Knowledge	2, 3	0123 22 and 33	03.04	05.09

Staff details			
Name	**Position**	**Met on**	**CV approved?**
Jean Haverham	IQA and centre co-ordinator	03.04	Y
Phil Scholey	Tutor/Assessor	03.04	Y
Terri Mandalay	Tutor and Trainee Assessor	03.04	Y

Contact log		
Date	**Mode of contact***	**Details**
19.03	T	Discussed qualification application and arranged approval visit date.
03.04	V	Met staff and completed qualification approval documents. E-mailed documents to AO and centre.
15.06	T	Rang Jean to check on progress of learners – no problems so far. Ten registrations on each level of the Certificate, and all taking the knowledge units.
09.07	E	E-mailed AO update to Jean. Asked her to forward to other staff.
13.08	T	Jean rang to arrange a visit as most units were complete. Checked with AO for approval to plan a visit.
05.09	V	EQA visit – see completed documents and report to support release of certification for 0123 (01, 02, 22 and 33). 0123 (03 and 04) have not been completed yet. See report for action points.
15.03	R	Remote monitoring activity of 0123 (03 and 04) – see completed documentts and report to support release of certification. No action points but a few improvement points.

*T – telephone call, E – e-mail, F – fax, L – letter, R – remote monitoring activity, V – visit

- records: minutes of meetings, standardisation records, appeals and complaints, initial and diagnostic assessment results, interview and induction records, tutorial review records, analysis of evaluations and questionnaires.

This information is usually in the form of a sample plan document (see Table 6.1 in Chapter 6 for an example) which must be sent to the centre within a given timescale before any activities will be carried out. Most AOs will supply templates for you to use.

Extension Activity

Obtain the sample planning documentation that you will use for your next centre visit. Complete it according to the AO requirements and then ensure you can sample a good cross section of the items in the previous bulleted list.

External quality assurance activities

External quality assurance (EQA) activities are not just about sampling learners' work which has been assessed. The process should include observing assessors' and internal quality assurers' (IQAs') practice, talking to learners and others (for example, workplace witnesses), sampling documents such as minutes of meetings and standardisation records, and checking policies and procedures are up to date.

> The EQA checks that the IQA process is fit for purpose and samples evidence to show that it is being implemented appropriately. For example, you would check that observed assessments are carried out in line with the IQA policy, and that any problems identified are followed up and resolved.
>
> (Read, 2012, p104)

Whichever activities are chosen, they should be fit for purpose and you should ensure that something from each IQA and each assessor is sampled during the visit. If there are too many staff to sample on the day, you should plan to ensure you will sample them all over a period time. It is about quality, not quantity. The size of the sample will be based on the centre's risk rating and your planned strategy.

You should always remain professional and not let any personal issues affect the sampling process or the activities carried out. For example, you should not expect a centre to do something that is not a requirement, i.e. create and use a particular document, or carry out an observation of a learner a certain number of times if it is not a requirement. When asking a centre to do something, it must always be based on a written requirement and not just on your opinion. You can offer opinions if you have ideas to help your centre, but these would be classed as *improvement* or *development* points and not *action* points. Improvement points are for guidance, whereas action points are based on requirements and are monitored. Action points can affect a centre's risk rating if they are not met by an agreed date.

Your AO will inform you how regularly you will need to visit a centre, usually based upon their risk rating, i.e. low, medium or high. A low risk centre might be operating well, and you could therefore carry out a remote monitoring activity instead of a visit. A remote monitoring activity involves the centre posting documents to you, rather than you visiting them.

Never arrange any activity without obtaining the approval of the AO first as, depending upon your contract, you might not be paid for any work that has not been authorised. You might also not get paid for any activities you carry out until you submit a report to the AO. A separate claim for any expenses such as travel costs might also need to be submitted, along with receipts.

The activities you might be required to carry out include:

- an approval visit for an organisation to become a centre and/or offer a qualification

- an advisory visit to give support and guidance

- a routine monitoring visit to meet staff, sample learners' work, observe assessment and internal quality assurance (IQA) practice, and sample other relevant documents

- a remote monitoring activity to sample learners' work, assessment and IQA documents.

Once it has been agreed with the AO that you can carry out an activity, you can confirm your requirements to the centre. Some activities are free of charge for centres, whereas others are chargeable. This will differ between AOs and you might like to find out what these are. For example, a centre might have one free monitoring visit per year, but have to pay for any additional visits.

Approval visit

All centres have to start somewhere; therefore a new centre will need an approval visit to ensure they have systems and procedures in place to operate as a centre, as well as to offer qualifications. An existing centre might just need an approval visit to add another qualification to their portfolio.

New centre approval
If a centre is currently accredited via another AO, the process should be quite straightforward as they will have recognised systems and procedures in place. Your AO might ask you to view at least two recent EQA reports from the other AO to check that the centre is being compliant and has no sanctions or serious action points. If the centre is not accredited with another AO, you will need to carry out a thorough check of all systems, procedures and resources to ensure they meet the AO and qualification requirements. Your AO will give you guidance as to what you need to see and do.

Aspects to carry out for centre approval include:

- meeting relevant staff, such as managers, administrators, IQAs and assessors

- looking at policies and procedures to ensure they meet all requirements, such as appeals, assessment, complaints, evaluation, equality and diversity, health and safety, initial assessment, quality assurance, safeguarding

- looking at the assessment and IQA system and documents to ensure they meet all requirements

- seeing the record-keeping system, whether manual or electronic, and ensuring data protection and confidentiality requirements will be met

- ascertaining details of other locations, for example different sites or workplaces where delivery and assessment will take place.

Based on the aspects listed and anything else you have reviewed, you will need to make a decision as to whether the centre can be approved or not. You will need to complete a centre approval report which will be supplied by your AO. The report might include some action points, such as to update and e-mail you a revised appeals procedure, which the centre will need to address by a set date.

During a centre approval visit, you can take the opportunity to discuss other aspects. These might include use of the AO's logo, qualification and credit framework (QCF) requirements, malpractice, the AO's guidance for registration and certification of learners, accessing updates via the website and anything else that is relevant at the time.

If the centre does not meet all the requirements, and there are several action points, an advisory visit might be necessary to give advice and support before centre approval is granted.

Qualification approval

You could carry out a qualification approval at the same time as a centre approval, providing everything you need to see is in place. Your AO will give you guidance as to what you need to see and do.

Aspects to check for qualification approval include:

- checking CVs of relevant staff, continuing professional development (CPD) records and original qualification certificates to ensure they meet the requirements to deliver, assess and quality assure the qualification

- looking at resources such as training rooms, equipment, library and computer facilities to ensure they meet the requirements of the qualification

- reviewing particular documents that relate to the qualification, for example assessment and IQA documents and strategies, delivery materials, recruitment and marketing materials, schemes of work if relevant

- reviewing the initial assessment, induction, review and evaluation procedures and documents.

Based on the above, and anything else you have reviewed, you will need to make a decision as to whether the centre can be approved to offer particular qualifications. You will need to complete a qualification approval report which will be supplied by your AO. The report might include some action points, such as to update and e-mail you the revised initial assessment procedure, which the centre will need to address by a set date.

If the centre does not meet all the requirements, and there are several action points, an advisory visit based on the particular qualification requirements might be necessary to give advice and support before qualification approval is granted.

Activity

If you are asked to carry out a qualification approval visit to a centre, how can you ensure the staff and resources meet the relevant requirements? What would you be looking for regarding your particular subject?

Advisory visit

An advisory visit can take place at any time and can be requested by the centre or the AO. It could be prior to a centre or qualification approval, or at some other time, perhaps because a centre feels they need some particular advice and support, for example when qualification criteria change. Your AO will give you guidance as to what you need to see and do, and you will need to complete a report as to what activities you carried out.

Monitoring visit

This type of visit is to monitor the practice of current centres. Never feel obliged to sample what the IQA or assessor wants you to, as you will only ever see what they want you to see and could easily miss something that is not meeting the requirements. It is useful to carry out an additional *random sample* in addition to what you have planned to carry out. This could be to check if a trend is occurring, for example all assessors interpreting the requirements incorrectly.

Example

Xavier, the EQA, had chosen to sample Unit 4 from two different learners who had been assessed by the same assessor. In both samples, the assessor had made an incorrect decision. Xavier decided to carry out a random sample of the same unit, but from two other learners, who had been assessed by a different assessor. He noticed the second assessor had also made the same mistake. This identified to Xavier that both assessors needed guidance. This was a serious matter as the IQA had not noticed this when carrying out her sample. Fortunately, the learners were still working towards their qualification and could be reassessed. However, they had been disadvantaged due to the assessors' mistake.

Activities you could carry out during a visit include:

- watching an IQA observing and giving feedback to an assessor
- observing teaching and training sessions
- observing assessment practice and feedback given to learners
- observing a standardisation activity taking place
- talking to staff, learners and other people such as workplace witnesses
- sampling learner work which has been assessed formatively and summatively, some of which has been internally quality assured and some of which has not
- sampling minutes of meetings, standardisation records, appeals and complaints, initial and diagnostic assessment results, interview and induction records, tutorial review records, analysis of programme evaluations and questionnaires
- reviewing statistics such as number of starters and completers, the amount of time taken between learners starting and completing, the time taken between learners commencing and being registered with the AO, success and progression rates for the programme

- monitoring policies and procedures and when they were reviewed/updated

- discussing Ofsted or other report findings if applicable.

Your AO will give you guidance regarding the activities you will need to carry out during a centre visit. However, it will be down to you to decide how much you will sample, and who you see. This will be based on your knowledge of the centre, any outstanding action points, and any risks you feel could occur to disadvantage the learners.

The following checklist might help you during a centre visit.

EQA checklist

☑ Arrive on time, have your identification available and/or wear a name badge, sign in as necessary and follow the centre's safety and security procedures.

☑ Act professionally at all times.

☑ Follow all AO and regulatory requirements.

☑ Be helpful and supportive.

☑ Keep records of everything you do, i.e. observations, discussions, sampling.

☑ Follow your plan. However, this might change as you progress through the visit, for example due to staff commitments or depending upon what you find when sampling.

☑ Carry out further samples if you identify any risk, for example incorrect assessor decisions regarding a particular unit.

☑ Talk to learners – you might get a different perspective to that given to you by assessors and IQAs.

☑ View training rooms, learning resource and library facilities, other resources and equipment as necessary.

☑ Contact the AO if you identify a serious risk, for example malpractice (don't alert the centre at this point).

☑ Identify an appropriate risk rating – usually low, medium or high.

☑ Complete the AO report accurately.

☑ Remain objective with your decisions and back up everything *by the book*, i.e. don't ask a centre to do something which is not a written requirement.

☑ Give constructive and developmental feedback to staff, and allow time for their questions.

☑ Agree relevant action points and appropriate target dates, along with any improvement points.

☑ Explain how the centre will receive the report and when the next monitoring activity will be carried out.

Remote monitoring activity

When you plan to carry out a remote monitoring activity, you must be very clear about what you wish to sample, as you may not have the opportunity to ask for additional documents on the day. If you do need to carry out a more detailed sample, you will need to arrange another date when the centre can get this information to you. However, if you are accessing the information and documents electronically, you might be able to carry out an additional sample if necessary. Always ensure you have been given any relevant passwords and guidance as to how to access a centre's online system.

There are also other issues with a remote monitoring activity, such as the sample not arriving by the due date, the package being left with a neighbour who has since gone out, misunderstandings regarding what was asked for, and items getting lost in the post. Electronic access may therefore make the process easier and rule out problems with using postal services if the centre operates in this way.

Activities you can carry out during a remote monitoring activity include:

- sampling learner work which has been assessed formatively and summatively by different assessors, and which has or has not been internally quality assured

- sampling minutes of meetings, standardisation records, appeals and complaints, initial and diagnostic assessment results, interview and induction records, tutorial review records, analyses of evaluations and questionnaires

- using the telephone and/or internet for communicating with staff and learners.

Example

Annabelle, the EQA, was completing a remote monitoring activity at home and noticed that the units she had requested from the centre had not been provided. She also noticed there were no IQA records. She telephoned the centre contact, who explained that they had substituted the learners' work due to absences. They also said the IQA had gone on holiday and had not left his records behind. This gave Annabelle cause for concern as these issues should have been notified to her beforehand. Annabelle then telephoned the AO, who told her not to go ahead with the sample, but to wait until the centre could send her what she had originally requested, plus a further sample. In the meantime, the centre was placed on a sanction so that they could not claim any certificates.

Not everything will always go smoothly when carrying out a remote monitoring activity as you will not have direct access to staff, learners and documents. However, if you have ongoing communication with your centre, most issues can be resolved before they become serious. It is about being proactive, not reactive.

Sampling learners' work

When sampling learners' work, you are not reassessing or remarking it, but checking if the assessor has adequately planned and documented the assessment activities, made a correct decision, and given constructive and developmental feedback. Otherwise, the learners might be disadvantaged through no fault of their own.

When sampling work from different assessors, if you are sampling the same aspects, you can see how consistent the different assessors are. You can then note any inconsistencies and feedback this to the centre staff. For example, if one assessor is giving more support to learners, or expecting them to produce far more work than others, then this is clearly unfair. Some assessors might produce detailed assessment plans and other plans might be minimal; the same might apply to the amount of feedback given. You need to ensure the staff are consistent by standardising their approach. If not, this would become an action point for the centre to address.

Sampling learners' work is also a good opportunity to check for certain aspects, for example plagiarism. You should also check whether the learners have had the opportunity to be assessed in another language which is acceptable, for example Welsh, or bilingually. Other aspects to check include the use of holistic planning and assessment. There is no need for an assessor to observe all the different units separately if one or two well-planned holistic observations will do. Another area to check is the RPL. If a learner already holds an approved or accepted unit from another qualification, they should not have to repeat it.

Because you are only sampling aspects of the assessment and IQA process, there will be some areas that get missed. This is a risk as you cannot sample everything from everyone. You need to build up your confidence in your centre staff to know they are performing satisfactorily. If you find a problem when sampling, or have any concerns, you will need to increase your sample size. You can always carry out an additional random sample at any time and ask to see something which is not on your original plan. (Usually, the AO sample plan document will have some small print to state that this might occur.) However, your decision can only be based upon what you have sampled and seen, not on any feelings you might have which are not substantiated.

Make sure you keep notes of what was sampled and update your report as you progress. If you are completing an electronic report, make sure you save it regularly and make a backup copy.

Other sampling activities

Other activities you can carry out during a centre visit include observing practice and interviewing staff and learners. You should always notify your centre of your plan and who you wish to see so that they can be available. If someone is not available on the day, the centre should inform you beforehand so that you can choose someone else, rather than the centre choosing for you. If the centre chooses, this could be because they don't want to bring your attention to an issue.

The AO might supply you with checklists to use for your other sampling activities. In this way, you have a formal record of what was carried out. If they don't, you could design your own to ensure you are keeping full and accurate records.

Examples include:

- observation checklist for IQA practice
- observation checklist for training delivery
- observation checklist for assessment practice
- interview checklist with an IQA
- interview checklist with an assessor
- interview checklist with a learner.

The following tables give examples of checklists you could use. They have been completed as though an EQA has used them. Records can often be completed electronically and might not need a signature. You should check with your AO what records and checklists they provide, if signatures are required and how they expect you to distribute and/or file them.

Table 7.2 Example observation checklist for IQA practice

Observation checklist for internal quality assurer practice		
IQA: Jean Haverham	**EQA:** Paulo Hancock	
Assessor: Terri Mandalay (trainee assessor)	**Date:** 05.09	
Checklist	**YES NO N/A**	**Comments/action required**
Did the IQA put the assessor at ease and explain what they were going to do?	Y	Jean explained she was giving feedback regarding Terri's judgement for Unit 4. This unit had been checked and countersigned by Phil.
Did the IQA give feedback to the assessor in a constructive and developmental way?	Y	Jean was very detailed with her feedback and gave advice as to how the forms should be completed according to company requirements.
Were appropriate records referred to?	Y	All assessment and IQA records were available.
Were questions appropriate and asked in an encouraging manner?	Y	Jean asked open questions to ensure Terri could give appropriate responses.
Was the assessor encouraged to ask the IQA questions and clarify points?	Y	Terri felt able to ask questions and did interrupt Jean on occasion with very pertinent questions.
Did the IQA give adequate support to the assessor?	Y	Good support was given, particularly regarding record keeping and the company requirements.
Was the IQA's decision correct?	Y	Jean's decision supported Terri's judgement.
Did the IQA agree any action points or development points with the assessor?	N	The opportunity should have been taken to discuss Terri's progress towards the assessment units.
Were all IQA records completed correctly?	Y	The IQA sample plan, tracking and reports were all complete and up to date.
Did the IQA perform fairly and satisfactorily?	Y	Jean performed well considering I was observing the discussion.
Does the IQA have any questions?	Y	Q – Do I need to retake my IV qualification now that it is known as IQA? A – No, as long as you are demonstrating the requirements of the IQA current standards.
Feedback to IQA:		
This was a very good feedback session. You put Terri at ease and guided her through the requirements of assessment of the unit and the organisation's systems. Don't forget to ask how she is getting on with her Assessor units.		

Table 7.3 Example observation checklist for training delivery

Observation checklist for training delivery		
Tutor/Assessor: Phil Scholey	**EQA:** Paulo Hancock	
Units/aspects being observed: Unit 3	**Date:** 05.09	
Checklist	**YES NO N/A**	**Comments/action required**
Were the aims and objectives of the session clearly introduced?	Y	Clear objectives were stated – there were ten learners in the group.
Do learners have action/assessment plans?	Y	All learners have individual action plans to denote units and target dates for assessment.
Is there a scheme of work and session plan?	Y	Both documents are available and relevant to the session being taught.
Are the resources/environment safe and suitable?	Y	Classroom is suitable, resources are adequate and plentiful for the group size.
Are the learners actively engaged?	Y	Learners were involved in group activities, paired and individual work.
Are open questions used to check knowledge?	N	Closed questions were used too often – try to use open questions more.
Are all learners able to ask questions and contribute to the session?	Y	Learners were encouraged to ask questions throughout.
Was clear feedback given?	Y	Group feedback was given after the activity; individual feedback was given throughout the session.
Was the session formally summarised?	N	No summary took place linking to the objectives of the session.
Was the next session explained? (if applicable)	Y	The topic which would be covered next week was clearly explained.
Did individual learners know what they had achieved during the session and how it relates to their qualification?	Y	Feedback linked achievements to the qualification's unit.
Are all relevant records up to date?	Y	Course folder was checked – all relevant records were seen.
Do any learners require additional support?	Y	No learners had disclosed any particular needs – tutor could tactfully ask them.
Did the tutor/assessor perform fairly and satisfactorily?	Y	The session was well planned and delivered.
Does the tutor/assessor have any training needs?	N	Tutor does not have any training needs.

Feedback to assessor:

This was a well-planned session. However, don't forget to involve your learners by asking open questions (e.g. ones that begin with who, what, when, where, why and how). You need to summarise your session at the end and link to the objectives.

Table 7.4 Example observation checklist for assessment practice

Observation checklist for assessment practice		
Assessor: Terri Mandalay (trainee assessor) **Units/aspects being assessed:** Unit 5	**EQA:** Paulo Hancock **Date:** 05.09	
Checklist	**YES** **NO** **N/A**	**Comments/action required**
Was the learner put at ease and aware of what would be assessed?	Y	You prepared the learner well by explaining what you would observe and how you would do it. This helped relax your learner.
Was an appropriate assessment plan in place?	Y	You had a detailed assessment plan in place which had been agreed in advance.
What assessment activities were used and why?	Y	Observation – to confirm performance. Questions – to check knowledge.
Were the resources and environment healthy, safe and suitable for the activities being assessed?	Y	All resources were appropriate and suitable.
Were questions appropriate and asked in an encouraging manner to all learners?	Y	You asked open questions to confirm knowledge.
Were current and previous skills and knowledge used to make a decision?	Y	You took into account the fact that your learner had already achieved an aspect of the unit prior to this assessment.
Was constructive and developmental feedback given and documented?	Y	Feedback was very positive and constructive. You asked your learner how they felt they had done – this prompted a few questions.
Was the assessor's decision correct?	Y	Your judgement was correct and accurate.
Did the learner's evidence meet VACSR requirements? *(valid, authentic, current, sufficient and reliable)*	Y	You checked VACSR for all the aspects you assessed.
Were all assessment records completed correctly?	N	Complete the observation report as soon as you can after the observation and give a copy to your learner.
Did the assessor perform fairly and satisfactorily?	Y	Yes, apart from not completing the observation report due to time limits.
Does the assessor have any questions?	Y	Q – How long do my decisions need to be countersigned? A – Until you are qualified as an assessor.

Feedback to assessor:

I liked the way you were unobtrusive during the observation, yet asked open questions to confirm knowledge as the learner carried out their job role. I appreciate you did not want to fully complete the observation report due to time constraints. However, you did confirm verbally how your learner had done. Once the observation report is completed, please give a copy to your learner.

Table 7.5 Example interview checklist with an IQA

Interview checklist with an internal quality assurer	
IQA: Jean Haverham **Qualification:** Customer Service	**EQA:** Paulo Hancock **Date:** 05.09
Checklist	**Comments/action required**
How long have you been internally quality assuring this qualification?	Nine years at this organisation and three years at my previous organisation – I have seen three changes in standards.
What qualifications do you hold, e.g. IQA Award/Certificate, subject specific qualifications? (EQA to see certificates/CVs.)	Level 4 Customer Service Level 4 Learning and Development D34 Internal Verifier Award
How do you maintain your CPD?	I updated my IV Award by attending an in-house event. I ensure I am working at the current IQA standards. I have used the standards as a checklist to confirm this.
How many assessors are you responsible for and how do you allocate learners to them?	Two – Phil is experienced and qualified; Terri has been working in customer service for many years but is new to assessing. Phil is currently countersigning Terri's decisions. Terri has fewer learners than Phil until she becomes qualified as an assessor.
How do you induct new assessors and what documents do you give them?	I have a meeting with them and use an induction checklist to ensure I cover all the necessary points. Each assessor is given a copy of the Company Handbook.
What is your sampling strategy for this qualification?	• Observe each assessor every six months. • Talk to a sample of learners and witnesses. • Sample all units from each assessor across a mix of learners over a period of time (new assessors will have a higher sample rate). • Chair a team meeting every eight weeks. • Facilitate a monthly standardisation activity to cover all units over a period of time. • Maintain full records of all IQA activities. • Implement EQA action points.
Which assessors have you observed since my last visit and why? (EQA to see records.)	I observed Phil two months ago and Terri one month ago. I have a plan which shows the dates I intend to observe them as part of my strategy.
Have you formally spoken to learners about the qualification process? (EQA to see records.)	Yes, I always speak to at least two learners from each assessor and I use a learner interview checklist to document this.
Have there been any appeals or disputes against your assessors or yourself?	No – we did have an appeal against an assessor for the old standards, but he has now left the organisation.
Have there been any changes to staff/resources since my last visit?	Since your approval visit there have been no changes.
How often do you hold team meetings and standardisation activities? (EQA to see records.)	There is a team meeting every eight weeks, and standardisation events are monthly. Records are kept of all units standardised and minutes are kept of meetings.
Do you have any questions?	Q – When are you due to visit again? A – When the level 3 and 4 Diploma has been completed. Please keep in touch to update me on progress.

Table 7.6 Example interview checklist with an assessor

Interview checklist with an assessor	
Assessor: Phil Scholey **Qualification:** Customer Service	**EQA:** Paulo Hancock **Date:** 05.09
Checklist	**Comments/action required**
How long have you been assessing this qualification?	Eight years – I assessed the previous version before the standards recently changed.
What qualifications do you hold, e.g. Assessor Award/Certificate, subject specific qualifications? (EQA to see certificates/CVs.)	Customer Service, Management and Retail Diplomas at level 4. A1 Assessor Award with an update to ensure I am working at the current standards.
How do you maintain your CPD?	The company organise monthly training events on various topics; the last one was about e-assessment. We also have regular standardisation activities.
How many learners do you have? Are they based at different sites?	Ten on each level. They all come into the organisation for knowledge training and are assessed in their place of work regarding performance.
How do you induct your learners and what documents do you give them?	There is an induction checklist to ensure all points are covered. Each learner is given a copy of the Learner Handbook and the Qualification Handbook.
What documentation do you use for the assessment process and why?	Assessment plans, observation reports and question records – to ensure all aspects of the units are planned and assessed according to the unit requirements.
How do you take into account prior learning and experience?	By discussion with the learner and viewing evidence provided by them. I try to assess holistically when I can, for example where aspects of units overlap.
How often do you review the progress of each learner?	Every six weeks in the workplace.
Have there been any appeals or disputes against your decisions?	Not that I am aware of.
How often do you attend team meetings and standardisation activities? (EQA to see records.)	We have a team meeting every eight weeks and standardisation events are monthly. Records are kept of each activity.
How is your assessment practice monitored?	I am observed assessing and giving feedback every other month. The IQA talks to my learners and samples my records.
Do you have any questions?	Q – When will the standards be changing again? A – I'm not sure. I will find out and get back to you.

Table 7.7 Example interview checklist with a learner

Interview checklist with a learner	
Assessor: Terri Mandalay (trainee assessor) **Learner:** Marie Maine	**EQA:** Paulo Hancock **Date:** 05.09
Checklist	**Comments/action required**
Are you aware of your progress and achievements to date?	Assessor explained these well to the learner.
Did you discuss and agree an assessment plan in advance?	Always done in advance.
Did you have a copy of, and understand what you are being assessed towards?	Has a full copy of the standards for each unit. Assessment for Unit 5 was fully explained.
Did you have an initial assessment and/or were your previous skills and knowledge taken into account?	Had told assessor what had been achieved previously – this was taken into account.
Were you asked questions to test your knowledge and understanding?	Assessor asks questions when appropriate.
Did you receive helpful feedback?	This was verbal but needs to be formally documented – assessor to follow up.
Is your progress regularly reviewed?	Once every 6–8 weeks during a one-year programme.
If you disagreed with your assessor, would you know what to do?	Assessor to explain the appeals procedure to learner and ensure they have a copy of the Learner Handbook.
Do you have any learning needs or require further support?	Learner happy with current support given.
Is there anything you would like to comment on that we have not discussed?	No, thank you.
Do you have any questions?	Q – When do I get my certificate? A – Three weeks after successful achievement.

Feedback to assessor after discussion with the learner:
Your learner was very pleased with the way the assessment was conducted. However, she is unsure of the appeals procedure. Please direct her to the Learner Handbook which contains a copy.

Find out what documents and records you need to use on behalf of the AO you will work for. Are they available in hard copy format, or can you access and use them electronically? What other documents will you need to use which might not be supplied, for example various checklists? What are the time limits for submitting sample plans to centres and reports to the AO?

Making decisions

You will need to make several decisions based on what you have sampled and seen during your monitoring activities. These will be based on whether the centre staff have performed satisfactorily and followed all relevant requirements of both the qualification and the AO. As the learners are registered with your AO, you have a duty to ensure they are being treated fairly and are not being disadvantaged in any way.

Making a decision: observing practice

A good way of ensuring assessment and IQA practice are adequate is to see this in action. Not only will this give you the opportunity to see the decisions made, but you will also be able to talk to the staff and learners afterwards. Using a checklist will help you to focus on various aspects and enable you to document what you have observed and discussed.

If what you see meets the requirements of the qualification, you can document this in the AO report. If not, you will need to explain to the centre staff what needs correcting and agree an action point, which must be added to the report with a target date.

Making a decision: sampling assessed work

You need to sample according to your plan. However, you can sample more if you need to, for example if you find something wrong. You need to follow a robust process and you should be able to confirm what you have sampled was safe, valid, fair, reliable and ethical.

- Robust: the activities are strong and will endure the test of time.

- Safe: there is little chance of plagiarism by learners, the work can be confirmed as authentic, confidentiality is taken into account, learning and assessment is not compromised, nor is the learner's experience or potential to achieve. (Safe in this context does not relate to health and safety but to the assessment methods used.)

- Valid: the activities used are based on the requirements of the qualification.

- Fair: the activities used are appropriate to all learners at the required level, taking into account any particular learner needs. All learners should have an equal chance of an accurate assessment decision.

- Reliable: the activities used would lead to a similar outcome with similar learners.

- Ethical: the assessment takes into account confidentiality, integrity, safety, security and learner welfare.

Activity

What do you feel might affect the decisions you make, either when visiting a centre or carrying out a remote monitoring activity? Do you think you could be influenced by anyone for a particular reason, and if so, how would you deal with them?

When sampling, you might find the following checklist useful to help you make decisions.

☑ Access – is the centre preventing you from accessing certain records or locations? If they cannot give a valid reason, this is cause for concern.

☑ Action from the previous report – has this been completed? If not, why not? If the centre has not communicated their reasons to you, it might place them on a higher risk rating.

☑ AO guidance and regulations – is the centre aware of and following these? Is the centre receiving regular updates and information (for example via the AO website) and passing these onto relevant staff?

☑ Appeals and/or complaints received – why is this happening, is there a pattern? Is the centre's policy and procedure adequate?

☑ Assessment methods and types of evidence provided by learners – do they meet the requirements? Are any assessors over- or under-assessing? Do learners have adequate assessment plans/action plans? Do they receive developmental feedback? Is initial, formative and summative assessment correctly carried out? Have assessors used appropriate or alternative methods, for example asking oral questions rather than issuing written questions for a learner who has dyslexia? Is holistic assessment carried out where possible? Is RPL used and documented where applicable? If written questions are developed by the centre, are sample answers used to standardise learners' responses? Is equality and diversity taken into account? Are special assessment requirements taken into account?

☑ Assessment strategy and requirements for assessors – has everyone interpreted these in the same way? Are all assessors qualified, or countersigned if they are working towards an assessor qualification (if required)? Are staff changes notified to you and the AO? Is there a high turnover of staff? If so, why?

☑ Authenticity of learners' work – do you suspect plagiarism? Have all learners signed a document to state the work is their own?

☑ Centre – has it been established for a while or is it new? Have they offered this qualification for a long time, i.e. how experienced are they or are they becoming complacent?

☑ Certification – if the centre has direct claims status, are they claiming the certificates according to the AO requirements and in a fair amount of time after completion? Are certificates being claimed before learners have been assessed and quality assured? Are certificates issued to learners in a timely manner?

☑ Communication – how do the staff communicate with you (between visits and during a visit)? Are they defensive when you ask questions, or open to listening to you?

☑ Consistency – are IQAs being fair to assessors, and assessors fair to learners? Are they making consistent decisions, or is there any bias towards some more than others?

☑ Data – is this kept safe and secure? Does it comply with the Data Protection Act?

☑ Decisions – do all assessors' and IQAs' decisions meet the relevant requirements? Are records maintained?

☑ Evaluation – does evaluation take place, i.e. can learners give feedback? Is this documented and acted upon?

☑ Induction – are all learners adequately inducted? Are records maintained?

☑ IQA expertise, knowledge and competence, whether new, experienced, qualified or working towards an IQA qualification (and being countersigned if relevant) – staff should have appropriate job descriptions and development plans. Check CVs and original certificates. Check CPD records and how staff maintain their knowledge and competence.

☑ IQA practice – is there an adequate and up-to-date IQA rationale and sampling strategy? Are all IQA records up to date and do they meet AO requirements? Does the IQA give support and developmental feedback to assessors? Do various IQA activities take place throughout the learner journey as well as at the end (interim and summative)?

☑ Language barriers, for example English as a second language, Welsh and bilingualism should be taken into account where relevant.

☑ Learning support – are learners given adequate and appropriate support as necessary? How has it been identified?

☑ Locations and allocations of learners and assessors/IQAs – are staff accessible and can they be located? Are the allocations fair, i.e. does one assessor have more learners than others for no reason? If there is more than one IQA, are they allocated fairly to their assessor? Do the staff from different locations standardise their practice?

☑ Logo – is the centre using the AO's logo without permission?

☑ Malpractice – do you suspect something is seriously wrong? For example, signatures not matching, assessors signing off units which are incomplete, IQA activities being documented but not taking place, if so you must contact the AO.

☑ Meetings – are these taking place regularly and are minutes distributed to all? If an assessor misses a meeting, how are they updated?

☑ Policies and procedures – are these current and relevant, for example appeals, health and safety, equality and diversity?

☑ Pressure – do IQAs or assessors feel under pressure to pass learners who are borderline, perhaps due to funding, targets or employer expectations? Do you feel under pressure, i.e. not having enough time to carry out your role effectively on the day to make a valid decision? If so, you may have to arrange a further visit via your AO. Never feel pressured because your centre is wanting direct claims status or rushing you to make a decision.

☑ Qualification criteria – are these new or have they recently changed? Are all staff aware of the changes?

☑ Records – you could compare assessment records across all assessors. Are some more detailed than others? If so, this is a standardisation issue. Are records manual or electronic? How does the centre authenticate them? Do dates on tracking sheets agree with those on feedback records? Are there any causes for concern with electronic records, for example access to learner work and assessment records, use of visual recordings of observations? Are all records kept confidential, safe and secure (usually for three years)?

☑ Registration – are all learners registered with the AO? How soon after they commenced does this take place? (You should not sample from a learner who is not registered with your AO.) If there is a long time gap, is this in breach of AO guidelines?

☑ Reviews of progress – do learners have the opportunity for regular reviews of their progress? Are they documented?

☑ Risk rating – what was the previous risk rating? If it was medium or high, has the centre addressed the issues? Can they now be on a lower rating and have their direct claim status back?

☑ Risks – are any assessors experiencing problems or do they have concerns (i.e. access to their learners for assessment purposes, learner issues, plagiarism, cheating, etc.)? Risk in this context relates to assessment risks, not health and safety risks.

☑ Sampling – have you sampled work from all assessors and all locations, some of which has been internally quality assured and some of which has not? Have you observed IQA feedback to assessors and seen the practice of trainers and assessors? Have you spoken to learners and others, for example witnesses? Has the centre prevented you from sampling anything you have requested? If so, can they adequately explain why?

☑ Standardisation – are activities taking place regularly and are records maintained?

☑ Time wasting – do centre staff keep you talking or offer to take you out for lunch? If so, they could be trying to distract you or waste your time.

☑ Training – do learners receive adequate training prior to assessment? If the course is formally delivered, is there an adequate scheme of work and appropriate session plans? Do staff have relevant training and development opportunities?

☑ Trends – is there a pattern, i.e. are most learners making the same mistakes? If so, it could be that the assessor has misinterpreted something. You may have to widen your sample if you find a trend or pattern.

☑ Type of qualification being assessed – are there any problem areas or units that could be misunderstood?

☑ Witnesses – are the statements reliable? Do the witnesses really exist and are they competent to make a decision?

Reviewing all the assessment and IQA documentation will help you gain a clear picture of how the centre operates. If witnesses are used, you should contact a sample of them to confirm their authenticity and that they understand what their role entails. If a qualification relies heavily on the use of witness statements as evidence, you will need to ascertain how the centre supports them.

You need to ensure that all supporting assessment and IQA tracking dates and records are seen for the learners' work you have sampled. Dates on assessment and IQA records must agree with those on the tracking sheets. If they don't, you will need to ascertain why; it could simply be an error or there could be a problem which will need following up. You should be able to follow a clear audit trail from when a learner commences to when they leave.

You might come across something that causes you concern. If so, you will need to tactfully discuss it with the centre staff. As a result, you may need to adapt your visit plan to deal with the situation. This might include amending your sample, observing more staff and/or talking to more learners. If this is the case, make sure you document in your report the reasons why you did not follow your original plan. Your AO might want to know why you did not do something that you had originally planned to do. It could be that a learner you had asked to interview is away at the time of your visit. Ideally, the centre should have informed you of this in advance to enable you to choose another learner. If the centre substitutes a learner without informing you, you will need to know why. It could be a genuine situation, such as the learner being absent due to illness, or the centre might not want you to talk to a particular learner for some reason.

You need to get a feel for how your centres operate and how you can trust what they tell you. As you only sample aspects of a centre's operation, you are likely to miss some things. Therefore, getting to know the staff, how they operate, and encouraging them to communicate with you regularly will help you understand if they are doing something intentionally or not.

Agreeing action and improvement points

Even if a centre is low risk, you might have identified some areas which require action, improvement or development. This could be due to the way they complete their records, a policy which needs updating or a handbook which is out of date. You should agree specific, measurable, achievable, relevant and time bound (SMART) action points with the centre staff and clearly document these in your report (see Chapter 2 for further information on SMART).

Action points
An action point is something specific which relates to the operation of the centre or the delivery, assessment and IQA of a qualification. An action point can only be given when something does not meet relevant written requirements. It cannot be given just because you want the centre to do something in a particular way. You must always be able to substantiate your action points by showing the centre in a relevant policy document the aspect to which it applies.

Example

Michael, the EQA, had asked to see records of standardisation during his visit and the centre could not supply them. They said they held meetings but did not keep records. The action point on the report therefore read: 'The internal quality assurer must hold monthly standardisation meetings with all assessors. This is to ensure all units of the qualification are standardised during a yearly cycle. Records must be e-mailed by the internal quality assurer to the external quality assurer within one week of the activity taking place.'

Improvement and development points

An improvement point can be given to a centre to help and support them to improve a particular aspect. A development point can be given to help a centre develop their practice generally. Some AOs use the term *improvement*, whereas others use the term *development*.

Example

> *Michael noticed the centre was completing two separate forms for assessment, when one would be adequate. He advised the centre how to do this, so that they could still meet the qualification requirements. The improvement point therefore read: 'The assessor will amalgamate the two current assessment forms within one month to create one form which will meet the requirements of the qualification.'*

Awarding organisation report

Your AO will provide you with a report template which should be completed during or shortly after you carry out the sampling and monitoring activities. The report will probably be electronic, allowing you to key in text into various areas, but not change the questions. You should answer all the questions objectively, based on fact and not on opinions. You should check for spelling and grammar errors to ensure your report is completed professionally. Don't get so tied up with completing the form that you don't allow enough time to give feedback to the centre staff.

You must be able to back up any statements afterwards in case there is a query, a complaint or an appeal by the centre. The report should be passed onto the AO within their timescales. Some AOs will forward it to the centre; others will request that you do this. Make sure you keep your own copy safe and use a filing system that enables you to access your records easily.

After the monitoring activity, you should:

- ensure your report has been completed correctly and forwarded to the AO within their timescale, and inform the centre how and when they will receive their copy

- ensure all your records are up to date, for example centre contact log

- keep in touch with the centre, particularly if there are action points

- keep in touch with the AO as necessary

- keep track of centre activity, for example registrations and certifications – you might be able to do this via the AO's intranet

- evaluate your practice to identify how you can improve.

Disputes and appeals

Most centres comply with all the requirements. However, you might come across a centre that breaches these. This could be due to ignorance, or it might be deliberate. Sadly, some centre staff feel pressured due to targets and funding, and might commit fraud, such as completing some of a learner's work for them. If you find this during a visit or remote monitoring activity, you should contact your AO and discuss it with them first. While you can recommend a sanction, the AO has the final say, as they can access the track record of the centre to see if similar problems have occurred in the past.

The staff might dispute your decision; therefore it is crucial that you keep full and accurate records of everything you find, not only by completing the AO's report, but also when writing your own notes. If a centre does dispute your decision, the AO might ask another EQA to carry out a sample from the centre to see if there is a pattern emerging.

Another type of dispute might be within the centre, and you could become involved to help them resolve it.

Example

Jeremiah, the EQA, was talking to a learner, Adam, during a visit to a centre. Adam stated he had failed an assignment because he felt the assessor did not like him. Adam had complained to the IQA but had not received any feedback. Jeremiah looked at the assignment and agreed the assessor was right, but that he had not clearly explained to Adam what the requirements of the assignment were. Jeremiah asked to see the centre's appeals procedure, which could not be located. Jeremiah therefore gave the centre an action point to ensure the procedure was up to date, with all learners being told how they could access it.

You should always check that the centre has an up-to-date appeals policy, and that all staff and learners are familiar with it. It might be included in a learner handbook or a centre manual, or be accessible via the centre's intranet or website. When talking to learners, this is a good time to ask them if they know what to do if they disagree with their assessor's decision. You should also ask a centre if they have had any appeals and if so, look at the records. It might be that one particular assessor is receiving far more appeals than others. If so, you would need to find out why.

It is best to be proactive and keep in touch with your centres between activities, encouraging them to communicate any concerns or issues they may have. This will enable you to support them and not be reactive when something more serious occurs.

Extension Activity

Reflect upon your most recent visit to a centre. Were you happy with the way it went? Did you remain professional or did you get too friendly with the staff? Did you find anything wrong and have to give an action point? If so, were you able to back this up by showing the centre staff the written requirements? What would you have done differently if you had the chance?

Providing feedback to centre staff

Feedback should be given throughout the sampling process during a visit, for example after an observation of an assessor, as well as at the end of the visit. If you are carrying out a remote monitoring activity, you could telephone the centre part-way through if you have any queries. Feedback should be based on what was sampled and monitored. It can be used to confirm compliance and competence, and to motivate and encourage centre staff. It can also be used to highlight areas for improvement, development and action.

You should give ongoing feedback at each opportunity; this can highlight good practice and be used as a basis to discuss any areas for concern. Always remain professional when giving feedback, and ensure you have valid evidence regarding what you have seen and any action points you recommend. At all times, remain objective and don't let any personal factors influence your decisions.

> The EQA will often give informal verbal feedback throughout the day, and this should be helpful to the centre as it means that there will be no 'nasty surprises' during the formal feedback at the closing meeting. However, it is important that even this informal feedback is captured on the report as otherwise it is likely to be forgotten or overlooked by all parties.
>
> (Pontin, 2012, p156)

See Chapter 2 for information regarding different feedback methods such as evaluative or descriptive, constructive or destructive and objective or subjective.

If you find something that a person could improve upon, don't be critical but state the facts based upon what you have seen. After an observation, you could ask the person to reflect upon their performance before you give feedback. In this way, they might realise any mistakes before you have to point them out. You can then suggest ways to improve. You might not find anything wrong, in which case you still need to give feedback, which will be positive and confirm that what they are doing is right. Always allow time for them to clarify anything you have said and to ask questions. Don't interrupt them when they are speaking and avoid jumping to any conclusions. Use eye contact, observe body language and listen carefully to what they are saying. Show that you are a good listener by nodding your head and repeating key points.

Example

> Josh, the EQA, carried out an observation of Donna, the assessor, with one of her learners in the workplace. He used an observation checklist to note what he had seen and to enable him to give constructive feedback. He noticed Donna was really detailed at giving developmental feedback, but forgot to state which aspects her learner had achieved. He asked her afterwards if there was anything she would do differently, and she did mention this point. As the learner was still available, Donna went to explain to him what he had achieved.

If you are carrying out a visit to a centre, you could give ongoing feedback, perhaps when you identify good practice, and then give further feedback at the end. Some centres might prefer you to give feedback to one named person, perhaps a manager or an IQA. Others might be happy for you to feedback to the full team.

You need to be tactful when giving feedback, particularly if you have identified some concerns, as some staff might take things personally and become defensive. Although you will be on your own at the centre, never allow anyone to persuade you to change your decision, or intimidate you with statements such as staff losing their jobs as a result of your findings. You must remain objective and do everything according to the written requirements. You can always telephone the AO for advice, or simply say that you have to leave if you feel threatened.

Record keeping – external quality assurance

Records must be maintained to satisfy the AO and the regulatory bodies, for example Ofqual. It is important that EQA reports, either manual or electronic, show a full audit trail of what has been monitored and sampled. To create a visual audit trail of everything you sample, you could use a coloured pen to date and initial the documents. If records are not kept, there is no proof the EQA process took place. This includes your own records and checklists as well as the reports you complete for the AO. This will usually be for a set period, for example three years, and should be the original records, not photocopies or carbon copies, to guarantee authenticity. Records should always be accurate, dated and legible.

There may be a standardised approach to completing the records and reports, for example the amount of detail which must be written, whether the records should be completed manually or electronically, whether they should be written in the first or third person, and how they are completed, i.e. written, word-processed or online. The AO should invite you to regular standardisation activities with other EQAs. This is an opportunity to see how they complete their records and carry out their role.

When completing any records, if signatures are required, these should be obtained as soon as possible after the event if they cannot be signed on the day. Any signatures added later should have the date they were added, rather than the date the form was originally completed. If you are completing documents electronically, you will need to find out if an e-mail address or electronic signature is required or not.

All records should be kept secure and should only be accessible to relevant staff. You also need to ensure you comply with organisational and statutory guidelines such as the Data Protection Act (1998) and the Freedom of Information Act (2000) (see Chapter 2 for further details).

Managing information

Records should always be kept up to date and include all communication and activities carried out with a centre. This will include which staff you have met and which learners' work you have sampled. You should monitor all staff over a period of time and should not assume that experienced staff will be performing adequately. It is easy for staff to become complacent. However, when standards change, new practices may have to be implemented by the centre to ensure everyone is aware of the changes.

Records might include:

- AO reports

- records of contact and communications with centres

- EQA sample plans sent to centres

- observation records of IQAs, trainers and assessors

- interview records, for example with learners and witnesses.

You must never trust your memory but should document all communication with your centres between visits, as well as keeping records of what was carried out during an approval or advisory visit.

Reasons for keeping records include:

- to satisfy the AO, i.e. you must be able to show a valid audit trail for all your activities

- to keep track of communication with centres

- in case of a complaint or appeal against your decision

- for standardisation and quality assurance purposes

- in case of malpractice in a centre, for example plagiarism

- to monitor qualification activity within a centre.

Records should always be accurate and based on what you have seen. They should be legible and kept safe, secure and confidential. Most records can be kept manually or electronically. Backing up your data and records is important, particularly if you have electronic records, for example in the case of power failures.

Confidentiality

Confidentiality should always be maintained regarding all information and data you use. You might work from home, in which case you should ensure all your records and data are safe and secure. You also have to ensure your centres are following confidentiality requirements for their records.

Extension Activity

Find out what the policies and procedures are for your AO. These might include: access to documents and regulations, appeals, assessment in other languages/ bilingualism, confidentiality, data protection, disputes, professional conduct, record keeping and report completion. Make sure you are familiar with them all.

Summary

In this chapter you have learnt about:

- external quality assurance planning

- external quality assurance activities

- making decisions

- providing feedback to centre staff

- record keeping – external quality assurance.

Evidence

Evidence from the completed activities within this chapter, plus the following, could be used towards the Externally assuring the quality of assessment unit, for example:

- EQA strategy for your centres

- centre contact record

- two completed assessor observation checklists

- two completed learner discussion checklists

- two completed EQA reports

- records of two standardisation activities with other EQAs

- CPD record

- critical reflections of own practice

- written statements cross-referenced to the unit's assessment criteria

- answers to questions issued by your assessor

- records of discussions with your assessor.

Coss-referencing grid

This chapter contributes towards the following assessment criteria, along with aspects of the National Occupational Standards for Learning and Development. Full details of the learning outcomes and assessment criteria for each unit can be found in the Appendices.

Unit	Assessment criteria
Understanding the principles and practices of externally assuring the quality of assessment	2.1, 2.2, 2.3, 2.4 3.1, 3.2, 3.3 4.1, 4.2, 4.3, 4.4 5.1 6.1, 6.2, 6.3
Externally assuring the quality of assessment	1.1, 1.2, 1.3 2.1, 2.2, 2.3, 2.4, 2.5 3.1, 3.2 4.1, 4.2, 5.1, 5.2,
Plan, allocate and monitor work	1.1, 1.2, 1.3, 1.4 3.1
National Occupational Standards	**Reference**
9 – Assess learner achievement	KU16, KU17, KU18 9.8
11 – Internally monitor and maintain the quality of assessment	KU1, KU2, KU5, KU6, KU7, KU11, KU13, KU14, KU15, KU16, KU17, KU18 11.1, 11.2, 11.3, 11.4, 11.5, 11.7, 11.8, 11.9, 11.10
12 – Externally monitor and maintain the quality of assessment	KU4, KU5, KU6, KU7, KU8, KU9, KU10, KU11, KU12, KU13, KU14, KU15, KU16 12.1, 12.2, 12.3, 12.4, 12.5, 12.6, 12.7

Theory focus

References and further information

Ofqual (2008) *Regulatory Arrangements for the Qualifications and Credit Framework.* Coventry: QCA.

Ofqual (2012) *General Conditions of Recognition.* Coventry: Ofqual.

Pontin, K (2012) *Practical Guide to Quality Assurance.* London: City & Guilds.

Read, H (2012) *The Best Quality Assurer's Guide.* Bideford: Read On Publications Ltd.

Roffey-Barentsen, J and Malthouse, R (2009) *Reflective Practice in Education and Training* (2nd edition). London: Learning Matters SAGE.

Scales, P, Pickering, J, Senior, L, Headley, K, Garner, P and Boulton, H (2011) *Continuing Professional Development in the Lifelong Learning Sector.* Maidenhead: McGraw Hill.

Wilson, L (2012) *Practical Teaching: A Guide to Assessment and Quality Assurance.* Andover: Cengage Learning.

Wood, J and Dickinson, J (2011) *Quality Assurance and Evaluation in the Lifelong Learning Sector.* London: Learning Matters SAGE.

Websites

Confidentiality of information: www.yourrights.org.uk/yourrights/privacy/confidential-information.html

Continuing Professional Development: www.ifl.ac.uk/cpd

Data Protection Act: www.legislation.gov.uk/ukpga/1998/29/contents

Equality Act: www.homeoffice.gov.uk/equalities/equality-act/

Evaluation: www.businessballs.com/kirkpatricklearningevaluationmodel.htm

Health & Safety At Work etc Act: www.hse.gov.uk/legislation/hswa.htm

Ofqual General Conditions of Recognition: www.ofqual.gov.uk/for-awarding-organisations/96-articles/611-the-general-conditions-of-recognition

Plagiarism: www.plagiarism.org and www.plagiarismadvice.org

Reflective practice: www.learningandteaching.info/learning/reflecti.htm

Sector Skills Councils: www.sscalliance.org/

8 PLAN, ALLOCATE AND MONITOR WORK

Introduction

In this chapter you will learn about:

- producing and using a work plan
- identifying and allocating responsibilities to team members
- monitoring the progress of others and the quality of their work
- communication skills
- updating the work plan.

Within the chapter there are activities and examples which will help you to reflect on the above and to develop and enhance your understanding of how to plan, allocate and monitor work. Completing the activities will help you to gather evidence towards the *Plan, allocate and monitor work* unit. This unit is based on the National Occupational Standards for Management and Leadership. At the end of each section is an extension activity to stretch and challenge your learning further.

At the end of the chapter is a list of possible evidence which could be used towards the *Plan, allocate and monitor work* unit.

A cross-referencing grid shows how the content of this chapter contributes towards the relevant TAQA units' criteria, the National Occupational Standards, and the Management Standards. There is also a theory focus with relevant references, further information and websites to which you might like to refer.

This chapter relates to the management of others and as such contains various leadership, management and communication theories. Planning, allocating and monitoring the work of others is a management function which you will carry out with your team of internal quality assurers (IQAs) or external quality assurers (EQAs).

Producing and using a work plan

If you lead a team of IQAs or EQAs you should be in a managerial role and as such have the authority to go with it. You will need to plan, monitor and review the progress and the quality of your team's work within the context of their roles. If you are an IQA or EQA, you will be leading a team of other IQAs or EQAs. Your role will therefore be to ensure they are all carrying out their roles satisfactorily.

To help you do this, you should use a work plan to organise the various activities you need to do. This will ensure your team works effectively and everyone performs the requirements of their roles. A work plan is a visual reminder of what needs to be done and when. You might produce a work plan for yourself to show what you will do as part of your role, for example, to plan, monitor and review the IQA process in accordance with organisational requirements. Your work plan would then list certain activities such as, create an IQA sampling plan and plan dates for team meetings. See Table 8.1 for an example work plan for a lead IQA. The shaded boxes are the months in which the activities will take place; the dates can then be added when the activities have occurred.

If you are delegating tasks to team members, using a work plan will help ensure you allocate work fairly and effectively. Monitoring and reviewing the tasks will ensure appropriate progress is being made. The tasks that staff carry out should lead to an improvement in the quality and standards of the product or service being offered. The product could be a qualification, and the service would be how the staff perform, for example how IQAs support their assessors. Records should always be maintained of all activities for audit purposes and external inspections.

Your aim as a manager should be that your own work, and the work of your team, is carried out effectively. Your starting point will be your job description or role specification. This should state what you are expected to do, enabling you to create a work plan and put it into action. If you don't have a job description or role specification, working towards the requirements of the qualification unit will ensure you are performing your role adequately.

Activity

Have a look at the learning outcomes and assessment criteria of the unit in Appendix 8 to see what you need to do to perform this role. If you are working towards this unit, use the assessment criteria as a checklist and note down what you currently know and can do to meet them.

As a manager you should be familiar with and committed to the vision and mission of your organisation. You should also know what part you have to play in achieving them. You need to make sure your team members are also aware of how their job role fits into the overall organisational requirements, and what they need to do. The vision and mission must be achievable and all staff should understand what they are and be committed to them. However, if they are unrealistic, staff might not be motivated to achieve them. If the latter is the case, you will need to discuss issues and concerns with someone in authority; otherwise staff morale may become low, which could lead to staff not performing their roles correctly and disadvantaging learners.

Table 8.1 Example work plan for a lead IQA

Objective	To plan, monitor and review the IQA process in accordance with organisational requirements												
IQA	H Rahl												
Activities	Jan	Feb	Mar	Apr	May	Jun	Jul	Aug	Sep	Oct	Nov	Dec	Comments
Produce IQA sampling plan	5th												
Produce IQA observation plan	5th												
Plan team meeting dates and delegate the role of the chair on a rota basis	12th												
Plan standardisation activities and dates, delegate to team		18th											
Prepare for EQA visit			▓										Inform all staff and hold an additional meeting before and afterwards
Meet with EQA				▓									Reserve a room
Review assessment/IQA policies/procedures					▓								
Review assessment and IQA documentation						▓							
Carry out staff appraisals									▓	▓			
Produce report and statistics regarding appeals and complaints											▓		Could be done in December
Write annual IQA report for directors											▓		Distribute two weeks before annual meeting
Attend annual directors' meeting												▓	

Activity

Obtain and read your organisation's vision and mission statements. Analyse how they will impact upon your role in producing a work plan for your area of responsibility. If you don't have a job description, make a list of what you consider your management roles and responsibilities to be. Locate all the relevant policies and procedures that underpin your job role and find out if there is any legislation that you need to follow, for example health and safety, equality and diversity, employment law.

Using the *who, what, when, where, why and how* (WWWWWH) approach will help you produce your work plans. All tasks and activities you set for yourself and your staff should have objectives which are specific, measurable, achievable, relevant and time bound (SMART).

Information you need to help you create a work plan includes:

- details of your team members, what their experience, knowledge and skills are, what they are expected to do and when

- documentation, policies and procedures relevant to the role

- financial information such as budgets for carrying out various activities

- information regarding what is being assessed and quality assured

- job specification – for yourself and others you are responsible for

- organisation vision and mission

- priorities, targets and expected success criteria

- relevant requirements for accredited qualifications (if applicable)

- resources: physical and human, and others such as transport

- the locations and contact details of your team members, and other relevant staff.

If you carry out internal or external quality assurance activities as well as manage a team of staff, you might already be using some types of work plan such as:

- an observation plan

- a meeting and standardisation plan

- a sample plan and tracking sheet.

However, you might have other responsibilities which need to be planned for, or activities you need to delegate to others. When delegating, don't impose the activities, but discuss and agree them to ensure you are utilising a person's strengths for the task. A work plan will help you prioritise and keep track of all activities.

The work plan can be produced and updated electronically, for example as a spreadsheet, and then e-mailed to all staff. Alternatively, it can be printed and displayed on a notice board as a visual reminder. If it is electronic, it is best to save any updates as a different version number to allow the original to remain accessible. Alternative styles of work plan could be used such as wall planners, which can be purchased from stationers, or templates such as Gantt charts, which are available free via an internet search or as part of some computer programs.

Supporting your team

You might have staff who are employed full time, part time, or on a voluntary or peripatetic basis (i.e. working for several organisations). You will need to know who all your team members are and keep their contact details handy. There will be occasions when you might not all be able to get together at the same time for a meeting; therefore using electronic methods of communication can ensure you all stay in touch regularly.

You will need an in-depth knowledge of all relevant policies, procedures and documentation that will be used by yourself and your team. You should support your team members in a proactive rather than a reactive way, encouraging them to talk to you when they need to. If they have a concern, it will need to be dealt with straight away rather than it escalating into a major problem due to a lack of communication. However, there might be occasions when you have to deal with poor practice, in which case you will need to ascertain all the facts and remain impartial with any decisions.

You might need to carry out coaching and/or mentoring activities with your team members, carry out staff appraisals and training needs analyses, and countersign the decisions of unqualified staff. These are all managerial roles and you could consider taking a management qualification as part of your continuing professional development (CPD). You might also be responsible for producing and/or updating staff and learner handbooks and other documentation such as policies and procedures.

Table 8.2 lists the skills required to help you perform your job role and support your team. If there are any you are uncertain of, you could research them further.

Table 8.2 Example job role skills

Skills to perform your role and support your team	
• analysing • appraising • being assertive • budgeting • coaching • communicating • computing • consulting • data analysing • decision making • delegating • leading • listening • managing: people, conflict, stress, time • mentoring	• monitoring • motivating • negotiating • planning • prioritising • problem solving • providing feedback • questioning • reading and writing • record keeping • reviewing • setting SMART objectives • speaking • supporting others

When planning activities for your team members to carry out, you will need to match their skills, qualities and locations against certain activities, objectives and priorities. You will need to know your staff well to be able to do this, or talk to them to find out their strengths and limitations. You might need to work within specific time or financial constraints, such as deadlines or lack of a budget. All activities will still need to take place and be monitored, but they could be carried out at a different time or location. Your work plan can be updated and amended at any time to take into account any changes or unforeseen events.

> The Leitch Review was established in December 2004 to consider the skills profile the UK should aim to achieve by 2020 in order to maximise growth, productivity and social justice. The UK must aim to improve its prosperity and fairness in a rapidly changing global economy. The Review has found that these changes are decisively increasing the importance of skills. Skills are an increasingly central driver of productivity, employment and fairness. The UK must achieve a world class skills base if it is to improve its prosperity and fairness in the new global economy.
>
> (Leitch, 2006, p27)

Improving your own skills and those of your team members will help everyone perform their job roles to the best of their ability and contribute towards their CPD. There might be instances where your team members have become demotivated or demoralised by circumstances beyond their control, for example a recent spate of redundancies at the organisation or family issues at home. Your own personal qualities and skills can help motivate and enthuse your team members.

Activity

Make a list of the personal skills and qualities you feel you possess. While doing this, consider your roles and responsibilities and the management duties you will be performing. Analyse these and consider how you can develop them further to achieve the requirements of your job role.

Some people are naturally good managers, have a helpful and pleasant personality and are good at communicating with others. However, if you have to identify and improve the performance of others and monitor their progress, appropriate training will help you. You should get to know your team members and realise that they may perceive your tone of voice and body language in a different way to that which you intended. Communication is important and it should always be carried out in a professional manner. You might also need to appreciate that your personal values and beliefs might be different to those of your team members, and not impose yours upon them.

You might have to deal with staff complaints, appeals and grievances, either directly or indirectly. If this is the case, you must remain impartial and maintain confidentiality throughout the investigation process.

Personality styles and preferences

Understanding a little about your personality style or preference will help you develop your personal qualities and skills. There are many models that can be used to ascertain personality types. The following are a few examples.

In the 1950s, a test was devised by cardiologists Friedman and Rosenham to identify patterns of behaviour considered to be a risk factor for coronary heart disease. This placed people as *Type A* or *Type B* and this is still used today to analyse personality types. Type A individuals can be described as impatient, excessively time conscious, insecure about their status, highly competitive, hostile and aggressive, and incapable of relaxation. They are often high achieving workaholics who multitask, drive themselves with deadlines and are unhappy about the smallest of delays. Due to these characteristics, Type A individuals are often described as *stress junkies*. Type B individuals, in contrast, are described as patient, relaxed and easy-going. There is also a Type AB mixed profile for people who cannot be clearly categorised. Knowing which type you are could help you change if necessary, for example becoming less stressed.

Other personality style tests include the Myers-Briggs Type Indicator (MBTI) and Keirsey's Temperament Sorter, which are based on the work of Carl Jung (1875–1961). Both involve a personality questionnaire. An MBTI report will give preferences for each of four pairs, known as E & I, S & N, T & F, J &P as in the bold letters below.

1. **E**xtrovert – sociable, get lonely when not surrounded by others, the life and soul of the party, need to be the centre of attention, get energy from being with others.

2. **I**ntrovert – territorial, need mental and physical space, pursue activities on their own, can feel lonely in a crowd, often work well with people.

3. **S**ensing – need things to be realistic, trust their experience and senses, are down to earth, good at picking out details; often good doctors, nurses and police officers.

4. I**n**tuitive – see things as wholes rather than details, trust hunches, enjoy ideas, challenges and change; good inventors, innovators and pioneers.

5. **T**hinking – make decisions based on principle, logic or objectivity; they like words such as analysis, principle, objective and firmness.

6. **F**eeling – base decisions on their personal impact; they like words such as values, personal, persuasion, appreciation.

7. **J**udging – like things settled, orderly, planned and completed; they make lists and follow them, they get things moving, use systems and routines.

8. **P**erceiving – don't like planning, preparing or cleaning up, are flexible and adaptable, delay making decisions hoping something better will turn up, are spontaneous, open-minded and tolerant.

There are 16 possible personality preferences based on combinations of the above. The benefits of knowing the preferences enable you to have some knowledge of how people function. They enable you to realise that other people have aims and needs, feelings and values which may differ from your own. Never assume that your team members are as highly motivated or as capable as you are.

Kiersey's model has four main temperament groups:

*   Artisan – concrete in communicating about goals, flexible and accommodating about achieving them

*   Guardian – concrete in communicating about goals, logical, good at facilitating projects

- Idealist – abstract in communicating, co-operative, good interpersonal skills

- Rationalist – abstract in reasoning, utilitarian in achieving goals.

The temperament groups can be further subdivided into character types. There are also eight technical terms which are the same as in the MBTI, for example extrovert and introvert. The questions used in the test will reveal a person's temperament and character type.

You might like to carry out a personality style test and encourage your team members to do so too. However, they should always adhere to a code of ethics. Reviewing your personality style should help you see aspects you might need to change, improve or develop, and can help you become more effective as a manager. Knowing people are of different types should help you realise how individuals act and react in different situations.

Taking personal responsibility for your own actions, supporting your team members and not apportioning blame should lead to a healthy working atmosphere for all concerned. This in turn should lead to an improved service for the learners and an improved reputation for the organisation.

Extension Activity

Create a work plan for your area of responsibility for a particular job role. Consider if you will need additional work plans for other tasks you will delegate to your team members. Decide on the activities that will be carried out along with appropriate target dates to meet your objectives.

Identifying and allocating responsibilities to team members

Once you know who your team members are, along with their experience, knowledge and skills, you can begin allocating activities to meet various objectives. You will, of course, need to identify what the objectives are, along with appropriate activities to enable you to know when they have been achieved. The objectives should be based on the job roles of yourself, your team members and the requirements of the organisation and qualification. You will need to decide what you will do yourself and what you will delegate. It could be that you plan a yearly calendar of team meetings and prepare the agendas, but don't chair them all. Delegating some meetings to other team members on a rota basis will give them responsibility and help them take ownership of agreed actions.

You will need to identify and make a list of all the activities you expect yourself and your team members to carry out. You can then create a work plan for yourself and others in conjunction with the relevant team members. Wherever possible, you should delegate tasks to your team members based upon their strengths. You could ask your team members to carry out something called a SWOT analysis to assist this process. SWOT stands for strengths, weaknesses, opportunities and threats. It can be used on people, products, services and projects to identify favourable and unfavourable contributing factors. You could also carry out one yourself.

Raj has a team of six IQAs who each have four assessors for the Health and Social Care qualification. One, Cameron, is new and working towards his IQA qualification. Raj could have allocated any of the other three experienced staff to countersign Cameron's decisions. After he asked his staff to complete a SWOT analysis, he allocated Tom due to the fact he was a very patient and approachable person and was also a qualified mentor. Raj felt these strengths would further support Cameron's development and help him achieve his qualification more quickly.

Once you get to know your team members and their strengths, you will feel confident delegating various activities to them. However, never assume they will always be carried out. You will need to monitor what your staff are doing, perhaps by asking them to give you a written, electronic or verbal report at agreed times.

At some point, you might experience some hostility between your team members, for example if they feel they should or should not be carrying out various activities. Getting people to work as a team can be problematic, particularly if there is a high staff turnover in your organisation. If this is the case, you would need to find out why staff are leaving and meet with relevant managers in your organisation to do something about it. Gaining feedback from the staff who have left should help you ascertain the reasons why.

Team working

A team is a collection of individuals and each person will have different ideas and ways of performing. Team building activities can be good fun and lead to staff having a better working relationship with each other. However, some staff may feel they are a waste of time, or there might not be a suitable budget available. If you expect your team members to work together collaboratively on certain activities or projects, you might like to familiarise yourself with Tuckman's *group formation* theory of forming, storming, norming, performing and adjourning, which he formulated in 1965 and amended in 1975.

- *Forming* – this is the *getting to know you* and *what shall we do* stage. Individuals may be anxious and need to know the boundaries and code of conduct within which the team will work.

- *Storming* – this is the *it cannot be done* stage. It is where conflict can arise, rebellion against the leader can happen and disagreements may take place.

- *Norming* – this is the *it can be done* stage. This is where group cohesion takes place and norms are established. Mutual support is offered, views are exchanged and the group co-operates to perform the task.

- *Performing* – this is the *we are doing it* stage. Individuals feel safe enough to express opinions and there is energy and enthusiasm to complete the task.

- *Adjourning* – this is the *we will do it again* stage. The task is complete and the group separates. Members often leave the group with the desire to meet again or keep in touch.

Being aware of the stages that groups go through, and informing your team members of each, should help you all see why things happen the way they do. Depending upon the activity, the stages might happen over a short- or long-term time frame. You might even see all the stages occur during one meeting where the team is new and have a tight deadline for an activity. Alternatively, you might have a team that gets stuck at one of the stages and you will need to intervene to move them on.

Activity

Plan an activity that you could carry out with your team, for example creating or revising a document or handbook. Carry out the activity and watch how the team develops through the stages. How many stages did it go through? Was the activity achieved within the time allocated? Did you have any staff members who were disruptive or worked well with particular team members and not others? If so, what could you do next time to ensure everyone is performing on task?

Many other group formation theories are available. You could try one of the following with your team, or research others.

Coverdale (1977) stated the essence of team working is that individuals have their own preferred ways of achieving a task, but that in a team they need to decide on one way of achieving this. In a team, three overlapping and interacting circles of needs have to be focused upon at all times. The *task needs,* the *team needs* and the *individual needs.*

Figure 8.1 Team working needs

When setting activities for your team members to carry out in groups, consider the following.

To achieve the task ensure:

- a SMART objective or target is stated

- responsibilities are defined

- working conditions are suitable

- supervision is available.

To build and maintain the team ensure:

- the size of the team is suitable for the task
- health and safety factors are considered
- consultation takes place
- discipline and order are maintained.

To develop the individual ensure:

- responsibilities are defined
- grievances are dealt with
- praise is given
- individuals feel safe and secure.

Individual personalities, and the roles that they take on when part of a group, may impede the success or the achievement of the task. As a manager, make sure you supervise your team members' work carefully to keep all individuals focused.

You might need to agree ground rules with your team members when working on group activities, for example switching off mobile devices and respecting others' opinions to help the group progress effectively. If new members join the team, they should be made to feel welcome and introduced to everyone. Allocating a mentor to them, or acting as a mentor yourself, should help them settle in. Hopefully, they will not feel isolated as they have a named person they can go to with any questions.

As the manager of the team, you should lead by example and promote an environment based on respect. If a team member has made a mistake, don't directly blame them, but find out what went wrong and why. It could be that the same mistake might be made by others. You could use the situation as a learning experience and share your solutions with your team members to ensure it does not happen with them too. Your staff should feel comfortable in talking to you about any concerns they have.

Team age ranges

The age range of your team members might affect the way they work or their attitudes towards work. The demographics of the country are continually changing.

- The *veteran* generation (aged 65 plus) may have been with the same employer for a long time and be thinking of retiring, have probably paid off their mortgage, and have children who have left home and therefore have different priorities from the other generations.
- The *baby boomers* (aged 48–64) might be working fewer hours and increasing their leisure pursuits, have grown-up children and a low mortgage. This generation will increase over the next few years which will lead to a larger number of older than younger people in the workplace.

- *Generation X* (aged 30–47) might be mid-career, have had several jobs, and perhaps experienced redundancy and unemployment along the way. They might have a large mortgage and a growing family.

- *Generation Y* (aged 18–29) might be unemployed, be in training, be first or second job-bers, could still be living with their parents, have few responsibilities and possibly have a large debt. They use technology a great deal and the line between work and social use can become blurred.

With these different generations come different aspirations, expectations, attitudes and values towards work. You might have team members from the different generations who have experienced these differences first hand. As a result, their attitude might be different towards their peers or indeed towards you as their manager.

A new generation is now growing up known as *Generation Z* (or the *i-generation*, meaning the internet generation). They have had lifelong access to technology, the internet and commu-nication tools such as instant messaging, blogs, text messages, Twitter, online videos and social networking. Access to multimedia to such an extent can lead to a change in communication methods, which to other generations can look like a lack of social manners. Communication becomes via technology rather than face to face and can lead to poor spelling and grammar. Personal aspects often take priority over work due to the *immediate* and *switched on* lives they lead. The opposite may also occur such as the desire to check work e-mails in their own time. This generation has been subjected to a fame culture through the many reality television shows and is often influenced by celebrities and fashion. However, an economic downturn may lead to a change in this generation's attitudes, for example their concern for the environment; not being as indulgent as their parents were, and recycling and reusing products.

Example

Marla is an assessor in her late 50s and extremely competent at assessing her subject of Hospitality and Catering. Her organisation wants all staff to use electronic assessment records but Marla is apprehensive as she has not used a computer before. Jon, her manager, asks another assessor, Robbie, who is in his 20s to help her. Robbie is pleased to do this as he has been using computers for many years. Marla was initially concerned and had even considered leaving. However, she finds she gets on very well with Robbie and also learns how to use an e-mail program and the internet. In return she shares a lot of Hospitality and Catering knowledge with him which helps his job role.

One of the greatest differences between Generations X and Y seems to be what they want from work. Generation X is enticed by freedom and independence and get on with their jobs without asking too many questions. Generation Y is more money and lifestyle ori-ented, focused on their own interests and used to 24-hour access to products and ser-vices. Another difference between the two generations relates to the use of technology. Generation Y have been brought up with technology and see it as embedded in, and inte-gral to, their life. They have had the opportunity to use the internet, e-mail and various computer programs at school, and expect to use them at home and work. They embrace new technology with ease, expect instant access to information, use social network sites, and often don't have independent thought or retain information as it is so quick and easy to locate elsewhere. Self-development or self-gain is often part of their motivation and many are reward oriented. To them, their social life comes first. Generation X, in contrast, mainly use technology for convenience, for example online banking and shopping, but it does not play a big part in their social lives.

Having an awareness of these differences might help you understand your team members' strengths and limitations. For example, graduates might be academically qualified but be lacking relevant experience. Older people, although very experienced, might not have the technological skills required. Being aware of this will help you appreciate the different aspirations, expectations, attitudes and values of the different age ranges within your team.

Extension Activity

Research various management theories regarding team work, for example John Adair (2002: John Adair's 100 Greatest Ideas for Effective Leadership and Management), Meredith Belbin (2010: Team Roles At Work) and Handy and Constable (1988: The Making of Managers). You could compare their similarities and differences. Understanding more of the theories of why individuals act the way they do will help you plan the workload to the strengths of your team members.

Monitoring the progress of others and the quality of their work

You must regularly monitor the progress of your team members to ensure they are performing satisfactorily and meeting relevant objectives. Your staff should be aware of what you are monitoring and when, which can be done formally by following your work plans.

When monitoring the progress of staff, you will be looking at the quality of their work, for example how they complete various documents and the amount of detail they write. Records of all formal activities should always be maintained, which can then be used as a basis for improvement and standardisation activities. When monitoring progress, you should talk to your staff and give regular feedback to:

- boost motivation

- build trust and respect

- confirm staff are doing their job correctly

- help overcome resistance to change

- help to avoid potential problems

- help to build a sense of ownership and responsibility

- identify any training and development needs

- improve communication

- reduce potential conflict.

Activity

How will you monitor the work of your staff and what records will you maintain? What will influence how you do this, for example relevant polices and legislation?

There will be internal and external policies, procedures and legislation which will need to be followed. For example, if you lead a team of IQAs, your organisation might require you to observe each one twice per year whether they are experienced or not. You might consider this wrong in that inexperienced staff should be observed more often. Or you might consider it good practice in that everyone is being treated fairly. You will also need to know the limits of your own role and what you can and cannot do in the timescales you have.

Whatever monitoring methods you are using, you are ultimately ensuring your staff are being consistent and accurate with their job role requirements, and are interpreting the qualification criteria correctly (if applicable). The learner is the customer and needs to be treated fairly and ethically by everyone who is in contact with them. You also need to make sure everyone understands and complies with all internal and external requirements. This is particularly important if you are quality assuring accredited qualifications on behalf of an awarding organisation (AO).

Although you are managing a team, you also need to ensure your own performance is meeting the required standards. If there are other IQAs or EQAs in the same subject area as yourself, you can monitor each other. If not, you could ask for feedback from others to help you improve. For example, it could be that you are performing your role adequately, but some staff feel you need to be more accessible when they have urgent questions.

You might have heard of the term *360 degree feedback*, which is a way of evaluating performance. It can contribute to staff appraisals and the self-evaluation process. It includes obtaining feedback from an employee's immediate work circle, for example their subordinates, peers, team members, supervisors and managers. It can also include feedback from external customers, for example via questionnaires and surveys. The rationale for 360 degree feedback is that managers might not always fully understand the workload and contributions of their staff. Feedback from others can be as valuable as traditional hierarchical feedback from managers.

Activity

How do you seek the views of others? Do you have any evidence of obtaining feedback and acting upon it? You could consider issuing a questionnaire to your team members. The results might help you revise the ways you monitor your team and how you delegate activities.

When standards are not maintained

Standards might not be maintained due to a lack of skills or knowledge by team members, or a lack of communication from managers. Identifying any issues early on can enable staff training and development to take place. The issues can then be used to standardise practice within the team to ensure it does not happen again. When allocating work to staff, you need to identify any individual skill shortages. This could mean you cannot deploy someone as you would like to, or they could be placed in a difficult situation that they cannot manage.

It is good practice to consult your team members regarding the ways you will monitor their performance. You also need to be clear about what will happen if they don't meet the standards or are performing poorly. It could simply be a need for further training and development, or it could be a more serious matter.

Monitoring your team members' performance and progress will help ensure the learners are receiving a good quality service. It should also identify any concerns that can be dealt with immediately to alleviate any learner appeals or complaints.

Unsatisfactory performance

Unsatisfactory performance could be due to many reasons, perhaps personal or professional. This could be an individual's fault, for example not being honest with regard to their knowledge when they applied for the position, or it could be the fault of the organisation by not conveying crucial information, for example when a policy has changed. Recruiting and retaining staff who have the necessary experience, knowledge and skills will hopefully keep staff turnover low. Investing in training and ongoing support for your team members should enable them to carry out their job role effectively. However, there may be times when an individual does not perform satisfactorily.

There should be a policy within your organisation for dealing with unsatisfactory performance which might lead to disciplinary action if an individual does not conform. If an individual's performance is not up to standard, an informal discussion could take place first to establish the reasons and agree necessary action. If the action cannot be reasonably achieved due to individual circumstances, the staff member should be given the opportunity of support, such as further training or assistance. In more serious circumstances, they could be offered a reduction in their workload, or counselling or stress management.

Disciplinary action could occur if the individual's performance constitutes misconduct. There will be organisational procedures to follow and the process might be linked to performance appraisals and reviews. Formal records should always be maintained and relevant employment law followed.

Hopefully, your staff member will improve, make progress and meet the standards required. However, if you don't wish to follow your organisation's disciplinary procedure, you might be able to offer them a different job role or look at reducing their workload or hours. There are many reasons why someone might not be performing well and these should all be taken into consideration. You will need to liaise with relevant personnel in your organisation, such as those from Human Resources, to ensure any contracts and/or terms of employment/equality legislation have not been breached.

Unsatisfactory performance of an individual could reflect badly on you and your organisation. It is therefore important to identify any issues quickly, discover the causes and put an action plan in place to rectify the problem. If staff members are not performing adequately, there will be an impact upon others.

Activity

What do you consider to be poor performance and how would you deal with it? What relevant policies are in place for you to ensure the satisfactory performance of your staff?

Armstrong (2003) suggests the following guidelines for defining effective individual performance.

- Measures should relate to results, not efforts.

- The results must be within the individual's or team's control.

- Measures should be objective and observable.

- Data must be openly available for measurement.

- Existing measures should be used or adopted wherever possible.

Performance measures should always be discussed during staff appraisals and you should monitor the progress of individuals and teams towards them. There is no point making these measures unobtainable as you could be setting your staff up to fail. You are there to support your staff, not make things difficult for them.

Extension Activity

How do you decide upon the standards of performance for the individuals and teams you have responsibility for? Do you discuss them with your staff and give them a copy? What methods do you use to monitor them and how effective do you think your methods are?

Communication skills

Communication is the key to effective management of your team. The four skills of language are *speaking*, *listening*, *reading* and *writing*. Using these effectively in various ways should help with the achievement of the activities you expect your team members to carry out. Different methods of communication can be used depending upon the situation or person, for example if a staff member does not have access to e-mail.

Methods of communication include written and oral, for example:

- e-mail, texts or social networking – to quickly pass on information to the full team

- face to face – meetings or staff appraisals, in person or electronically

- intranet, web or cloud based – updated documents, policies and procedures

- newsletters – bulletins and updates (hard copy or electronic)

- notice boards – displaying work plans and information for staff

- telephone – a call to check on a team member's progress

- written – letters, memos, reports and minutes (hard copy or electronic).

Example

Imran needs to notify his team quickly of a change to a meeting date. He e-mails and sends a text to all the team members. He also telephones two members who he knows don't have direct access to e-mail or text messages. In this way he has used several communication methods to meet the needs of his team.

You will need to develop the skills which enable you to use all the methods of communication which are practical, and to decide which is the most suitable for a particular situation and person. You should weigh up the advantages and limitations of the different methods and consider if you need any training, for example in using new technology. In some cases, more than one method of communication may be needed. For example, you might have an informal discussion with team members and follow this up with an e-mail to confirm what was decided.

The way you communicate with your team might be influenced by your personality. For example, you might prefer to use e-mails rather than the telephone or text messages. Whichever method you use, you need to make sure that what you convey is understood and acted upon by everyone. You need to be seen as a respected and trusted source of accurate information. You might not be liked by everyone in your team. However, you are performing a professional role and you are not there to be everyone's friend. Don't take it personally if you feel someone does not like you; it is probably the situation they don't like rather than you as a person.

You need to be aware of your verbal and non-verbal body language, for example not folding your arms when speaking as this could look defensive. You also need to take into account the way you speak and act, as your mannerisms might be misinterpreted by others.

Activity

Think back to the last time you communicated with your team members, perhaps during a meeting. How did you act and react to different people and situations? Why was this, and would you do anything differently at the next meeting?

Records should always be maintained of all formal communications. This will enable them to be referred to at a later date, for example if there is any doubt about what was actually said in a meeting or if actions which should have been completed have not been. Informal communications can be more personal and may be quicker if you need to get your team members to react immediately to new information. However, not having a record could prove disadvantageous if a team member has no recollection of you asking them to do something. This would be of particular importance if any issues result in disciplinary action.

Skills of communicating effectively include the way you speak, listen and express yourself, for example with non-verbal language. Understanding a little about your own personal communication style will help you create a lasting impression upon your team members.

Interpersonal and intrapersonal skills

A way of differentiating between interpersonal and intrapersonal skills is to regard interpersonal skills as *between people* and intrapersonal skills as *being within a person*. Understanding and using these skills will help you develop a range of creative communication techniques appropriate to the activities you require your team members to perform.

Interpersonal skills are about the ability to recognise distinctions between other people, to know their faces and voices, to react appropriately to their needs, to understand their motives, feelings and moods, and to appreciate such perspectives with sensitivity and empathy. Possessing interpersonal skills will help you develop personal and professional relationships.

Ways to improve interpersonal skills include:

- being a mentor to others

- getting organised

- meeting new people at work, social groups, clubs, meetings, etc.

- participating in workshops or seminars in interpersonal and communication skills

- spending time each day practising active listening skills with friends, family, colleagues, etc.

- starting a support/network group.

Intrapersonal skills are about having the ability to be reflective and access your inner feelings. Having this ability will enable you to recognise and change your own behaviour, build upon your strengths and improve your limitations. This should result in quick developments and achievements as people have a strong ability to learn from past events and from others.

Ways to improve intrapersonal skills include:

- attending courses, for example Neuro Linguistic Programming (NLP), Transactional Analysis (TA) and Emotional Intelligence (EI)

- creating a personal development plan

- developing an interest or hobby

- keeping a reflective learning journal

- meditation, or quiet time alone to think and reflect

- observing people who are great leaders, motivators or positive thinkers

- reading self-help books

- setting short- and long-term goals and following these through.

Howard Gardner (1993) defines intrapersonal intelligence as: *sensitivity to our own feelings, our own wants and fears, our own personal histories, an awareness of our own strengths and weaknesses, plans and goals* (1993, p263). He is best known for his theory of multiple intelligences of which there are eight, interpersonal and intrapersonal being two of them. The other six are:

- linguistic – the ability to use language to codify and remember information; to communicate, explain and convince

- logical (also known as mathematical intelligence) – the capacity to perceive sequence, pattern and order, and to use these observations to explain, extrapolate and predict

- musical – the capacity to distinguish the whole realm of sound and, in particular, to discern, appreciate and apply the various aspects of music (pitch, rhythm, timbre and mood), both separately and holistically

- naturalist – the ability to recognise, appreciate, and understand the natural world; it involves such capacities as species discernment and discrimination, the ability to recognise and classify various flora and fauna, and knowledge of and communion with the natural world

- physical (also called kinaesthetic intelligence) – the ability to use one's body in highly differentiated and skilled ways, for both goal-oriented and expressive purposes; the capacity to exercise fine and gross motor control

- visual-spatial – the ability to accurately perceive the visual world and to re-create, manipulate and modify aspects of one's perceptions.

According to Gardner, individuals possess all of these intelligences. However, they are not all present in equal proportions (in extreme circumstances it may appear that an individual is severely lacking in one or more). The particular combination of intelligences and their relative strengths can form a profile that is unique to each individual. Some people are more intelligent than their peers; others appear superior at certain tasks, are more capable of manipulating information or more readily see the solutions to problems. Others are more expressive or more capable of learning new tasks quickly.

Being aware of differing intelligences within your team members, and in yourself, will help you consider alternative ways of communicating with your staff. Gardner's eight intelligences have been debated and amended by many other theorists over time. They can be compared to various learning preference theories, for example Honey and Mumford's (1986) Activist, Pragmatist, Reflector and Theorist.

Extension Activity

Consider how you will communicate with your team members. Do you prefer a formal or informal approach and why? Review the theories mentioned so far in this chapter and state how they might influence the way you act and react with your staff.

Updating the work plan

Your original work plan may need updating at some point due to unforeseen circumstances such as a team member leaving or an external inspection. All changes will need to be communicated to your team members via the next team meeting or by another quicker appropriate method such as telephone or e-mail.

As a manager you should keep up to date regarding what is happening in your area of responsibility and within your organisation. This also means keeping up to date with changes to the qualification or the subject being assessed and quality assured. If your team is working with accredited qualifications, you will need to ensure they all read the latest updates from the AO. It is useful to sign up for newsletters and check websites regularly. Any developments should be discussed at team meetings and minutes distributed.

Examples of factors that will necessitate a change to your work plan include:

- a report requiring immediate action
- an increase in learners and/or staff
- changes to funding
- developments with resources, i.e. new technology
- external inspections
- financial or budget constraints
- organisational developments, i.e. additional locations for assessment
- policy and procedural changes
- qualification changes
- staff turnover
- targets not being met
- updated documentation.

Activity

What situations might occur within your organisation which would necessitate a change to your work plan? How would you update your work plan and how would you communicate the changes to your team?

If you are involved in communications from those in higher positions than yourself, you should be kept up to date with what is happening in your organisation. If you don't attend all the meetings or read e-mails and updates, you might not know about any important developments. When changes do occur, it is best that you convey them to your team members rather than have them hear rumours that might not be true, for example a takeover bid or possible redundancies.

When amending your work plan, if it is a hard copy, try not to use correction fluid, but cross out and rewrite any changes to allow the original information to still be seen. This is useful in case of any queries as to why activities were changed or what the original dates were. If you are using an electronic work plan, you can resave it as a different version with a new date. However, do keep a note of which is the latest version in case you accidentally refer to an outdated one.

Your work plans should be regularly reviewed to make sure that they are still fit for purpose, and updated to meet changes and new circumstances. When amending your plans, you are likely to be more successful if you include your team members in the making of major decisions rather than imposing changes upon them. As their job roles will be affected directly, discussing these and communicating with your team on an ongoing basis could help alleviate future problems.

Example

Celina needed to amend her observation work plan for her team of ten assessors due to her relocation to the company's European site for two months. She sent an e-mail to all those whom she was due to observe during that time giving them a new date. Almost immediately, she received replies from nearly all her assessors stating the dates were not suitable. On reflection, Celina should have asked her team members first for suitable alternative dates. She would then not have had to deal with several annoyed individuals as well as wasting her time making rearrangements.

Communication is a two-way process and at some point you will have to reallocate staff responsibilities. However, if you can do this by agreement rather than imposition you should maintain the respect and support of your team members. If you do have to impose a change on an individual, try to do so with tact and diplomacy. Tell your team members why you are making the changes and that you need their support. Some people might resist change as they are comfortable with the way they currently do things. During meetings you could stress that change is inevitable in training and education and that you all need to react to it in a positive way. Treating change as an opportunity for improvement can be enlightening and motivating. Ensuring your team members, including you yourself, remain current in their practice should help towards a smoother transition when any changes do take place.

When staff decide to leave your organisation, you will need to plan who will take over their workload and ensure there is a smooth transition so as not to disadvantage anyone.

Feedback and conflict

You should give ongoing informal feedback to your team members as well as formal feedback. If there is a culture of giving constant feedback, your team members are more likely to listen and respond to your comments. Feedback should always be constructive and developmental and should be given individually when possible, and to teams perhaps during a meeting.

There is a chance that in some organisations feedback is only given in formal situations, such as staff appraisals after an observation or a sampling activity. If this is the case, individuals might come to dread the formal meeting as they may feel they have done something wrong. Giving praise and clarifying situations when you have the opportunity should help motivate your staff. Individuals need to know what they are doing right, as well as what they are doing wrong. Creating a culture of giving and receiving regular feedback will help break down barriers, increase motivation and encourage staff to feel valued. This can contribute to positive working relationships and can make more formal feedback sessions, such as staff appraisals, run more smoothly.

Example

Keiran was walking past a training room and noticed a group of learners who were becoming rather disruptive. He saw Alfons, their assessor, immediately deal with the situation. When Keiran next saw Alfons in the corridor, he said how pleased he was that the situation had been dealt with in a quick and amicable manner. This left Alfons feeling that what he had done was worthwhile and had been noticed.

According to Kermally (2002), apart from being ongoing, feedback should also be a development tool. It should allow skills gaps in teams and individuals to be identified and provide opportunities for the necessary skills to be acquired. Carrying out staff appraisals should be seen as a positive way of discussing a person's job role, any concerns they might have and identifying any training needs. If action points are agreed, these should always be followed up by both parties.

Conflict can arise when an individual or a group believe that someone has done (or is about to do) something with which they disagree. It could be something minor, such as an individual sitting in another's usual seat at a meeting. Or it could be more serious, such as a dispute over who carries out certain tasks. There could be challenges and barriers that your staff might face which you were not aware of, for example transport issues. This might involve you reallocating staff to make the location more accessible to them. A team member might have a complaint or grievance against another team member and it might be your responsibility to deal with it. You should always base your judgement upon facts after listening to both sides, remain impartial, and be fair and ethical with your decision. Make sure you keep records for future reference in case of any queries.

Mullins (2004) identified a range of potential sources of conflict with individuals, groups and organisations.

Individuals may come into conflict because they have different attitudes, personality styles or particular needs. In some instances, the situation might be aggravated by stress or illness. One team member, for example, may perceive quality assurance activities in a different way to another. A reason for different attitudes can be the age gaps between different individuals. An older person might feel they have the necessary skills, knowledge and experience, but the power and responsibility might lie with a younger person.

Groups might come into conflict because individuals have different skills, attitudes and ways of working. Team members might interpret tasks in different ways, new staff might feel excluded or a key person might be absent. Organisation characteristics, for example the hierarchy structure, management or leadership styles, can create conflict. This could result in differences and disagreements between departments or teams within the organisation.

Sometimes, simple situations can easily lead to conflict if they are not dealt with immediately or are misinterpreted. Ongoing communication and feedback should help confirm your expectations of your team members and their expectations of you. Always establish the root cause of any situation that leads to conflict to work out a strategy that will resolve it. Opportunities should be taken to clarify any misunderstandings and the whole team should be informed to ensure everyone is working to the same ethos. Allowing conflict to worsen over time can lead to a situation becoming much more difficult to resolve. Conflict can also affect others who are not directly involved in the original situation. For example, if you don't take any action, your own manager might perceive you as being ineffective. This could affect the confidence they have in you as a manager, and it could also affect the respect you have from your team members.

Extension Activity

Refer to your original work plans created earlier on in this chapter. What changes would you make to them now that you have been using them for a while? What developments might occur in the future which would require you to amend them? Will you act differently with your team members now that you have gained further knowledge of communication techniques?

Summary

In this chapter you have learnt about:

- producing and using a work plan
- identifying and allocating responsibilities to team members
- monitoring the progress of others and the quality of their work
- communication skills
- updating the work plan.

Evidence

Evidence from the completed activities within this chapter, plus the following, could be used towards the *Plan, allocate and monitor work* unit, for example:

- detailed work plans with reviews and amendments
- reports you have produced
- list of priorities, SMART objectives and success criteria for team members

- list of your own and team members' responsibilities
- records of monitoring and evaluating team members' work towards agreed targets
- minutes of team meetings
- records of standardisation activities
- list of resources (human and physical)
- records of communication with staff such as e-mails, memos, etc.
- records of giving support, advice and guidance to staff
- records of problems or critical incidents with actions taken
- written statements cross-referenced to the unit's assessment criteria
- answers to questions issued by your assessor
- records of discussions with your assessor.

Cross-referencing grid

This chapter contributes towards the following assessment criteria, along with aspects of the National Occupational Standards for Learning and Development, and the Management Standards. Full details of the learning outcomes and assessment criteria for each unit can be found in the Appendices.

Unit	Assessment criteria
Principles and practices of internally assuring the quality of assessment	2.1, 2.3 4.1 6.1, 6.3
Internally assuring the quality of assessment	1.1, 1.2 2.1, 2.2 3.1 4.1 5.1, 5.3, 5.4
Plan, allocate and monitor work	1.1, 1.2, 1.3, 1.4 2.1, 2.2 3.1, 3.2 4.1, 4.2
National Occupational Standards	**Reference**
9 – Assess learner achievement	9.3, 9.4, 9.8 KU3, KU8, KU10, KU15, KU16, KU17, KU18

(Continued)

(Continued)

11 – Internally monitor and maintain the quality of assessment	11.1, 11.2, 11.3, 11.4, 11.5, 11.7, 11.8, 11.9, 11.10, 11.11 KU1, KU2, KU3, KU7, KU8, KU11, KU13, KU14, KU15, KU16, KU17, KU18
12 – Externally monitor and maintain the quality of assessment	12.3, 12.4, 12.5, 12.6, 12.7 KU4, KU5, KU6, KU8, KU10, KU11, KU13, KU14, KU16, KU17

Management standards	Reference	
D5 – Allocate and check work in your team	Outcomes	1, 2, 3, 4, 5, 6, 7, 8, 9, 10, 11, 12, 13
	Behaviours	1, 2, 3, 4, 5, 6, 7, 8, 9, 10
	Knowledge and understanding	1, 2, 3, 4, 5, 6, 7, 8, 9, 10, 11, 12, 13, 14, 15, 16, 17, 18
D6 – Allocate and monitor the progress and quality of work in your area of responsibility	Outcomes	1, 2, 3, 4, 5, 6, 7, 8, 9, 10, 11, 12, 13, 14
	Behaviours	1, 2, 3, 4, 5, 6, 7, 8, 9, 10, 11, 12
	Knowledge and understanding	1, 2, 3, 4, 5, 6, 7, 8, 9, 10, 11, 12, 13, 14, 15, 16, 17, 18, 19, 20, 21

Theory focus

References and further information

Adair, J (2002) *John Adair's 100 Greatest Ideas for Effective Leadership and Management*. Mankato: Capstone.

Armstrong, M (2003) *A Handbook of Human Resource Management*. London: Kogan Page.

Armstrong, M (2008) *How To Be An Even Better Manager* (7th edition). London: Kogan Page.

Bacal, R (1998) *Performance Management*. New York: McGraw-Hill.

Belbin, M (2010) *Team Roles At Work* (2nd edition). Oxford: Butterworth-Heinemann.

Berne, E (1973) *Games People Play: The Psychology of Human Relationships*. London: Penguin Books.

Coverdale, R (1977) *Risk Thinking*. Bradford: The Coverdale Organisation.

Douglass, M and Douglass, D (1993) *Manage Your Time, Your Work, Your Self*. New York: Amacom.

Friedman, M (1996) *Type A Behaviour: Its Diagnosis and Treatment*. New York: Plenum Press.

Gardner, H (1993) *Frames of Mind: Theory of Multiple Intelligences*. New York: Basic Books.

Handy, C and Constable, J (1988) *The Making of Managers*. London: Longman.

Honey, P (2001) *Improve Your People Skills* (2nd edition). London: CIPD.

Honey, P and Mumford, A (1986) *Manual of Learning Styles*. Coventry: Peter Honey Publications.

Kennedy, C (2007) *Guide to the Management Gurus* (5th edition). London: Random House.

Kermally, S (2002) Appraising Employee Performance. *Professional Manager*, 11(4): 30–31.

Leitch, S (2006) *Review of Skills: Prosperity For All in the Global Economy; World Class Skills*. London: HM Treasury.

Mullins, LJ (2004) *Management and Organisational Behaviour* (7th edition). London: Prentice Hall.

Skinner, BF (1968) *The Technology of Teaching*. New York: Appleton, Century & Crofts.

Wallace, S and Gravells, J (2007) *Leadership and Leading Teams*. London: Learning Matters SAGE.

Wallace, S and Gravells, J (2007) *Mentoring*. London: Learning Matters SAGE.

Websites

360 degree feedback: www.cipd.co.uk/hr-resources/factsheets/360-degree-feedback.aspx

Carl Jung: www.cgjungpage.org/

Gantt charts: www.mindtools.com/pages/article/newPPM_03.htm

Institute of Leadership and Management: www.i-l-m.com

Kiersey temperament theory: www.kiersey.com

Myers-Briggs Type Indicator: www.myersbriggs.org

SWOT analysis: www.businessballs.com/swotanalysisfreetemplate.htm

Tuckman: www.infed.org/thinkers/tuckman.htm

Work plans: http://cec.vcn.bc.ca/cmp/modules/pm-pln.htm

Skype: www.skype.com

Webex: www.webex.com

UNIT I: Understanding the principles and practices of assessment

LEVEL 3 (3 credits)

Learning outcomes The learner will:	Assessment criteria The learner can:	
I. Understand the principles and requirements of assessment	1.1	Explain the function of assessment in learning and development
	1.2	Define the key concepts and principles of assessment
	1.3	Explain the responsibilities of the assessor
	1.4	Identify the regulations and requirements relevant to the assessment in own area of practice
2. Understand different types of assessment method	2.1	Compare the strengths and limitations of a range of assessment methods with reference to the needs of individual learners
3. Understand how to plan assessment	3.1	Summarise key factors to consider when planning assessment
	3.2	Evaluate the benefits of using a holistic approach to assessment
	3.3	Explain how to plan a holistic approach to assessment
	3.4	Summarise the types of risks that may be involved in assessment in own area of responsibility
	3.5	Explain how to minimise risks through the planning process

Learning outcomes The learner will:	Assessment criteria The learner can:	
4. Understand how to involve learners and others in assessment	4.1	Explain the importance of involving the learner and others in the assessment process
	4.2	Summarise types of information that should be made available to learners and others involved in the assessment process
	4.3	Explain how peer and self-assessment can be used effectively to promote learner involvement and personal responsibility in the assessment of learning
	4.4	Explain how assessment arrangements can be adapted to meet the needs of individual learners
5. Understand how to make assessment decisions	5.1	Explain how to judge whether evidence is: • sufficient • authentic • current
	5.2	Explain how to ensure that assessment decisions are: • made against specified criteria • valid • reliable • fair
6. Understand quality assurance of the assessment process	6.1	Evaluate the importance of quality assurance in the assessment process
	6.2	Summarise quality assurance and standardisation procedures in own area of practice
	6.3	Summarise the procedures to follow when there are disputes concerning assessment in own area of practice
7. Understand how to manage information relating to assessment	7.1	Explain the importance of following procedures for the management of information relating to assessment
	7.2	Explain how feedback and questioning contribute to the assessment process
8. Understand the legal and good practice requirements in relation to assessment	8.1	Explain legal issues, policies and procedures relevant to assessment, including those for confidentiality, health, safety and welfare
	8.2	Explain the contribution that technology can make to the assessment process
	8.3	Evaluate requirements for equality and diversity and, where appropriate, bilingualism in relation to assessment
	8.4	Explain the value of reflective practice and continuing professional development in the assessment process

UNIT 2: Assess occupational competence in the work environment

LEVEL 3 (6 credits)

Learning outcomes The learner will:		Assessment criteria The learner can:
1. Be able to plan the assessment of occupational competence	1.1	Plan assessment of occupational competence based on the following methods: • observation of performance in the work environment • examining products of work • questioning the learner • discussing with the learner • use of others (witness testimony) • looking at learner statements • recognising prior learning
	1.2	Communicate the purpose, requirements and processes of assessing occupational competence to the learner
	1.3	Plan the assessment of occupational competence to address learner needs and current achievements
	1.4	Identify opportunities for holistic assessment
2. Be able to make assessment decisions about occupational competence	2.1	Use valid, fair and reliable assessment methods including: • observation of performance • examining products of work • questioning the learner • discussing with the learner • use of others (witness testimony) • looking at learner statements • recognising prior learning

Learning outcomes The learner will:	Assessment criteria The learner can:	
	2.2	Make assessment decisions of occupational competence against specified criteria
	2.3	Follow standardisation procedures
	2.4	Provide feedback to learners that affirms achievement and identifies any further implications for learning, assessment and progression
3. Be able to provide required information following the assessment of occupational competence	3.1	Maintain records of the assessment of occupational competence, its outcomes and learner progress
	3.2	Make assessment information available to authorised colleagues
	3.3	Follow procedures to maintain the confidentiality of assessment information
4. Be able to maintain legal and good practice requirements when assessing occupational competence	4.1	Follow relevant policies, procedures and legislation for the assessment of occupational competence, including those for health, safety and welfare
	4.2	Apply requirements for equality and diversity and, where appropriate, bilingualism, when assessing occupational competence
	4.3	Evaluate own work in carrying out assessments of occupational competence
	4.4	Maintain the currency of own expertise and competence as relevant to own role in assessing occupational competence

UNIT 3: Assess vocational skills, knowledge and understanding

LEVEL 3 (6 credits)

Learning outcomes The learner will:		Assessment criteria The learner can:
1. Be able to prepare assessments of vocational skills, knowledge and understanding	1.1	Select methods to assess vocational skills, knowledge and understanding which address learner needs and meet assessment requirements, including: • assessments of the learner in simulated environments • skills tests • oral and written questions • assignments • projects • case studies • recognising prior learning
	1.2	Prepare resources and conditions for the assessment of vocational skills, knowledge and understanding
	1.3	Communicate the purpose, requirements and processes of assessment of vocational skills, knowledge and understanding to learners
2. Be able to carry out assessments of vocational skills, knowledge and understanding	2.1	Manage assessments of vocational skills, knowledge and understanding to meet assessment requirements
	2.2	Provide support to learners within agreed limitations
	2.3	Analyse evidence of learner achievement
	2.4	Make assessment decisions relating to vocational skills, knowledge and understanding against specified criteria
	2.5	Follow standardisation procedures
	2.6	Provide feedback to the learner that affirms achievement and identifies any further implications for learning, assessment and progression

Learning outcomes The learner will:	Assessment criteria The learner can:	
3. Be able to provide required information following the assessment of vocational skills, knowledge and understanding	3.1	Maintain records of the assessment of vocational skills, knowledge and understanding, its outcomes and learner progress
	3.2	Make assessment information available to authorised colleagues as required
	3.3	Follow procedures to maintain the confidentiality of assessment information
4. Be able to maintain legal and good practice requirements when assessing vocational skills, knowledge and understanding	4.1	Follow relevant policies, procedures and legislation relating to the assessment of vocational skills, knowledge and understanding, including those for health, safety and welfare
	4.2	Apply requirements for equality and diversity and, where appropriate, bilingualism
	4.3	Evaluate own work in carrying out assessments of vocational skills, knowledge and understanding
	4.4	Take part in continuing professional development to ensure current expertise and competence in assessing vocational skills, knowledge and understanding

UNIT 4: Understanding the principles and practices of internally assuring the quality of assessment

LEVEL 4 (6 credits)

Learning outcomes The learner will:		Assessment criteria The learner can:
1. Understand the context and principles of internal quality assurance	1.1	Explain the functions of internal quality assurance in learning and development
	1.2	Explain the key concepts and principles of the internal quality assurance of assessment
	1.3	Explain the roles of practitioners involved in the internal and external quality assurance process
	1.4	Explain the regulations and requirements for internal quality assurance in own area of practice
2. Understand how to plan the internal quality assurance of assessment	2.1	Evaluate the importance of planning and preparing internal quality assurance activities
	2.2	Explain what an internal quality assurance plan should contain
	2.3	Summarise the preparations that need to be made for internal quality assurance, including: • information collection • communications • administrative arrangements • resources
3. Understand techniques and criteria for monitoring the quality of assessment internally	3.1	Evaluate different techniques for sampling evidence of assessment, including use of technology
	3.2	Explain the appropriate criteria to use for judging the quality of the assessment process

Learning outcomes The learner will:	Assessment criteria The learner can:	
4. Understand how to internally maintain and improve the quality of assessment	4.1	Summarise the types of feedback, support and advice that assessors may need to maintain and improve the quality of assessment
	4.2	Explain standardisation requirements in relation to assessment
	4.3	Explain relevant procedures regarding disputes about the quality of assessment
5. Understand how to manage information relevant to the internal quality assurance of assessment	5.1	Evaluate requirements for information management, data protection and confidentiality in relation to the internal quality assurance of assessment
6. Understand the legal and good practice requirements for the internal quality assurance of assessment	6.1	Evaluate legal issues, policies and procedures relevant to the internal quality assurance of assessment, including those for health, safety and welfare
	6.2	Evaluate different ways in which technology can contribute to the internal quality assurance of assessment
	6.3	Explain the value of reflective practice and continuing professional development in relation to internal quality assurance
	6.4	Evaluate requirements for equality and diversity and, where appropriate, bilingualism, in relation to the internal quality assurance of assessment

UNIT 5: Internally assure the quality of assessment

LEVEL 4 (6 credits)

Learning outcomes The learner will:		Assessment criteria The learner can:
1. Plan the internal quality assurance of assessment	1.1	Plan monitoring activities according to the requirements of own role
	1.2	Make arrangements for internal monitoring activities to assure quality
2. Internally evaluate the quality of assessment	2.1	Carry out internal monitoring activities to quality requirements
	2.2	Evaluate assessor expertise and competence in relation to the requirements of their role
	2.3	Evaluate the planning and preparation of assessment processes
	2.4	Determine whether assessment methods are safe, fair, valid and reliable
	2.5	Determine whether assessment decisions are made using the specified criteria
	2.6	Compare assessor decisions to ensure they are consistent
3. Internally maintain and improve the quality of assessment	3.1	Provide assessors with feedback, advice and support, including professional development opportunities, which help them to maintain and improve the quality of assessment
	3.2	Apply procedures to standardise assessment practices and outcomes

Learning outcomes The learner will:	Assessment criteria The learner can:	
4. Manage information relevant to the internal quality assurance of assessment	4.1	Apply procedures for recording, storing and reporting information relating to internal quality assurance
	4.2	Follow procedures to maintain confidentiality of internal quality assurance information
5. Maintain legal and good practice requirements when internally monitoring and maintaining the quality of assessment	5.1	Apply relevant policies, procedures and legislation in relation to internal quality assurance, including those for health, safety and welfare
	5.2	Apply requirements for equality and diversity and, where appropriate, bilingualism, in relation to internal quality assurance
	5.3	Critically reflect on own practice in internally assuring the quality of assessment
	5.4	Maintain the currency of own expertise and competence in internally assuring the quality of assessment

UNIT 6: Understanding the principles and practices of externally assuring the quality of assessment

LEVEL 4 (6 credits)

Learning outcomes The learner will:	Assessment criteria The learner can:	
1. Understand the context and principles of external quality assurance	1.1	Analyse the functions of external quality assurance of assessment in learning and development
	1.2	Evaluate the key concepts and principles of external quality assurance of assessment
	1.3	Evaluate the roles of practitioners involved in the quality assurance process
	1.4	Explain the regulations and requirements for external and internal quality assurance in own area of practice
2. Understand how to plan the external quality assurance of assessment	2.1	Evaluate the importance of planning and preparing external quality assurance activities
	2.2	Explain what an external quality assurance plan should contain
	2.3	Summarise the preparations that need to be made for external quality assurance activities, including: • information collection • communications • administrative arrangements • resources
	2.4	Explain how to adapt external monitoring and evaluation approaches to meet customer need without compromising quality standards

Learning outcomes The learner will:	Assessment criteria The learner can:	
3. Understand how to externally evaluate the quality of assessment and internal quality assurance	3.1	Explain the procedures for externally monitoring and evaluating internal quality assurance arrangements and practices
	3.2	Interpret the requirements for externally monitoring and evaluating internal assessment arrangements and practices
	3.3	Evaluate different techniques for externally sampling evidence of assessment, including those that use technology
4. Understand how to externally maintain and improve the quality of assessment	4.1	Critically compare the types of feedback, support and advice that internal assessment and quality assurance staff may need to maintain and improve the quality of assessment
	4.2	Evaluate standardisation requirements relevant to the external quality assurance of assessment
	4.3	Explain the importance of providing feedback, support and advice to internal assessment and quality assurance staff that is consistent with standardisation requirements
	4.4	Explain the relevant procedures to follow when there are disputes concerning quality assurance and assessment
5. Understand how to manage information relevant to external quality assurance	5.1	Evaluate the requirements for information management, data protection and confidentiality in relation to external quality assurance
6. Understand the legal and good practice requirements relating to external quality assurance	6.1	Evaluate legal issues, policies and procedures that are relevant to external quality assurance, including those for health, safety and welfare
	6.2	Critically compare different ways in which technology can contribute to external quality assurance
	6.3	Evaluate requirements for equality and diversity and, where appropriate, bilingualism, in relation to the external quality assurance of assessment
	6.4	Explain the value of reflective practice and continuing professional development in relation to external quality assurance

UNIT 7: Externally assure the quality of assessment

LEVEL 4 (6 credits)

Learning outcomes The learner will:		Assessment criteria The learner can:
1. Be able to plan the external quality assurance of assessment	1.1	Plan procedures for the external quality assurance of assessment
	1.2	Communicate procedures for external quality assurance to the organisations and individuals concerned
	1.3	Ensure arrangements and resources are in place for external monitoring and evaluation
2. Be able to externally evaluate internal quality assurance and assessment	2.1	Carry out monitoring activities to quality requirements
	2.2	Evaluate the quality of internal quality assurance systems
	2.3	Evaluate the quality of internal administrative arrangements
	2.4	Evaluate the quality of internal staffing and internal staff expertise and competence
	2.5	Determine whether assessment arrangements, methods and decisions meet quality requirements
3. Be able to maintain and improve internal quality assurance processes	3.1	Provide staff with feedback, advice and support which help them maintain and improve the quality of assessment
	3.2	Apply procedures for the standardisation of assessment practices and outcomes

Learning outcomes The learner will:	Assessment criteria The learner can:	
4. Be able to manage information relevant to the external quality assurance of assessment	4.1	Apply procedures for recording, storing and reporting information relating to external quality assurance
	4.2	Apply procedures to maintain confidentiality of information relating to external quality assurance
5. Be able to maintain legal and good practice requirements when externally monitoring and maintaining the quality of assessment	5.1	Apply policies, procedures and legislation relevant to the external quality assurance of assessment, including those for health, safety and welfare
	5.2	Apply requirements for equality and diversity and, where appropriate, bilingualism, to the external quality assurance of assessment
	5.3	Critically reflect on own practice in externally assuring the quality of assessment
	5.4	Maintain the currency of own expertise and competence as relevant to external quality assurance

UNIT 8: Plan, allocate and monitor work in own area of responsibility

LEVEL 4 (5 credits)

Learning outcomes The learner will:		Assessment criteria The learner can:
1. Produce a work plan for own area of responsibility	1.1	Explain the context in which work is to be undertaken
	1.2	Identify the skills base and the resources available
	1.3	Examine priorities and success criteria needed for the team
	1.4	Produce a work plan for own area of responsibility
2. Allocate and agree responsibilities with team members	2.1	Identify team members' responsibilities for identified work activities
	2.2	Agree responsibilities and SMART (*Specific, Measurable, Achievable, Realistic and Time bound*) objectives with team members
3. Monitor the progress and quality of work in own area of responsibility and provide feedback	3.1	Identify ways to monitor progress and quality of work
	3.2	Monitor and evaluate progress against agreed standards and provide feedback to team members
4. Review and amend plans of work for own area of responsibility and communicate changes	4.1	Review and amend work plan where changes are needed
	4.2	Communicate changes to team members

formal assessments 28–9, 86–7
  ensuring authenticity 62, 64, 77–8, 81, 106–8
formative assessment 14, 29, 85, 111, 160
  activities 21, 86, 87, 91
  questioning techniques 103–6
Freedom of Information Act (2000) 79, 127, 178

G

Gardner, Howard 165, 246
General Conditions of Recognition (Ofqual) 176
Goleman, Daniel 165–6
grades
  analysing learner achievement 110–12
  awarding 62, 105, 106
Grinder, John 164, 165
group work 64, 87

H

health and safety 23, 26, 128, 178, 181
holistic assessment planning 58–9
homework 106

I

ICT 108–9, 141–2, 186–7
  see also technology
improvement points 188, 202, 219–20
inclusion 56–7, 61, 103–4
informal assessments 28–9
information management, EQAs 224–5
initial assessment 29
  occupational competence 50, 52, 54–5
interim sampling 157
internal moderation 160
Internal quality assurance of assessment processes
  and practice: Level 4 Award 5
internal quality assurance (IQA)
  appeals and complaints 142–3
  definition 27, 122–3
  evaluation 143–8
  key concepts 126–8
  key principles 128–9
  maintaining and improving quality of assessment
    139–41
  monitoring assessment activities 153–60
  process 130–3
  rationale 129
  record-keeping 170–1
  regulations 125
  role of ICT 141–2
  sampling 133–9, 157, 160–1
  strategy 132–3
  see also internal quality assurers (IQAs); planning IQA
internal quality assurers (IQAs)
  communication with assessors 163–7
  decision making 160–3
  providing feedback 156, 157, 168–70
  qualifications 4–5, 124
  roles and responsibilities 123–5, 151–2
Internally assure the quality of assessment (Unit 5)
  4–5, 151, 262–3

internet see technology
interpersonal and intrapersonal skills 245–6
interview checklists (EQA) 212–14

J

job specifications
  assessors 17–20
  EQAs 199
  IQAs 151–2
  managers 229
  workplace assessment 14

K

Keirsey's Temperament Sorter 234–5
Kermally 249
knowledge-based units 2, 4, 5, 7
  assessment 29, 56

L

Leading the external quality assurance of assessment
    processes and practice: Level 4 Certificate 6
Leading the internal quality assurance of
    assessment processes and practice: Level 4
    Certificate 5
learners
  accommodating needs of 57–8
  feedback from 75, 98
  inclusion 56–7, 61, 103–4
  reviewing progress 96–9
  support for 99–103
  talking to for IQA 155–7
  see also feedback; peer assessment
learning domains 88, 90
learning outcomes 8
learning preferences 101
Learning and Skills Improvement Service (LSIS) 3
legislation relating to records 79–80
Likert scale 145

M

malpractice 191–2
management 228
  allocating activities 42, 235–40
  communication skills 243–6
  feedback and conflict 248–50
  monitoring progress and quality 240–3
  personality styles and preferences 233–5
  skills 232, 233
  supporting the team 232–3
  work plans 228–32, 235, 240, 247–8
Maslow, AH, Hierarchy of Needs 98–9
meeting and standardisation plans (IQA) 134, 136,
  137, 141, 158–60
mentors
  assessors 19, 96, 169
  EQAs 178
  learners 94
  management 238
methods of assessment 25, 29, 32–4, 35–46
  in the work environment 56–9
monitoring visits 205–6